MENTAL ILLNESS: A HOMECARE GUIDE

Dr. Aristide H. Esser
Sylvia D. Lacey

WILEY

John Wiley & Sons

New York • Chichester • Brisbane • Toronto • Singapore

This publication is designed to provide accurate and
authoritative information in regard to the subject
matter covered. It is sold with the understanding that
the publisher is not engaged in rendering legal, accounting,
or other professional service. If legal advice or other
expert assistance is required, the services of a competent
professional person should be sought. *From a Declaration
of Principles jointly adopted by a Committee of the
American Bar Association and a Committee of Publishers.*

Library of Congress Cataloging-in-Publication Data

Esser, Aristide H., 1930–
    Mental illness: a homecare guide/
    edited by Aristide H. Esser and Sylvia D. Lacey.
        p.   cm.
    Bibliography: p.
    Includes index.
    ISBN 0-471-61158-1.—ISBN 0-471-61157-3 (pbk.)
    1. Mentally ill—Home care.   I. Lacey, Sylvia D. (Sylvia Denny),
1947– . II. Title.
RC439.5.E77   1989   89-9011
362.2'4—dc20   CIP

Printed in the United States of America

10 9 8 7 6 5 4 3 2 1

DEDICATION

This book is dedicated to the chronic mentally ill, who taught us what we know.

CONTENTS

Foreword, by *Rosalynn Carter*   vii
Preface   ix
Acknowledgments   xiii

PART ONE   BEING AT HOME WITH MENTAL ILLNESS   1

  1 What Is Mental Illness?   3
  2 The Decision to Provide Homecare   31
  3 Choosing the Homecare Coordinator and the
    Primary Care Physician   50
  4 The Role of the Primary Care Physician
    and the Homecare Team   62
    by *John W. Lacey, III, M.D.*

PART TWO   BASIC PLANNING   91

  5 Planning Homecare   93
  6 Transition From Hospital to Home   117
  7 Medication   134

PART THREE   INDIVIDUAL PROBLEMS   157

  8   The Recovering Person   159
  9   Sexuality   176
 10   Behavior in Public Places   188
 11   Crisis Intervention   197

**PART FOUR   SOCIETY AND THE RECOVERING
                PERSON**   **211**

    12 Support From the Community   213
    13 Long-Term Planning   223
    14 A Look Toward the Future   233

APPENDICES   **253**

    National Alliance for the Mentally Ill (NAMI)   253
    National Mental Health Association (NMHA)   256
    National Mental Health Consumer Self-Help
    Clearinghouse   259

Recommended Reading   265

Index   267

FOREWORD

Like other national health problems, mental illnesses have causes (many of which are largely unknown at present), prognoses, and, for several, successful treatments. Though mental illnesses are biological diseases, they are stigmatized by our society. The stigma is so great that people often do not seek treatment. Families with mentally ill relatives may also deny the illness, despite the devastation untreated illness may cause the entire family.

Shunned by society, the mentally ill are viewed as a threat to other people, although they are no more violent than the population at large. Many mentally ill persons are forced to live on the streets, in jails, in run-down housing, or in public shelters, where their quality of life is an affront to our modern, civilized way of living.

Those of us who work with the mentally ill recognize the tremendous need for education concerning both those who suffer from mental illness and the kind of care they receive. Because the responsibility for that care falls mainly on the family, this book addresses both the practical day-by-day care required and the necessary coordination of team effort. The high quality of information contained in this publication will narrow the educational gap concerning the stigmatization of the mentally ill.

ROSALYNN CARTER

PREFACE

This book owes its origins to our colleague, Nathan S. Kline, M.D., who had been planning such a work with Sylvia Lacey prior to his untimely death. Dr. Kline left no notes about its contents, but he did leave us a legacy of abiding interest in helping families to cope with the problems of severely disturbed mentally ill relatives within their home settings. We met when Dr. Esser, a research associate of Dr. Kline, was supervising the patients Dr. Kline had left behind. At that time, we shared in the treatment and care of one of Dr. Kline's former patients and found a mutual interest in completing the project barely begun when Dr. Kline passed away.

When planning the contents of this book, we searched for a synergy of our own experiences working with the mentally ill in hospital and community settings. We wanted in particular to use our backgrounds in psychopharmacology, psychosocial rehabilitation, education, and restoration of interpersonal relations in chronic mental illness. We both have initiated homecare at different levels in varied settings. Aristide Esser directed the opening and maintenance of group homes to bring chronic hospital patients back to their home community. Sylvia Lacey developed and coordinated services to bring about a high quality of life for recovering mentally ill individuals living in family homes.

History has documented many approaches to the treatment of mental illness. The Koran, for example, states about the mentally ill ". . . speak to them gently, saying nice things." However, this attitude was not shared by many, for through the ages mentally ill persons were subjected to various inhumane treatments. These included persecution, complete neglect or abandonment, restraint by ropes or chains, imprisonment in attics or cellars, and harsh punishment or death for being accused of possession by evil spirits or witchery.

The first mental hospital was built in Valencia, Italy, in the year 1412. Since that time, mental hospitals were intended to be places where mentally ill persons would be housed and humanely cared for. The patient was expected to progress better in the structured environment of the hospital, away from the unstructured environment of the home.

It is our opinion that in many cases, mental hospitals have been used simply because families did not know how to cope with their mentally ill family members. This book does not advocate against hospitalization; instead, it shows a way to maintain a mentally ill member of the household at home. We believe that the health of the mentally ill person is enhanced within the home environment where supportive family and friends actively participate in the care of the patient.

Current societal forces give added urgency to our concerns about homecare treatment for the mentally ill. Since the late 1960s, deinstitutionalization has brought about a decrease in available psychiatric hospital beds. Shifts in budget priorities in the 1980s have retarded growth and changed service patterns of community mental health centers. The problems posed by the homeless mentally ill and by drug abuse in the streets have awakened the general public to many unmet mental health needs. And, last but not least, the ground swell of tens of thousands of families, who have become vocal about the lack of support available to them in caring for their mentally ill loved ones, has become an influence to be reckoned with. Their organized activities, in the form of the

National Alliance for the Mentally Ill (NAMI) and other grass roots movements, are making an impact in drawing attention to the fact that care for mentally ill citizens, like any other victims of serious illness, should be part of the national agenda.

It is estimated that 70% of the seriously mentally ill live with relatives or friends! This means that between 1 and 2 million households are in need of both advice and support services to cope with long-term mental problems. Yet this large part of our population is attended to by only a small part of a large variety of professional providers.

This book is an attempt to increase the awareness of homecare alternatives in psychiatric treatment of chronic emotional and mental problems. The authors hope also to contribute to a national debate regarding the efficacy and desirability of integrating the majority of even our chronic mental patients into the community. Our focus is on doing this while safeguarding the integrity of the home environment. We do this out of our conviction that without a place in which the recovering person can feel safe at all times, learning how to prepare for independent living is impossible, and everyone's quality of life is bound to deteriorate.

We hope that this book can be a guide to help families and households reach homecare treatment decisions more decisively and comprehensively, while remaining flexible in exploring various kinds of therapies and community support services. We show families what criteria to use in selecting professional services, how to help design a treatment program, how to cope with unforeseen circumstances, how to ensure self-preservation, and, most importantly, how to assist their disturbed relative or friend in living a productive and rewarding life. Throughout, the book focuses on practical and understandable step-by-step instructions for dealing with the day-to-day problems in the medical treatment and psychosocial education of the ill member of the household.

It is important to realize that homecare is not an easy task and that it often is excruciatingly painful just to regain or maintain control of household functioning after it was disrupted or had been threatened by a seriously ill member. However, we show you how you can locate understanding mental health professionals who can guide you in decision making. And we explain how you can broaden your insight and experience by sharing your problems with many others in existing local and national family networks. Once you have weighed the pros and cons and decided to try homecare, you may be surprised by how much your mentally ill loved one will benefit from your efforts.

New City, New York   ARISTIDE H. ESSER
Knoxville, Tennessee   SYLVIA D. LACEY
April 1989

ACKNOWLEDGMENTS

Our inspiration comes from communion. We are deeply grateful to many individuals whose interest, encouragement, and assistance helped us in the writing of this book. We wish to express our gratitude to the following: John W. Lacey, III, M.D., for writing Chapter 4, on the primary care physician, and for his advice on other chapters; Helen Singer Kaplan, M.D., Ph.D. and to Donald Klein, M.D., for sharing their understanding of effective management of chronic mentally ill persons; Laurie Flynn, national director of the Alliance for the Mentally Ill, for her interest and advocacy for the mentally ill; and Ada Reif Esser for her invaluable editorial assistance.

We particularly appreciate Mrs. Rosalynn Carter, who has continually strived to reduce the stigmatization of the mentally ill, and we heartily thank her for providing the Foreword to this volume. Others from whose friendship, advice, information, or example we have benefited include Vickie Baity; Moonyean Bell; Albert Brigance, Ph.D.; Elaine Cappuccino, R.N.; Maureen Carney; Sonja Claiborne; Elizabeth Collins; Steve Daves; Deborah Denney; Theresa Denney; Roberta K. Dorr; Jessica and Jonathan Esser; Piet Hein Esser, M.D.; Ruth Feeney, R.N.; Janice Fox; Maurice Green, M.D.; Virginia Hannon, Ph.D.; Darlene Hendricks; Layton Howell; June

Husted, Ph.D.; Joyce Judge; Marna Kline; Diane Kirby; James T. Kirkpatrick, III; James Kohl; Jennifer and John W. Lacey, IV; James Lockett, D.D.S.; Allison Lunden; Carol Madans; Francis Mas, M.D.; Becky Minchey; Dottie Peagler; Leary Puryear; Carrie Reynolds; Dolores Rouse; Alex Ruth, M.D.; Shirley and William Sacks, Ph.D.; Julie Seaton; Phyllis and Riley Senter, M.D.; Helen Stallard; Paul Talarico; Alex Taylor; Anne R. Tousek; Rev. Charles A. Trentham, D.D., Ph.D.; Paul Ullmark; Kenny Withers; Kent C. and Martha Ann Withers; Naomi Womble; Debbie Wood; Henry Wright; and Richard Yoakley, E.E.D. Last, but not least, we wish to express a deep appreciation for the guidance given us by our Senior Editor, Herb Reich. For their invaluable assistance during completion of this book we thank Shari Hatch and Maggie Dana.

PART ONE

BEING AT HOME WITH MENTAL ILLNESS

1

WHAT IS MENTAL ILLNESS?

[Home is] the place where
when you have to go there
they have to take you in.

Robert Frost, The Death of the Hired Man

FINDING OUT ABOUT MENTAL ILLNESS

Due to changes in governmental and private insurance reimbursement, advancements in medication, and a genuine belief that the family environment provides the best care situation, the days of long-term psychiatric hospitalization are over. Today, treatment is aimed toward getting the psychiatric patient out of the hospital as soon as possible. Therefore, mentally ill individuals are usually released within 60 days (the maximum number of days covered by most insurance policies). The majority of families do not have a choice as to where their mentally ill relatives will live. Suddenly, they are faced with the responsibility not only for care of ill relatives, but also for rehabilitation. The family may also be confused about both the illness and the family's role in helping. This book is intended (1) to explain mental illness and its treatment and (2) to inform family members about their roles in effective caregiving and rehabilitation.

In all likelihood, you gave little consideration to mental illness until someone close to you became mentally ill. Your bits of knowledge about mental disease probably came from superficial, inaccurate, or overdramatized newspaper articles, television shows, movies, or even gossip. In these accounts, the mentally ill person was probably portrayed as someone who was dangerous, violent, out of control, having a split personality, or coming from a "crazy"[1] family background. When the illness hit your home, you suddenly found that preconceived notions about the mentally ill are not necessarily true.

As a matter of fact, you may still be overwhelmed by how little you know about this disease. This lack of understanding fills you with questions and concerns: How did this happen? Whose fault is it? Why me? Am I to blame? Where did I go wrong? Did I not love enough? Did I love too much? How long will the illness last? Is there a cure? Should I tell anyone? Will I or other family members get this illness? Where will I get help? All these anxieties, and often anger and pain, are aroused when mental illness touches a family member.

At first, your family may deny that there is even a problem; you may make excuses or try to explain why the ill relative is acting this way. Some members of your family also may attempt to alleviate the problems either by showing more love or by being more lenient. It is often only after the members of the household have exhausted their patience or have experienced tremendous guilt and embarrassment that they finally seek medical advice.

---

[1]"Crazy" is not an appropriate descriptive term for mental illness. When used in this text, it signifies society's misunderstanding and stigmatization of mental illness.

FACTS ABOUT MENTAL ILLNESS

What is mental illness? *Mental illness* is a "malfunction" of the brain that causes a confusion of feelings, beliefs, motivations, interpersonal skills, and ideas that prohibit the ability to function in everyday life. A person with mental illness is unable to deal with the changing demands of daily living. Depending on the seriousness of the disease, the mentally ill person may (1) lose control of her/his own behavior, (2) do or say something which shows that he/she does not know what is going on or (3) react to something that does not appear to exist. We call the last behavior "out of touch with reality."

Someone is said to suffer from a *psychosis* when that person is unable to distinguish between what is and is not real and can no longer correct his/her behavior by "reality testing." When we dream, we are in a similar mental state. However, when we wake up (and sometimes even during the dream), we realize that it was only a dream, and we return to reality. But when an awake person can no longer evaluate his/her perception and thoughts in terms of what is really going on in the outside world, or the person can no longer change his/her mind even in the face of contrary evidence, this individual is said to show "psychotic symptoms." And, whether psychotic or not, when someone shows behavior that does not fit the circumstances and that persists over a period of time, we call it "an impairment of the brain" or "mental illness."

What causes mental illness? In many cases, we cannot find a clear cause. Though there is not one specific cause of all mental illness, there are several probable contributing causes: heredity, organic diseases, physical and chemical agents, and environmental factors such as stress, destitution, and family problems.

Who becomes mentally ill? Knowing no boundaries, mental illness affects persons from all ages and from all economic, social, religious, or ethnic backgrounds. It is believed by many professionals to be the most common type of illness occurring today. Some form of it affects the life of nearly everyone.

How many people are affected? Recent surveys estimate at least 20 people in 100 are personally affected by mental illness. It is also estimated that more than half the patients seen by medical practitioners are suffering from some type of psychological disorder. These may present such physical complaints as headaches or stomach distress, or such psychological problems as anxiety, tension, or depression.

Where do mentally ill persons live? The National Institute of Mental Health (NIMH) estimates that approximately 3,000,000 people are seriously or long-term mentally ill. Of these, it is thought, approximately 1,200,000 live in households with their families or friends, and another 800,000 live in nursing homes, residential care facilities and hospitals. The remainder of the chronic mentally ill live alone, in public shelters, in jail, or—worst of all—on the streets.

How severe is mental illness? Degrees of severity range from a short-term mild illness, such as a brief bout of depression, to a lifelong disabling disorder, such as schizophrenia. To understand severity, we should try to think in terms of both how appropriate behavior may disappear when the brain is unable to function normally (absence of "normal" behavior) and how inappropriate behavior may appear when the brain functions abnormally (presence of "abnormal" behavior).

Almost a century ago, the English neurologist Hughlings Jackson increased our insight into the types of abnormal behavior by suggesting that when the brain is not able to respond with higher level behavior, it will try to respond on a lower level. For instance, when someone has had a stroke and cannot speak, we may instead see gestures as a response to questions. The nature and accuracy of such gestures depends on the level of the brain that is still functioning after the stroke. If the stroke was limited, the patient may be able to write or otherwise indicate what he or she means. But if a large part of the brain is damaged, the patient may react with angry movements that do not show an understanding of the meaning of our questions.

In the first case, we call the patient's symptoms "negative": From the *absence* of the ability to speak, we know that the patient has a problem. Otherwise, the individual is responding appropriately by trying to react to questions. In the second case, we call the symptoms "positive": From the *presence* of responses that have nothing to do with our questions, we know that the diseased brain is responding with abnormal behavior that does not show a relation to what we talked about. Note that in both cases, the patient's behavior can be considered abnormal; in the first case (negative), however, the malfunction shows in what the patient *does not do*, and in the second case (positive), in what he or she *does*. In treating mental patients, it is often easier to determine that they are sick because of what they do and not because of what they do not do. In other words, we initially notice mental illness because of the individual's positive symptoms.

Often, the mentally ill person with positive symptoms is considered severely mentally ill. This is because the things we do when our brains are confused or out of touch with reality are most readily termed "crazy" by others. Negative symptoms are often noted only over time, and even a severely mentally ill individual may appear normal during a brief encounter. Persons with these symptoms are often considered less ill because their behavior is socially less objectionable. However, even those mentally ill persons who only show negative symptoms may be severely and chronically disabled, as, for instance, is the case in the later stages of schizophrenia and dementia when they are nonresponsive and therefore sometimes insensitively compared to "a vegetable."

What are the types of mental illnesses? The many different types of emotional and mental disorders may differ in their symptoms, their degree of severity, and their effects on a person's life. The officially recognized types of mental disorders are categorized in the American Psychiatric Association's *Diagnostic and Statistical Manual of Mental Disorders* (third edition—Revised; DSM-III-R). This book focuses on those mental disorders that most often become a chronic problem and may need long-term attention, treatment, care, and rehabilitation. Chronic mental illness most often results from the following types of disorders: the schizophrenias; the mood (or affective) disorders, as well as anxiety disorders; the organic mental disorders; and some of the personality disorders and psychoactive substance use disorders (addictions).[2] Severe psychotic illnesses not caused by organic mental disorder (p. 17) are often called *functional psychoses*, for example, the schizophrenias and mood disorders.

KINDS OF MENTAL ILLNESS

This section describes the aforementioned groups of chronic mental illness that often require hospitalization and that tend to have a lasting influence on the mentally ill person's life.

The Schizophrenias

Schizophrenic disorders are perhaps the most frightening and incapacitating of all mental diseases. Their characteristics include those positive symptoms that most people would include in their description of being "crazy." The term *schizophrenia* can evoke as much terror and confusion as the

---

[2]Though DSM-III-R does not consider mental retardation a psychiatric disorder (it is a developmental disorder, meaning that the brain is considered never to have completed its normal development), it is a condition characterized by subnormal functioning, and many of its problems closely resemble those of mental disorders. The information found in this book will be helpful for families of those suffering from this defect in brain functioning as well.

disease itself. The word was coined in 1911 by the Swiss psychiatrist Eugen Bleuler and means "splitting of the mind." The mental split is between such functions as emotion and thought, or perception and behavior—unlike the popular belief that a schizophrenic has a split, or dual, personality, such as a Dr. Jekyll and Mr. Hyde. Therefore, schizophrenia often shows psychotic symptoms caused by disturbances of the ability to think and act rationally and to express or experience proper emotions, especially in its beginning. Also, most tragically, patients often retain for a long time such negative symptoms as the inability to make decisions and a loss of initiative and ambition.

Schizophrenia is not truly rare, for it affects about 1 or 2 out of every 100 persons. It is estimated that over 500,000 persons yearly are in need of active treatment for schizophrenia. Although it can affect anyone at any age, it most frequently occurs in young persons between the ages of 15 and 25. A specific cause of this group of illnesses is not known; however, many contributing factors have been identified. Although many treatments have been tried, and some medications have been proved effective in combating specific symptoms of this group of diseases (especially in recent decades), unfortunately, no totally effective cure is yet available.

We do not know what causes schizophrenia, and we cannot prevent it. As an illness, it can be as devastating as cancer, and it is as difficult to treat and manage. A relationship with personality disorders has been found, in that many of those suffering from schizophrenia were somewhat odd and eccentric while growing up. In particular, the paranoid and schizoid personality disorders often occur in persons diagnosed with schizophrenia. Another relationship often noted is the increase in schizophrenic symptoms either brought about by the use of alcohol, marijuana, or street drugs, or due to the fact that schizophrenia is diagnosed after a youngster has abused any of these drugs for some time. Again, why this is so is unclear. One might think of a general vulnerability of the brain in persons who are prone to becoming schizophrenic.

The important point to remember is that we have to take the condition of the person's body and nervous system into account when caring for those recovering from schizophrenia.

The disease mysteriously affects the sense of inner and outer reality and thus frequently makes the patient appear out of touch with reality. This psychosis, more than any other severe mental illness, impairs the functioning of the self ("I") and therefore often changes the whole personality. In typical cases, we begin to notice the disease through its positive emotional symptoms. It may be that a boy or girl starts to behave oddly, or that we find a person's emotions to be disconnected from his/her thought content or behavior. For instance, a person suffering from schizophrenia may giggle if told of a friend's accident or death. Other positive symptoms are thought and perception disturbances: For example, the individual may become suspicious or may complain of hearing voices or noticing things that others cannot verify. It is also possible that negative symptoms become noticeable first. We may see someone lose interest in former pleasurable activities and begin to withdraw gradually from relatives and friends. The feeling we often get from those afflicted with schizophrenia is that they don't care. Often, they make no eye contact, and their faces remain expressionless regardless of what we may talk about.

There are no laboratory tests to diagnose schizophrenia, but on the basis of the person's history and the clinical observations, we can come to an impression. (Some of the recent technologies that give hope for the future diagnosis of schizophrenia are cited in chapter 14.) Several symptoms characterize schizophrenia, and experience has shown that if these symptoms have existed for more than 6 months, a diagnosis of schizophrenia is likely. Most important is that the patient shows clear signs of disordered thinking in the absence of a disturbance in consciousness (such as a fainting spell or intoxication with alcohol). Because the patient may not show what he/she is thinking spontaneously, we must try to bring into the open such disturbances as hallucinations or delusional thinking, ideas of reference (see below), and other positive symptoms of brain malfunction. Elicitation of symptoms is particularly important in the acute phase of the disease. Once the disease becomes chronic, it becomes hard to distinguish inactivity based on disturbance of the brain function (due to a positive symptom such as hallucinating commands to sit completely still) from inactivity due to inertia, laziness, or boredom. In the case of positive symptoms, the patient may report hearing voices commanding that the patient do something. These command hallucinations may lead to bizarre and even dangerous behavior, such as being commanded to "jump out of the window" (see chapter 11).

The ill person often readily admits to hallucinations if we ask whether he or she hears voices or sounds when nobody is around. More rarely, patients see, smell, or feel others when no one is present. Often, the voice(s) tell the patient what to do, or the suffering person feels that his or her thoughts are being broadcast over radio or TV. A schizophrenic patient may also talk and gesture to him- or herself. When the disorder in perception is still less noticeable, the person may complain of thinking that people and events in the environment always affect or center on him/her. This symptom is called "having ideas of reference," such as when an ill person at a party sincerely tells you that all the other guests are talking about him/her when this is clearly not the case.

Delusions are falsely held beliefs that occur frequently in schizophrenia. For example, the patient "knows" that the FBI or others are watching him/her, talking about him/her, or perhaps even conspiring to harm him or her. Often, delusions are connected to hallucinations, as when an adult male tells us of being "programmed" by voices he hears through a dental filling during the night as part of a conspiracy to make him a homosexual prostitute. Obviously, many hallucinations and delusions are projections grossly out of touch with reality.

The ill person's speech is commonly disturbed, even to the

extent that it becomes meaningless to others. Often, spoken thoughts seem unconnected. Or the thoughts are too concretely expressed; for instance, in trying to say that someone looked at him, a patient remarked, "This fellow stood still in front of me." Sometimes the severely ill person may simply echo parts of the conversation, as when the response to "How have you been feeling today?" is "Have you been feeling today?"

Such exchanges show that many functions are disturbed and/or absent, though we may not notice such disturbance unless we make a special effort. A negative symptom might be a thought process having become so poor that if one asks "What are you thinking of now?" the answer may be "I am not thinking of anything" or "I feel empty." Another characteristic sign is that the mentally ill person may not do anything at all because he or she cannot come to a conclusion. The will and the ability to carry out plans is paralyzed, but the patient may not complain about this unless we specifically search for this negative symptom.

In certain cases, the activity level of the mentally ill may change; the patient appears either overly excited and restless or lethargic and inactive. The person may also show either bizarre or repetitive behavior, as in either taking clothes off in public or continually wanting to shake hands.

Once the acute phase of the illness is over, most positive symptoms disappear and the seriously ill person will predominantly show negative symptoms: He or she just sits around all day, thinking and doing nothing, saying little, neglecting his/her appearance and not being interested in socializing. At this time, the most disturbing symptoms may be the development of such bad or annoying habits as overeating or constantly wanting to smoke.

Because of the debilitating nature of the disease, schizophrenics may try to commit suicide. The reasons for such attempts vary. When there are many positive symptoms, it may come about through *command hallucinations*—voices tell the patient to kill him- or herself. When the mentally ill person experiences mostly negative symptoms, he or she may feel hopeless and depressed and abruptly decide to end life.

It is estimated that once a schizophrenic disorder is diagnosed, approximately 25% of those ill with the disease can recover with proper medication and support; with proper homecare, 50% will be able to lead a fulfilling life in the community, although they may experience periodic setbacks and hospitalization; while 25% will have a severe disability that may last a lifetime. Fortunately, there appears to be some improvement associated with age; growing older often brings about a decrease in symptoms.

Mood Disorders and Anxiety Disorders

We discuss these two classes of mental disorders together because they often occur together and may then make each other's symptoms more pronounced.

Manic–Depressive Disorder

Depression can be understood as a natural—although unpleasant—experience, which can vary in intensity and duration. But when it leads to persistent unhappiness, listlessness, feelings of unworthiness or excessive guilt, and a withdrawal from social functions, it interferes seriously with the patient's ability to function. Likewise, the opposite of depression—*manic behavior* ("feeling on top of the world")—is occasionally part of natural experiences. Yet, when it leads to inability to relax or keep quiet, a constant need to talk or do things without the competence of finishing anything, and recklessly spending money or making commitments that one cannot possibly keep, there results a disorder called mania, which may end disastrously if not treated. Depression and mania should not be confused with the temporary experience of a mood swing. All of us may feel depressed at times or become extremely happy, but to be called a mood or affective disorder, the mood should persist for several weeks, disrupt normal functioning, and be combined with several other signs and symptoms.

In some persons, episodes of depression and mania occur with regularity or alternate with each other. In this case, we call it manic–depressive, or bipolar, disorder (from the perceived swings between the opposite poles of feeling good and feeling bad), and increasing evidence suggests that this is caused by a genetic or inborn factor. Also, treatment available for most of those suffering from mood disorders is much more effective than treatment for schizophrenic disorders.

Anxiety Disorder

Fortunately, there are also many effective treatments for *anxiety disorders*—a large group of mental illnesses with symptoms that are similar to—but that go beyond—the occasional tension, stress, grief, or overwhelming emotional experiences of normal life. When apprehension and tensions interfere with a person's effective coping with family, job, school, or other demands of daily life, the condition must be regarded as a serious psychiatric disorder and requires treatment and care.

The anxiety disorders often manifest themselves through such physical symptoms as excessive perspiration, shortness of breath, palpitations and rapid heart beats, dizziness, tension headache, and many other accelerated or slowed down body functions. The topic of *somatization,* or the expression of emotional and mental problems in signs of physical illness, is further discussed in chapter 4.

Much can be said about anxiety disorders, especially the *phobias* (or extreme panics in certain situations, such as fear of high places). However, because descriptions of the feelings and sensations of anxiety are available through popular magazines and many other publications, we do not need to explore these deeply here.

Because signs and symptoms of depression and anxiety occur often for short periods of time under normal circumstances, it is important for us to recognize when such behavior becomes so persistent as to cause significant loss of function. Further, the incidence of depression and anxiety disorders is high; up to 20% of people at some time in their lives may be so affected that they lose both work and personal relationships, and develop low self-esteem and thoughts of suicide. Especially in persons suffering from depression, the search for some relief may end in a retreat into feelings of inadequacy, unworthiness, and finally, killing oneself.

Depression

Of all the psychiatric disorders, depression results in the highest rate of suicide. The incidence of depression is higher among women than men, with most attacks occurring first in persons between the ages of 25 and 35. But even young children, and certainly the elderly, are subject to this illness. Many signs and symptoms are associated with depression. The following examples indicate the increasing depth and degree of the illness: sadness and feelings of gloom; either insomnia, restless sleep, or sleeping too much; sense of failure and loss of interest; either loss of appetite or overeating; inability to concentrate and loss of memory; a sense of guilt and need for punishment; suicidal thoughts and actions. Less often, such positive symptoms are present as hallucinations (voices telling the patient that he/she is "bad" or "guilty" or "deserves to die"), or delusions (the depressed person may incorrectly believe he/she has hurt or killed somebody). Sometimes, those suffering from depression feel hopeless, believing that their symptoms will never get better. Others feel helpless because they think that nothing can be done about their condition, nobody is able to help them, and so on. At such times, it is always wise to think about hospitalization because without further warning, such feelings, coupled with their belief that they have failed or have done something heinously wrong, may result in suicide.

Many depressed persons coming in for treatment have been feeling bad for years. Their life has often become flat and meaningless for them. Sometimes they have been thinking about being hopelessly ill with a physical disorder, because body aches and pains are almost always intensified when we are depressed. Especially in anxiously depressed persons, the bodily symptoms may be in the foreground, as we saw in the description of anxiety. It is also true that many people suffering from a chronic physical illness become depressed because of it. It is therefore no wonder that many physically ill persons do not realize—or refuse to acknowledge—that they are depressed. About 25 to 50% of major depressive illness may go unrecognized in the medically ill and in the elderly. In addition, even with the availability of effective treatments for depression, mania, and the anxiety disorders, these conditions often require chronic care and treatment, just as schizophrenia does.

Posttraumatic Stress Disorder (PTSD)

One of the recognized anxiety disorders that often leads to depressed feelings and inability to work has gained increasing public attention: *posttraumatic stress disorder (PTSD)*, which appears after a psychologically traumatic event that is outside the usual range of human experiences. For instance, experiencing one or more serious threats to one's life or health (as in experiencing or witnessing a serious accident or natural disaster) may lead to recurring frightening and painful memories during specific daytime situations and also in dreams. Often, such persistent memories ("flashbacks") begin only after the trauma has long passed. Up to 20% of Vietnam War veterans (especially those exposed to combat or to torture and suffering such as in concentration camps) cannot reestablish themselves in normal civilian life. This is because the flashback becomes more and more frequent and more easily triggered, and the resulting anxiety can become debilitating. The person with PTSD may then try to avoid the memory of the traumatic event by not becoming involved in anything that may bring up associated thoughts or feelings. This leads to progressive restriction and loss of (1) contacts with other people, (2) daily activities, and (3) expectations about the future. The suffering person may begin to think that he/she cannot hold a job or develop a career, get married, build a life. In addition, the apprehension caused by the fear of reexperiencing the trauma leads to such physical symptoms as muscle tension, sweating, and overreaction. Treatment for PTSD is improving since more attention is being paid to this disorder. PTSD is a serious chronic mental disorder that may require the organization of homecare in addition to ongoing treatment on an outpatient basis.

Organic Mental Disorders

There are groups of mental symptoms (called "syndromes") and specific disorders that come from known changes in or damage to the brain tissue. The central feature of these disorders is a temporary or permanent psychological/behavioral abnormality due to a dysfunction of the brain as an organ of the body. Examination of the symptoms and their relation to psychological and laboratory tests can determine that the mental disorder is organic.

The oldest and best known of the organic disorders is *epilepsy*, or seizure disorder. Often, we can find signs of head injuries before or after birth, scars in the brain tissue, or malformations or tumors of the brain. In other seizure patients, it is not known exactly what is wrong in the brain or where it is localized. However, in all cases of epilepsy, sudden massive discharges of electrical energy occur in the brain, and we call the resulting behavior a "fit" or a "seizure." Between seizures, the person may function normally. Because epilepsy is quite manageable with antiepileptic medication and many books have been written about it over the years, we do not further discuss this brain disorder, which occurs in 1% of the population.

Fortunately, many organic mental disorders and syndromes are transient, and the brain regains its full function. But when there is a serious head injury (such as in a traffic accident), the brain may never heal completely, and *dementia* (chronic loss of brain function) may occur. The same may happen after brain tumors, strokes, and other identifiable damage to the brain. It is impossible to review all causes of brain damage and their consequences. Herein we primarily discuss progressive dementia that results from slow degeneration of the brain. Most of the time, its beginning is not clear, although in multi-infarct dementia, a stroke may occur as a warning sign. *Degenerative dementia* begins with a nonspecific loss of intellectual functioning, and when it progresses, it may lead to severe problems that require well-planned homecare.

The essential features of dementia are negative symptoms, almost always beginning with forgetfulness, especially for recent events. Patients also show, in one or more ways, the loss of higher cortical functions, evidenced by such negative symptoms as impairment in thinking and inability to make plans or to judge a situation. The changes in personality particularly alarm family and friends. The person may become apathetic and withdrawn or be described by others as "not being him/herself." Or demented persons may become irritable and try to hide their loss of abilities by becoming cantankerous or by constantly complaining. A previously neat and precise person may become unconcerned with his/her appearance and may begin to speak and act in a slipshod manner. But often the diagnosis of dementia is made only after the aforementioned disturbances start to interfere with the ill person's functioning in work and social relationships.

In dementia, the damage to the brain first shows in the loss of intellectual functions, then it ends up in the decrease of body functions and death. The loss of memory makes it impossible for the deteriorating person to learn, understand, or reason. Slowly, orientation begins to slip away. The loss of orientation at first mostly concerns the sense of time; the individual no longer knows the date, the year, the time of day, or the season. Later, demented persons may no longer know where they are; and finally, they will even be unable to tell you who they are. The person may lose the ability to dress, eat, bathe, and go to the bathroom unattended. It is usually the latest skills learned or the more recent memories that are the first to go. Losses of acquired behavior may continue until the person is reduced to an infant-like stage.

Though negative symptoms dominate the picture in degenerative organic brain disorders such as dementia, we often see positive psychotic symptoms. Especially during periodic deteriorations, as may occur in multi-infarct dementia (see p. 20), the patient may temporarily be totally confused, hallucinating, or delusional. But overall, the picture of the demented person is one of loss of abilities and concern with what he or she can no longer talk about or do.

Dementia occurs mostly in the elderly, but as noted before, other disorders may bring about loss of intellectual functions at an earlier age. The course of dementia depends on the underlying brain disorder; for instance, if it is caused by a head trauma, it may remain unchanged for a long time. However, when it is caused by a degenerative brain disorder such as Alzheimer's disease, it may begin with barely noticeable symptoms, but over a period of several years, it leads to progressive loss of functioning and death. The degree of dementia determines whether homecare is possible. In general, when the activities of daily living are so impaired that continuous supervision and care are required (for example, when the person is not able to communicate or maintain minimal care of him/herself), homecare may be out of the question.

During the first stages of degenerative dementias, homecare can be arranged. This also provides time to prepare for the possibility that in later stages of the illness, care in a hospital or nursing home may be required. To determine the progression of care required, you should know the different characteristic progressions of the two most frequent types of dementia: Alzheimer and multi-infarct.

It is estimated that by age 65, 2–4% of the population shows degenerative dementia of the Alzheimer type and that 10% of all deceased elderly show brain damage from this disease.

In dementia of the Alzheimer type, we see a slow onset with a small loss of intellectual functioning, which then spreads over several months or years to many specific abilities, such as judgment, abstract thinking, and work activities, and it ends up in a total personality change. Finally, the bodily functions give way, often beginning with incontinence and ending up in not being able to eat or drink. In Alzheimer's disease, it is not known what causes the characteristic damage to the brain that is detectable in autopsies. Much research has been done in recent years to find a treatment for this illness, but thus far none of the hoped-for specific cures has been found effective.

Unlike Alzheimer-type dementia, multi-infarct dementia is caused generally by the degeneration of the blood supply to the brain, and it is often possible to determine the specific cause and appropriate treatment for living patients. For instance, high blood pressure, diabetes, or *atherosclerosis* (hardening of the arteries) may be found to exist and can be treated.

Also, in contrast to the more rapid rate of deterioration in the Alzheimer-type dementia, we see a stepwise progression in multi-infarct dementia, often stretched out over many years. An *infarct* is a scar in the tissue, which occurs after a blood vessel leaks or bursts, and *multi* means that it occurs more than once. Typically, the patient may have experienced a stroke and lost some function such as speech, which may not return after recovery. During and immediately after the stroke, the individual may show such positive symptoms as hearing voices or conversing with old friends or relatives who have died. Other strokes may follow, and gradually more functions drop out, and the negative symptoms increase. On the other hand, one may see the typical senile dementia, in which the person very gradually loses more and more intellectual functioning and then slowly loses physical functioning as well. All gradations of loss of function may be observed, and negative symptoms may appear in different sequences, depending on which brain regions are affected. The important thing to remember is that with advancing age, anyone's blood supply to the brain may be interrupted in spots, and they gradually can no longer be restored. It can therefore be understood that this type of dementia occurs in old people, mostly starting in their 70s.

In recent years, acquired immune deficiency syndrome (AIDS) has also become recognized as a cause for progressive dementia. This means that AIDS may show itself for the first time with mental symptoms and then progress to complete loss of intellectual function. We do not know how to predict the rate of progression, but homecare for the chronic mental problems of AIDS is possible, taking into account the knowledge of its infectious risks.

Personality Disorders and Psychoactive Substance Use Disorders

As was the case with mood disorders and anxiety disorders, these two classes of mental disorders often coincide and may exacerbate one another. Whereas the symptoms of the schizophrenias may seem far from the norm, those of the personality disorders are closer to home. All of us may at times lose control or become unreasonably stubborn and set in our ways or opinions, even if this is not in our own best interest.

Each of us has certain patterns of thinking, reacting, and relating to our environment. Sometimes, we call these patterns "attitudes" or predispositions to act or react in a certain direction. Such behavior patterns and attitudes form personality traits that make it possible for us to remain ourselves in a wide range of different social situations. But when these traits become inflexible and do not help in adaptation, they may cause loss of effective functioning and distress. Distress is more often experienced by persons in the patient's environment than by the patient him/herself, and persons with personality disorders often have a hard time understanding what is wrong with their behavior that hurts or offends other people.

Agatha, a 20-year-old unemployed woman, has been in trouble since age 12. Her parents, a well-to-do professional couple living in the suburbs of a large city, had noticed that she had acquired a smoking habit, and on one occasion, she had come home drunk after a junior high school party. Discussions of her behavior, restricting her freedom, and even sending her to a psychotherapist did not help. She appeared not to care about her parents, her home, or her school. While she could not understand "what the fuss is all about," she constantly looked for excitement and dangerous situations. She began to complain of tension spells, which often found relief in violent behavior. She believed that her parents and her former friends were against her. She gradually went from bad to worse, and by age 16, she was often truant from school, kept undesirable company (mostly delinquent teenagers), and abused alcohol and street drugs. Then began a pattern of public offenses and petty crimes: She was found intoxicated in a shopping mall, was picked up for soliciting, was involved in minor drug deals, and so on. She dropped out of school, and within the next 2 years, it became clear that she was dependent on alcohol and would do anything to obtain drinking money for her binges, at which times she would stay away from home for weeks on end. After several court appearances, she was ordered to be hospitalized for alcohol detoxification and subsequently placed in a 6-month program free of alcohol and other drugs. Afterward, her parents accepted her back home under condition that she attend Alcoholics Anonymous meetings and enroll in adult education classes. She also received medication to control her periodic bouts of tension and irritability, on an "as needed" basis. Together with homecare supervision and psychotherapy, this proved sufficient to have her gradually gain more control of herself.

This case of antisocial personality disorder shows the relationship between personality disorders and substance abuse. The association goes both ways: A person with personality disorder may have character traits that encourage pleasure seeking through substance abuse, and someone who begins to abuse alcohol or street drugs may subsequently develop maladaptive traits while searching either for money or for an occasion to get high again.

We can think of personality disorders in three categories: (1) persons who appear unpredictable, overly emotional, or acting in conflict with their environment (such as the antisocial and borderline personality disorders), (2) persons who fear social relations (for instance, paranoid and schizoid personality disorders), and (3) persons who are anxious and careful (such as dependent and obsessive–compulsive personality disorders).

When we look at the psychoactive substance[3] use disorders, there are two important categories: (1) dependence on alcohol or other psychoactive drugs; and (2) abuse of alcohol or other psychoactive drugs.

Data suggests that persons suffering from personality disorders and substance use disorders form the largest of the four groups of chronic mental disorders discussed here. About 1 in 8 persons show symptoms of these disorders at least once during their lifetime, and about 5–10% of those (up to 1.5 million in the U.S.) develop severe long-term problems. As with most of the chronic mental disorders, there are no clear causes. Although no direct hereditary influence has been shown to exist, personality disorders and alcoholism appear more often in some families than in others. Another general observation is that substance use disorders and feelings of either depression or anxiety are often related. Also, as mentioned earlier, diagnosed schizophrenics seem likely to exhibit paranoid and schizoid personality disorder, and schizophrenics also are often seen to have substance abuse problems. We do not review substance abuse and personality disorders at length in this book because, as was the case with anxiety disorders, many descriptions are available in the popular literature. Nonetheless, a brief overview of personality disorders may prove helpful.

---

[3]Psychoactive substances alter mood or behavior, and the effects vary according to the circumstances, such as the use of caffeine for stimulation, the use of alcohol for recreation, or the illegal use of street drugs. Such substances readily lend themselves to abuse, which may endanger physical or mental health.

Personality Disorders

The *antisocial type of personality* is perhaps the best known because it was often described in the past as "psychopathic" or "sociopathic" personality. Together with the borderline personality disorder (discussed next), this diagnosis most often leads to chronic severe mental illness, either through the debilitating combination with substance abuse, or through occurrence of psychotic episodes, especially in reaction to stressful conditions. In the case of Agatha, unwarranted suspiciousness was part of the personality disorder. Under the influence of alcohol or stress, this can easily deteriorate into a delusion of persecution, together with hallucinations of accusative voices and so on. The main points to remember about these persons with unpredictable behavior is that they can be in control of their behavior and in touch with reality at one moment and be out of control, angry, frustrated, and acting impulsively the next. They often have insight afterward and may make excuses, but this remorseful behavior will not lead to lasting social relationships, and it is in the area of social life that the symptoms of these disorders are most prominent. Antisocial personalities can seldom function as stable responsible partners or parents, can rarely sustain steady employment, can repeatedly get into conflict with the law, and can often fail to honor financial obligations.

Persons with *borderline personality disorders* straddle the border between normalcy and psychosis. They show a pattern of unstable but intensive relationships. They also feel uncertain about their identity and cannot stand being alone because they feel empty or bored, and they show marked shifts from normal mood to exhilaration, to irritability, or to anxiety and depression.

The *paranoid and schizoid personality disorders* show up in people who are fearful of others. Often, such persons are perceived as strange, or as cold and distant—difficult to approach or talk to. *Paranoid disorder* refers to a pervasive attitude of suspiciousness and mistrust of people. These persons are guarded or secretive, always expect harm, are hypersensitive and quick to take offense, are not able to relax, and often show an absence of feelings. *Schizoid disorder* refers to being withdrawn with both an emotional coldness or aloofness and an unwillingness to become involved. Such persons are unable to make social contacts and often end up being close to only one friend or relative. It is easy to see why all these character traits resemble symptoms found in the schizophrenias. As mentioned before, sometimes these personality disorders are seen in individuals who later develop a (paranoid) schizophrenia.

The dependent and the obsessive–compulsive personality disorders show patterns of worry and extreme caution in living and social relationships. *Dependency* consists of making sure that other people will take care of you. Persons with dependent disorder lack self-confidence and seek out partners, friends, or employers who will tell them what to do. Such persons avoid making decisions as much as possible and see themselves as helpless or stupid. Persons with an *obsessive–compulsive* style of living are also extremely reluctant to make decisions. But with them, it is for another reason: They are so intense and perfectionist that they want to master any detail and thus have a hard time finishing tasks. They are excessively careful, get hung up on rules or organization, and often insist that others follow exactly their way of doing things. Because of these traits, such individuals are vulnerable when sudden and unexpected changes occur in their lives.

Recently, *eating disorders* have become the focus of much interest. The two best-known examples are *anorexia nervosa* (starving) and *bulimia* (binge overeating and vomiting). It appears that in one third of the cases, both disorders overlap, in which case one may observe alternating cycles of binge eating, vomiting, and self-starvation with severe weight loss. These disorders are often described as not resulting from any other medical illness, but in fact, they mostly occur in people within the entire range of severe mental illness, from psychosis to anxiety disorder. Many people with eating problems suffer from other personality disorders. *Anorexia nervosa* is self-starvation in which the person willfully eats minimally and exercises often. The reason given is often a fear of becoming obese, but in anorexic schizophrenics, unrealistic comments such as "I have to purify myself and save the world" may be elicited. Anorexics are almost exclusively female, and once their weight loss exceeds more than 25% of their ideal body weight, the condition may become life-endangering. The treatment is difficult and best left to specialized clinicians. Similarly, bulimia is seen mostly in women and is also difficult to treat. However, in bulimia, a connection with mood disorders has been suggested, which would make treatment more feasible.

Psychoactive Substance Use Disorders

Although abuse of and dependence on alcohol and other psychoactive drugs are among the most frequently discussed and described mental problems, it is hard to define exactly when the behavior of the user becomes a disorder. We best describe abuse as excessive drug use that is not medical practice. Such excessive use often results in *tolerance*—an altered physiological state of the body whereby taking the same amount of the drug produces less response over time. Thus, the drug abuser needs progressively larger doses to produce the same drug effect.

In *drug dependence*, there is a psychological or physical compulsion to take a drug regularly either to experience its pleasurable effects or to avoid the discomfort of its absence. In such cases, when the drug is abruptly discontinued, symptoms of physical and mental disorder occur: the *abstinence syndrome*. Both tolerance and the abstinence syndrome force the drug abuser to continue searching for more drugs to use. The behavior becomes a mental disorder because it affects the patient's family and social relationships, health, employment, and it sooner or later brings about legal difficulties. The surest signs of substance abuse are a change in life style and habits: inability to keep appointments and regular hours, lying and cheating about money, and so on. Eventually, the drug abuser will have to violate other societal rules and laws, such as to steal and obtain drugs illegally or (see the case of Debra in chapter 3) to falsify prescriptions.

What causes people to abuse alcohol or other drugs? No single factor can explain why as many as 1 in 12 persons at some time during their life may become dependent on or otherwise abuse drugs. Yet this is understandable if we realize that psychoactive drugs produce all types of effects: they perk you up or calm you down; they give you a solitary "high" or make you feel more at ease with others; they increase your energy and concentration or take away your anxiety and sleeplessness; and so on. There are as many reasons for drug abuse as there are combinations of the chemical substances that cause one or more of the desired effects. Or the abuser may resort to using more than one drug simultaneously; we then talk of polydrug (or alcohol and other drug) abuse. This book does not describe all signs and symptoms of the different chemical substances that may be abused. Instead, it reviews the consequences of chronic drug or alcohol abuse and the often slow process of making the recovering person able to remain *abstinent*—that is, not use any of the addictive substances—which may require long-term homecare.

Among the important factors contributing to substance abuse are (a) the relative availability of drugs or alcohol; (b) the (street) culture in which the individual lives; and, perhaps most important, (c) the likelihood that the person suffers from other mental illness, especially the schizophrenias, anxiety and depression disorders, or antisocial and borderline personality disorders. For reasons discussed before, those who suffer from these disorders are (a) looking for relief from some of their feelings (boredom, tension, etc.) by using street drugs or alcohol, and (b) particularly vulnerable to the effects of chemical substances: The drugs make their symptoms worse. Persons with a mental disorder compounded by substance abuse are often identified as *mentally ill chemical abusers* (MICA) or suffering from *dual diagnosis*, although the latter term is also used to refer to mental retardates with mental illness. The MICA category is increasingly important. About 50% of psychiatric admissions in metropolitan areas involve people who are mentally ill *and* abuse alcohol or other drugs. The need for special programs to deal with these persons is being recognized, as it is clear that the clinical needs of the mentally ill with substance abuse problems may be extremely complicated.

However, returning to the individuals with substance abuse disorders, let us assume that the person has undergone a detoxification program in a hospital or has agreed to work with a clinic or a doctor to stay away from alcohol and the illegal use of other drugs. It should be clear that homecare must concentrate on keeping the environment absolutely free of alcohol and other drugs. The social relationships should also discourage contact with known abusers—in other words, promote a drug-free cultural life. And finally, any related mental illness should be treated and cared for, so that any subjective reasons that would tempt the recovering individual to reach out for the effects of alcohol or drugs are minimized.

DIAGNOSIS: UNDERSTANDING IS THE BEGINNING OF HOMECARE

The treatment, care, and rehabilitation of chronic mental patients, especially schizophrenics and substance abusers, is difficult and often painful and frustrating. As in any undertaking, one has to know what it is all about. In chronic mental illness, where so many different signs and symptoms may need different kinds of attention, one has to establish general guidelines. These come from understanding the particular needs of the recovering individual. These needs, in turn, are determined by the type of disorder, or combination of disorders, from which the person is suffering. The most important determination of what type of disorder one is dealing with is called the "diagnosis."

As a family member, uppermost in your mind is, "What's the matter? What is wrong with my relative?" And immediately afterward, you'll ask, "What causes it?" and "How will it come out?" Discuss the resulting diagnosis with the primary care physician, who will begin to clarify for you what is known about the following: the possible causes of the disease or the prevention of symptoms; the likely course of the disease; the effect you can expect from different treatments, especially from therapeutic drugs; and, most important, under what circumstances you can keep the member of your household at home and what plans you must make to provide effective homecare.

Many recovering persons and members of their households experience problems in discussing a diagnosis with their doctor, who may worry about the *differential diagnosis*— that is, the medical term for making distinctions regarding conditions that look alike so that even doctors find it hard to tell them apart. This is particularly important either when seeking the right treatment or when diagnosing serious illnesses that offer little hope for cure. Also, in chronic mental illness, many doctors are reluctant to talk about the diagnosis because it may mean a *stigma* for the person—a mark of shame or discredit whereby others may identify him/her with undesirable behaviors, incompetence, or failure.

The problems in confronting the recovering individual with a dim future or the urge to shield him/her from negative reactions may prevent doctors from making a firm diagnosis or from talking about it. Yet, if you and the other relatives and friends are to be effective in caring for the recovering person, you should know as much as possible to help in that task. The problem may pose a dilemma: You need to know specifics to determine whether you can provide homecare, yet you cannot find a doctor to help you make up your mind.

The next two chapters describe how to make a decision about homecare (chapter 2) and how to find a physician with whom you can work satisfactorily (chapter 3). You may not yet be absolutely certain that you will be able to provide homecare. If so, it is only by intuition and a leap of faith that you will be committing yourself to this most difficult act of love. If you choose homecare, you and your family members and friends must prepare to deal with any of the stresses and frustrations you can imagine. You may learn about some of these from others who have experienced having a mentally ill person in the household. You should realize from the outset that your life at home will change and that everyone, especially younger members of the household, will have to take notice of the impact on their lives. But you can gain strength from knowing that family members and friends are going to be able to be of great help in restoring the person's life, and one can gain strength from his/her religious faith. If people in the social environment can learn to show *empathy* (the willingness to identify with the needs, feelings, and thoughts of the recovering person) rather than anger and rejection, the individual may reward you by recovering more fully than anyone could have expected. It is with this in mind that we write this book of suggestions for homecare, including treatment and rehabilitation of serious and long-term disorders of the brain.

2

THE DECISION TO PROVIDE HOMECARE

So faith, hope and love abide, these three; but the greatest of these is love.

1 Corinthians 13:13

THE RETURN TO HOMECARE FOR THE MENTALLY ILL

In this chapter we assume that your family member has been diagnosed as having a serious mental illness belonging to one of the four categories mentioned in the previous chapter (with or without a hospital stay). Next, you must decide (a) whether you are going to keep the mentally ill member of your household at home, and if so, (b) how you will arrange your life and take care of the recovering person without overtaxing yourself and your family. If you decide to do so, you will experience the immense difficulty of living with someone who has a chronic mental illness, and you must be prepared to give up much of your previous lifestyle. In many respects, caring for a mentally ill person is like caring for a youngster: Unpredictable needs may arise in an instant, which will preclude your previous obligations, whether personal or business. Also, bear in mind that you are unlikely to receive a lot of appreciation for this—either from the family member or from others. Please consider that you'll have to give, and give again, and to continue giving; you'll also have to be forgiving, and above all, to be able to love.

Throughout history, persons who behaved abnormally were at best tolerated, but mostly discriminated against and even put to death by the community. "Crazy" behavior or talk threatens our expectations of daily life. Everyday actions are geared toward orderly and predictable events in which we can feel in control and can participate productively in ways that our particular community considers valuable. Anything unpredictable upsets the routine of daily living and therefore threatens our feelings of security. Upsets that are too big or too numerous render us emotionally incapable of functioning consistently, especially in our work. This fear of incapacitating our emotional stability lies behind the often-expressed reluctance to socialize with the mentally ill. The hidden anxiety is, "Are you sure it is not contagious?"

The threat of disruption of family function, especially in regard to interference with the employment of the caregivers, led to the public perception in modern societies that persons with severe mental illness should be maintained in large state hospitals. Thus, household functioning could continue for families who may have a chronic mental patient yet lack secure financial means to take care of the problem privately. About a century and a half ago, patients began to be placed far away from the industrial metropolitan areas, and, as often was the case, never returned home. However, the reverse process toward providing treatment in the community was initiated in the 1960s, and in the U.S. today, about 40% of those who suffer from schizophrenia are cared for at home, and approximately 70% of all the seriously mentally ill live in a household. European estimates for homecare are higher: Between 50 and 70% of chronic schizophrenics are discharged into the care of relatives or friends, and up to 90% of the seriously mentally ill live in households!

In the family, mental illness, especially if chronic, triggers emotional stress because it forces us to act or react to irrational demands. Mental illness in the family ranks with such overpowering stressors as death, divorce, loss of a job, serious accident, or catastrophic financial problems. Moreover, the occurrence of mental illness can cause these stressful events or can lead to other stressors, such as abuse of alcohol or other drugs.

The problems now caused by trying to care for mental patients at home have been found to be less harmful to society than the century-old placement of the patient in a state-governed hospital—which often led to "out of sight" becoming "out of mind." In particular, financial constraints have forced communities to keep their members out of expensive acute or long-term care hospitals as long as possible. Also, we are now learning to understand mental illness better and thus are better able to cope with its chronic manifestations. However, the decision to keep a mentally ill family member at home must be thought through carefully.

EVALUATING YOUR HOMECARE HOUSEHOLD

Before discussing some specific advantages and disadvantages of homecare for the mentally ill, let us consider the basic requirements for the homecare environment. Of primary concern are the family and friends in the home environment. Two aspects of life in an intimate social group are important for the mentally ill: its size and the attitude of its members. There is reason to believe that the chronic mentally ill are unable to handle effectively a large *social field* (that is, the number of intimate social relations). Especially, schizophrenics seem to do best when living in a household of no more than three to five relatives or friends. Sharing an apartment or house with this number of people is about the upper limit of closeness, or lack of privacy, that can be tolerated by an emotionally vulnerable person.

Assuming that your family household is of an appropriate size, your family members need no formal education to be able to interact with most of the mentally ill. However, you (and your family) should probably have a nonjudgmental attitude, an open mind, and a willingness to learn. This receptive predisposition should pervade your responses to emotional and behavioral problems during daily contacts with your mentally ill family member. These open-hearted interactions also promote your early recognition of (possibly recurring) positive symptoms and your constant vigilance and efforts required to overcome negative symptoms.

Positive and negative symptoms (described in chapter 1) are important for you to evaluate the patient's condition, so we mention those that are most often seen even after successful treatment. Positive symptoms should be minimal, but when you ask, a recovering person often will admit to hearing voices or having delusions, including the possession of unusual personal powers. Sometimes, you may hear the inverse: Individuals mention that they hear their own thoughts broadcast by the media or that their life is curtailed because others conspire against them. Be alert for any reported increase of such symptoms. Also, notice whether the person's behavior shows such typical preoccupations with his/her inner life, as shown either by talking and laughing to him/herself, or by watching too intently what others say or what comes over radio or television.

Especially in schizophrenia, negative symptoms are more likely to persist even after the patient has responded well to hospital treatment for positive symptoms. Some of the most common negative symptoms are apathy and lack of initiative, difficulties in paying attention and poverty of speech, narrowing of ideas and a *flat affect* (meaning that the person is often withdrawn, shows no curiosity for his/her surroundings, and does not react emotionally to sad or happy events). The problem is that all of us have periods in which one or more of these symptoms appear to affect us. However, in contrast to the mentally ill, such moods do not last long in normal people, and rarely do all symptoms manifest themselves at the same time. In the mental patient, the most disturbing and baffling symptom may be *anhedonia*—the inability to enjoy or experience pleasure. Nothing is more unnerving than bringing someone to a party or a picnic and never getting any reaction out of the person.

It is of the greatest importance to learn to look for these symptoms and learn to check for fluctuations in the ill person's behavior with an eye to preventing sudden relapses. Take advantage of improvements in negative behavior, initiative, and attention so that you will be able to spur the recovering individual on to greater participation.

DEVELOPING YOUR HOMECARE SKILLS

Some skills that may help the chronic mentally ill make a comeback into productive living are (a) acceptance and understanding of the illness and its requirements for treatment and care, (b) interpersonal skills, and (c) perseverance. The importance and value of your development of these can't be overstated.

Learning to accept and understand the illness, the treatment, and the care. All members of your household must try to understand the illness and must agree to the care and treatment, especially regarding maintenance medication, if prescribed. Unless you and other family and friends understand and agree with the planned therapeutic approach, your attitudes toward particular routines will send conflicting messages to the recovering individual and the resulting confusion may lead to rehospitalization. Try to listen to and learn from the doctor, the social worker, the rehabilitation counselor, and other professionals regarding different needs

of the ill person. Try also to tolerate any annoying consequences of remaining symptoms, but be firm in helping the
recovering person to overcome tendencies arising from his/
her illness, such as social withdrawal, lack of initiative, difficulties in coming to a conclusion, or reluctance to act. Also,
try to suppress irritation when noticing that the individual
does not seem to appreciate, enjoy, or even respond to an
event that you may have planned carefully for his or her
pleasure.

Interpersonal skills. Interpersonal skills are needed, primarily to communicate both with the patient and with all concerned with the illness, and to solve problems in a way that
balances diverse family interests. It's often hard not only to
think of the ill member of the household, but also to make
sure that everyone understands each other's particular
needs. Naturally, a solution-oriented (not blame-based) approach and a repertoire of problem-solving skills are key. It
also helps to consciously try to keep up a good mood and to
inject humor into the situation.

Related to your communication and problem-solving skills
is *emotional self-control*—the ability to keep cool under adverse
circumstances while remaining focused on mutually agreed-
upon expectations. When the recovering individual has
agreed to look for a job, do not lose your temper when this
promise is not promptly kept. Continue to try over and over
again to elicit his/her compliance with the agreement. Do
not offer any way out of this "chore" (see chapter 5). Firmly,
yet calmly, go over all previous considerations again—even if
you feel like screaming!

If you or another family member are not careful in expressing feelings regarding the recovering individual's behavior
or attitudes, the resulting emotional atmosphere can influence significantly the likelihood of relapse. In particular,
refrain from making critical comments, from showing anger
or hostility, and from becoming overinvolved with private
aspects of the mentally ill person's life. No matter how in-

sistent you have to be when communicating expectations to the ill member of the household, this should never lead to emotional overinvolvement. Similarly, do not openly voice critical comments about noticeably ill behavior or thoughts, and above all, never be hostile or rejecting. If you have to comment on objectionable behavior, do it in the form of expressing dissatisfaction rather than criticism. For instance, when the individual has failed to take a shower in the morning say, "I am sorry that you have not showered yet; please do it before you leave," rather than "Why have you not checked your schedule in order to remember to take a shower!"

Also, when, for the sake of privacy, you have to ignore the individual, don't do it at a time when it could be interpreted as punishment. Withhold social contact to give time to heal in private, but not to hurt or to show disinterest. This means that you must be prepared to deal in a creative yet factual manner with specific social problems caused by the individual's irritability or hypersensitivity, possible (sexual) aggressiveness, or obstinacy and negativism. Often, after problems have arisen, the person may be depressed or refuse to talk. Practice trying to lighten the situation or bring out some humorous aspect of the situation.

Further, try to educate family members to avoid judgmental attitudes and criticism because over the long term, the negative emotional atmosphere of a household may contribute to rehospitalization. Persons who express their negative feelings about a chronically ill member of the household generally have a low tolerance for disturbed behavior or even for what they consider undesirable personality traits. Such persons also tend to look at the social and employment problems resulting from chronic mental illness as willfullness or laziness. Learning new realistic attitudes may encourage the critical family member to learn new helpful behaviors.

Perseverance. Always remember that you are in for the long haul and that homecare may take much of your day at critical times. Rehabilitating the patient to take his/her place in the community is more of an art than a science and requires endurance and love above all.

ASSESSING YOUR HOMECARE LOCATION

Size. Not only are loving attention and time needed to help the mental patient get well; homecare also requires a safe, suitable place. We all need privacy at times, and constant exposure to mental and emotional problems can be exhausting. It would not do to share a small space (such as a one-bedroom apartment) with a mentally ill person because you or he/she must have your areas of retreat while keeping yourself available on short notice. In such a case, you would do better by moving to a larger place or renting an additional apartment in the same complex or close by.

Safety. The mentally ill person needs protection from those persons who could easily victimize the individual, from environmental dangers, and from the person's own impulses. For instance, life in a drug-infested neighborhood would be hazardous to a recovering person, especially if he/she has had an abuse problem. Likewise, living next to commuter railroad tracks or a main highway is not desirable. For demented persons with organic brain disease, the house must be secured. In particular, those suffering from Alzheimer's disease often show a stage in their progressive dementia in which they try to leave the house during all hours of night and day. You then will have to install special locks to prevent such persons from leaving and wandering away at times when you sleep or cannot pay attention.

A final consideration for the choice of location for homecare is the availability of cultural resources and other social supports in your community. This should fit in with the patient's cultural values in order to allow the patient opportunities to develop proper social networks. Help in this respect is also available through patient self-help groups and clubhouses (see chapter 12).

ADVANTAGES OF PROVIDING HOMECARE

Maintaining attachments. It can be very satisfying to act on the basis of deeply felt attachments to family or friends. Our intuitive notion of belief in the healing function both of life at home and of the continuation of experiencing love and friendship on a daily basis is basically correct. It often is a devastating experience for the patient to hear, especially after the acute phase of the illness has passed, that return to home is impossible. Further, social relationships must be maintained on a daily basis if we are to prevent their disruption. Once a relationship is broken, it takes much more time to restore it (if that is still possible) than it would have taken to maintain it. Parents and spouses often intuitively resist suggestions that a patient should not return home. Even if in some instances this initially may be good advice, it is generally possible to support an interest in homecare, given proper safeguards.

Sharing common goals. Caring for someone in the family may provide a life focus for family members and friends. Such a communal interest helps strengthen feelings of cooperation and willing sacrifice within a small group and often acts to prevent loss of contact and mutual interest when group members move away. As remarked before, it is important that all agree on the goals and methods of homecare treatment (see the case of Carlos in this chapter) and are willing to restrain their own feelings regarding aspects of the recovering person's life (see the case of Bernard in this chapter).

Fostering independence, initiative, and productivity. The quality of life at home is better than in an institution. A long-term stay in a large hospital or nursing home contributes to passivity, loss of initiative, decrease in self-esteem, and abandonment of good habits in grooming and other activities of self-care and daily living. Even a stay of a few months in an institution often contributes to the development of such undesirable behaviors as sloppiness in dress or habits, disregard for punctuality or completion of a task, and so on. Such behaviors in themselves can lead to a lowered level of expectations in the mentally ill person. Even if he/she recovers from the illness that led to hospitalization, this in itself may result in his/her wish for no more than food and shelter ("a hot and a cot").

The passivity of institutionalized patients occurs because patient care on a large scale *must* result in the feeling that following orders from staff is the only way to stay out of trouble. Food and shelter is provided at the convenience of staff schedules; many enterprising behaviors are not welcome because they disrupt the routine and may slow down the provision of services to large numbers of persons at the same time. It has been found that after a while, these symptoms of institutionalization become greater barriers to discharge and life in the community than the mental disorder itself. Belatedly, institutions have started spending efforts and financial resources to overcome these results of their own striving toward efficiency. A good patient (passive, predictable) on a hospital ward often does not show the type of behaviors expected in the community!

In the community a recovering person has greater chances to overcome some of the negative symptoms of his/her disease and begin to participate again in productive activities, which brings hope for the future. The wide variety of challenges and opportunities offered by living in the community provide the best antidote to feelings of hopelessness and passivity in the person with chronic mental illness.

Personal and emotional reasons for providing homecare may also move you strongly to want to offer it to your loved one. You may feel greatly uplifted to realize that successfully expressing your love to someone creates hope. But you'll have to weigh this against some potentially negative impacts on your household and personal life.

DISADVANTAGES OF KEEPING THE PATIENT AT HOME

The following powerful disadvantages, especially during an acute phase of the illness, or during times that one or more positive symptoms return, must be taken into account. Therefore, in order to minimize failure when acute symptoms are not fully controlled, preparation for homecare should always consider the timing and conditions of discharge (see chapter 6).

Potential for unhealthy conflict. A compelling disadvantage of homecare is the potential for violent conflict within the family because of the strong emotions that the disturbed behavior or communication of the patient may provoke. Unbearable stress may result, especially if family members or close friends have difficulties accepting the particular characteristics of the mental illness, or they fail to stick to realistic expectations about the recovering person's behavior.

Bernard, whose hospitalization had forced him to drop out of graduate school, came home early in summer as a transition from the hospital to a possible return to school. The father had a professional practice in which the mother used to assist on a part-time basis. Because of the increased attention needed for the household, in which two younger siblings of high-school age also resided, it was decided that the mother would temporarily stay home. This decision was not too difficult to make because the practice usually slowed down during the summer months anyway.

There was an expectation that Bernard would soon be able to spend time away from home by himself, either by getting a job or by beginning to attend some adult education classes as soon as possible. However, he failed at a job as a sales aide, and subsequent job interviews did not lead to results. It then became clear that Bernard had little initiative and no motivation to leave his room, where he mostly slept or read, or the family room, where he watched TV. When encouraged to socialize or look into courses at local schools, Bernard found plausible reasons for inaction: He did not know too many people any more, he was reluctant to have strangers find out about his illness, and so on. It became increasingly evident that without further improvement, Bernard would continue to require the daytime presence of others in the household. When fall approached, the father became more and more exasperated by Bernard's increasing withdrawal and lack of progress. Pretty soon, the routine question of what he had done with his day became occasion for angry words, and when Bernard's homebound behavior one day led to an accusation by his younger brother of ruining a planned family outing, the resulting serious fistfight landed Bernard back in the hospital. There, it was determined that he had suffered a return of threatening auditory hallucinations that occupied him to the extent that he was afraid to leave the house.

This was a case of a positive symptom reappearing and thereby aggravating negative symptom behavior to which nobody in the home had been properly sensitive. Subsequent specific education of the family members (a) to be alert to such increases in symptoms and (b) to refrain from expressing their emotional reactions to Bernard's negative symptoms improved the home atmosphere. A more frequent schedule of psychiatric office visits after discharge also helped prevent further relapses of Bernard's illness.

Discord among family members. Disruption of relationships among family members and close friends may result from disagreement about one or another aspect of the patient's behavior. This may also lead to rehospitalization when it results in the individual's needs being neglected. As in the case of Bernard, education and agreement on realistic expectations help prevent this type of failure in the social network.

Carlos, a 25-year-old office worker of Hispanic descent, had been hospitalized briefly seven times since becoming mentally ill at age 22. He managed to hold onto his job, although this became more problematic after each hospitalization. He also obtained his own quarters in the same apartment complex in which his parents resided. Although his parents, older brother, and friends all stood by and assisted him in many respects, they continually differed in opinion regarding Carlos's taking his medication and attending Alcoholics Anonymous (AA) meetings. Whenever Carlos felt good, he would try by himself to do without medication, and he would be inclined to resume an unrestricted social life. But in view of the fact that his last three hospitalizations had been precipitated by alcohol abuse and concomitant neglect of taking his prescribed medications, his psychiatrist had given him the choice of taking disulfiram (Antabuse®) medication daily to prevent drinking or attending AA. Neither of these choices met with the approval of his brother or with their boyhood circle of friends, who wanted him to honor the values of their social club, which included drinking rituals. They thought little of medication and reminded Carlos repeatedly that the manly way to deal with his illness was to be strong, to stay out of the hospital, and to learn to tolerate alcohol. His parents, who were closest to him in terms of daily living, urged him to keep attending AA, or otherwise to try using Antabuse®. The recovering individual himself felt caught between behaving as part of his culture and peer group or following the advice of his psychiatrist. A full family therapeutic session, laying bare the reasons for the medical and more protective viewpoints of the psychiatrist and his parents, made it possible for Carlos's brother to accept the patient's need to abstain from drinking without diminishing his machismo.

In this case, it was clear that not everyone in the immediate environment of the patient shared the chosen treatment philosophy. Also, there existed unfamiliarity with the danger that mind-altering chemical substances (of which alcohol is the oldest!) pose to a person with serious mental illness. Apart from increasing insight into the illness, the case solution required a good deal of humor. The psychiatrist, using a light touch, brought the implied ludicrousness of the situation out into the open. He reminded one and all in the session (parents, brother, Carlos) of their shared wish to achieve one goal (staying out of the hospital), while giving the recovering individual diametrically opposed options: those of being a patient and those of being a proud Hispanic male! Education had succeeded when both Carlos and his brother could finally shake their heads and laugh about this dilemma.

Need for hospital services and resources. Sometimes, the patient needs proper therapeutic and environmental conditions that only a hospital can provide. The best example is the environmental supervision and treatment for a suicidal or violent patient. This again brings up the point that any discharge from an institutional environment should take place after staff, family, and patient all have come to agreement regarding the conditions of life in the community. Besides the potential danger to the patient's or other people's lives, carefully consider the continuity of treatment, care, and rehabilitation after discharge (see chapter 6).

FINANCIAL CONSIDERATIONS IN HOMECARE

It is not easy to estimate the financial consequences of homecare. There may be short-term disadvantages as well as long-term advantages. In the long run, successful homecare may save a substantial amount of money, estimated at up to 40% if compared with hospitalization. However, especially in the beginning stages, homecare can be expensive because provision of specific services by professionals or agencies at different sites are often not covered by private medical insurance. Therefore, in considering homecare, calculate the short-term and long-term financial impact on your family's private resources. If it turns out that you'll have difficulties providing the funds for continuing homecare, you would do well to check around for public financial support before your family member is discharged from the institution.

Because alternatives to hospital care have proven to be less expensive, social service agencies should be eager to help you maintain someone with chronic illness in the community. Basically, any person who has been ill and incapable of competitive work for more than a year, or who has been found to be disabled after previous employment, is eligible for federal and state aid. Consider that the recovering individual may qualify for the (part) coverage of medical costs through government aid in the form of Medicare (for those over 65) or Medicaid (for those considered truly indigent).

Another factor to consider are the nonmedical costs for room, board, transportation, and personal expenses. You may get an idea of these costs if you take into account the annual charges (ranging from $15,000 to $36,000) of few agencies that undertake to provide all-inclusive services for the mentally ill. These sizeable costs depend on where you live and whether your recovering family member is eligible for governmental support. Support may be in the form of public assistance ("welfare"), disability insurance benefits from the Social Security Administration (SSA; for those who contributed Social Security payments for a sufficient time), or Supplemental Security Income (SSI, for those 65 years and older, or those who are considered indigent because they are blind or disabled and do not qualify for SSA benefits). Again, it is important in the case of the chronic mentally ill to establish whether they would be eligible for SSI because this also may establish eligibility for other assistance programs. Medicaid was already mentioned, but SSI may also qualify the patient for vocational rehabilitation services, food stamps, and such programs as housing assistance. Details of governmental support differ from state to state and across the provinces of Canada. In addition to establishing contact with federal offices, obtaining information through such local networks as family support groups (see chapter 12) may turn out to be most effective.

Finally, keep careful records of any costs associated with the mental illness. According to the definition of the Internal Revenue Service, medical expenses are money paid for preventing, treating, and alleviating diseases or disabilities of a taxpayer and his/her dependents. And more than you think may therefore be tax deductible!

PRIORITIES AFTER YOU HAVE DECIDED ON HOMECARE

If you have made the decision to try homecare, you should assess your own priorities for which arrangements are to be completed—preferably before the member of your household is discharged. The following points need to be settled:

1. Who is to be the homecare coordinator? This is the most important consideration in regard to homecare. This individual will (a) be the one to communicate with the primary physician (see chapters 3 and 4), (b) coordinate all services rendered by fostering communication between the recovering person and the homecare treatment team members (see chapter 5), and (c) monitor the implementation of the homecare plan and the individual's progress. In most cases, the homecare coordinator will be the head of your household. But there are instances in which you might want to place these responsibilities in the hands of another person, preferably a mental health professional. Following this listing, two case histories show the importance of either an outsider or a household member in the role as coordinator of primary caregivers.

2. Who is the primary care physician? This is the second most important (and much more complicated) choice, discussed in chapter 3.

3. How will the physical *and* mental health needs be taken care of? This may depend on the choice of the primary physician, and it is discussed in detail in chapter 4.

4. How will the composition and functioning of the homecare team help the recovering individual to lead an active, and preferably productive, life in the community? This is discussed in chapter 5.

5. What will be the role of long-term medication in the recovery of the individual? This is discussed in chapter 7.

6. How will special needs of the recovering individual be taken care of? Because chronic mental illness disrupts interpersonal relations, may interfere with expressions of the sexual drive, and often distorts spiritual and

religious needs, chapters 8 to 12 are devoted to these topics.

FEATURES OF EFFECTIVE HOMECARE

We end this chapter by reviewing some determinants of effective homecare in the cases of William (son of well-to-do parents) and Zena (the wife of a low-income manager).

William is a young adult schizophrenic with a history of repeat hospitalizations during his 20s. Excessive expectations from his family after his two first discharges contributed to his subsequent relapses. After his third and last hospitalization, he was discharged with an excellent medication regimen, which completely suppressed his positive symptoms. By this time, the parents had decided to look for assistance outside their household to coordinate the convalescent care for their son. They succeeded in locating someone experienced in working with the mentally ill, who was also liked and ultimately fully trusted by their son.

The coordinator then established contacts in the community for the three main goals of aftercare. First, a roof over the head: It was decided that William should no longer live in the household of his parents but in an apartment nearby. The coordinator established relationships and secured understanding with the landlord and neighbors. Second, a daily focus of activity: William agreed to attend a psychiatric rehabilitation program and, after on-the-job training, he was placed in an office job working with computers. The coordinator, in cooperation with her team members (a rehabilitation counselor and the treating psychiatrist) prepared William for this career choice and provided information leading to the choice of medication proper for the final job placement. Third, a quality of life: William was encouraged to attend a church of his choice, to join a country club, and to expose himself to a variety of social settings. The coordinator initially accompanied William in a discreet manner, and she arranged for other members of the homecare team (William's parents and siblings, a golf pro, and a female friend from his high school days) to keep William socially involved.

Presently, William lives in his own apartment, is taking his medications, and monitors himself for the recurrence of symptoms. He is also working regularly, and he actually has not shown unscheduled absenteeism in over a year. His primary caregivers have also stimulated him sufficiently, in that he plays golf once a week (11 handicap), and goes to religious services and social events without much prodding.

All of these improvements in William's quality of life could not have been foreseen when he did so badly in the community that he had to be hospitalized for the third time. The basic insights that turned his life around were the realization by his parents that they would be unable to remain neutral in day-to-day living with their mentally ill son, and the good fit between the recovering person, his homecare coordinator, and the primary physician. One could say that all this was possible only because the parents were able and willing to pay for the services needed to allow their son to regain his place in the community. But the following case history shows that even with little money, and a homecare team limited to family members and friends, satisfactory results can be obtained.

Zena, a 56-year-old clerical worker, noticed one day that she could not distinguish right from left, which interfered with her work and daily life. Initially, she and her husband, who manages a gas station, were not concerned. But when the quality of her work and household functions began to deteriorate, they consulted their primary physician. After several months of testing and consultations with a neurologist and a psychiatrist, it became clear that Zena suffered from Alzheimer's disease. Apart from her specific problem in mental functioning, CAT scans (CAT refers to "computerized axial tomography") and skull X-rays showed enlarged ventricles of the brain, as well as shrinking of the cortex, all indicative of the Alzheimer diagnosis.

After diagnosis, the primary physician reviewed what the couple and their grown children, who lived independently nearby, should prepare for, in view of the unavoidable decrease of Zena's functions. In the first place, there were to be financial considerations, and then the family would have to decide how and for how long they would be able to care for Zena at home. All these issues were not discussed in one session, but over time the doctor discussed them and guided Zena and her husband in the decision making.

Financially, Zena's health benefits from her (by now threatened) job ceased shortly after the diagnosis. Also, she had to file for disability as soon as she lost her job. The doctor then suggested that she might want to prepare for psychiatric rehabilitation and find other, less mentally demanding, work, via the State Vocational Rehabilitation Services. Finally, once it became clear that Zena was no longer employable, she had to prepare to file for Medicaid.

Apart from these financial preparations, the conditions for keeping Zena at home were discussed each time new symptoms appeared. First, the only adjustments that needed to be made were that Zena obtain help from husband or children in shopping and doing household chores, while her husband had to begin handling all financial transactions and correspondence. Then, when Zena became less coordinated in her day-to-day activities and showed signs of being restless and disoriented, sometimes trying to leave the home at night, husband and children planned housesitting with Zena. Whenever they were not available, friends and neighbors took over. Finally, when Zena started to become incontinent, a nursing service was asked to make home calls.

This may not seem to be a success story, but consider what was accomplished. In the end, 5 years after the diagnosis was made, Zena had to be placed in a nursing home because the homecare team guided by the doctor and her husband could no longer take satisfactory care of her. Zena died after 2 more years, having outlived the average time of 4–5 years between diagnosis and death in Alzheimer's disease. And the majority of those years were spent within her own household while surrounded by her own family and friends! One could not hope for a better quality of life if one suffers from progressive dementia.

3

CHOOSING THE HOMECARE COORDINATOR AND THE PRIMARY CARE PHYSICIAN

Oh yet we trust that somehow good
Will be the final goal of ill

Tennyson, In Memoriam

WHY AND HOW TO CHOOSE THE HOMECARE COORDINATOR

After making the decision to keep a mentally ill family member or friend at home, your family must choose your homecare coordinator. The homecare coordinator coordinates the care by soliciting cooperation and input from the entire family (and from a network of helpers, the homecare team). Initially, the coordinator may have to work alone with the recovering person because it may take some time to redevelop rapport and trust between the ill person and other members of the family. Therefore, in the beginning, it is best for the mentally ill individual to rely on one person. Too many people with too many demands will cause the recovering person to react with anger and frustration. But, if the homecare coordinator explains what should and should not happen, the homecare team can refer to this information when relating with the recovering person. For example, when the recovering individual is doing something other than what is listed on a preplanned schedule (see chapter 5, Step 5), a team member might ask, "What does your schedule say that you should be doing?" This approach takes the onus off the team member and puts it on the recovering person and the schedule.

If relatives and friends are apprehensive about their capabilities in helping the recovering individual, they may want to hire a mental health provider as the homecare coordinator. The hired provider can also serve as a companion for outings with the family, to movies, to sporting games, or to restaurants. Consider the following qualities if you or a family member will be the homecare coordinator, or if a mental health provider is going to be hired for that role:

- Kindness and patience
- Willingness to work as an advocate for the rights of the ill person
- Egalitarian and collegial (The coordinator should see him/herself as a friend and not a sitter.)
- Easy to get along with and not overly aggressive
- Consistency (The ill person will have a hard time progressing if the caregiver is not consistent in what is said or done. A recovering person needs a consistent, structured program.)
- Humility (The coordinator should not see him/herself as being better or more intelligent that the recovering person or the family.)

- Mental stability (Don't overlook the hiring of a physically handicapped person, who, if emotionally stable, may relate well because of his/her own understanding of handicapping conditions.)
- Inoffensiveness (The coordinator must show no offensive mannerisms, gestures, or behaviors peculiar to that person only—if a mannerism bothers you, it certainly would bother the recovering person.)

The homecare coordinator may live in the same household or may simply spend scheduled time with the recovering person. The coordinator is responsible for helping to define goals and to decide the route to take in order to reach those goals. It is his/her job to set up and attend family meetings. Even if the coordinator is a hired person, he/she in essence becomes part of the family, functioning primarily on the behalf of the ill individual. It is also part of the coordinator's job description to see that the ill person is not isolated from the other family members. When possible, the coordinator should accompany the recovering individual on family outings and attend family meals. This will put both the family and the ill individual at ease with each other, and it will establish the grounds for understanding and accepting the handicapped person. It also makes the family more comfortable with the ill relative at times when the coordinator is not around. If you have decided to hire a coordinator, don't become too dependent, as he/she may suffer job "burnout." Make sure that you leave the door open for discussions about misunderstandings.

NOTE: Throughout the remaining chapters of this book, it is assumed that the reader is the family's homecare coordinator. Nonetheless, all family members would benefit from the information provided herein. If you, the reader, are not the coordinator, you will discover how to help the coordinator to provide the optimal environment for all members of the family, including your mentally ill family member.

WHY AND HOW TO CHOOSE A PRIMARY CARE PHYSICIAN

After selecting a homecare coordinator, give the highest priority to obtaining the services of the most suitable medical doctor available to monitor the proposed homecare. If you can find a qualified psychiatrist (or if the hospital psychiatrist is willing to continue treatment on an outpatient basis), so much the better. However, you may have to settle for any M.D. who is both interested in the recovering member of the household and willing to put up with the demands of homecare. In most cases, doctors (other than psychiatrists) available to act as the primary care physician are general or family practitioners or internists (see also chapter 4). Empathy for the patient and willingness to make a long-term commitment is as paramount for the treating doctor as it is for anyone else on the homecare team. Another important consideration is whether the M.D. is willing and able to play a role as part of your homecare team (see also chapter 5).

If the M.D. knows the individual and knows some of the mental problems existing before he/she was hospitalized, it is likely that the needed long-term commitment to treat can be obtained quickly. In many cases, however, the diagnosis of mental illness with chronic problems is reached in the institutional treatment setting without involvement of community physicians. In such cases, how do you locate a physician willing and able to participate in providing homecare?

About 2 million or more of the chronic seriously mentally ill do not reside in institutions (hospitals, nursing homes, jails, etc.). Of these (as we saw in chapter 1), perhaps one half are schizophrenic; one quarter suffer from mood disorders, severe anxiety, or phobias; and the others suffer from organic brain syndromes or severe dependence or abuse of alcohol and other drugs. Few M.D.s are willing to serve this population, and of those, few are familiar with the problems posed by homecare. All of us, therefore, need to encourage professional and popular interest in homecare.

HOW TO LOOK FOR A PRIMARY CARE PHYSICIAN

Recommended by other persons. When looking for a suitable mental health agency or private physician, begin by asking doctors, nurses, psychologists, social workers, and other health professionals for their recommendations. To check an M.D.'s credentials, you may look him/her up in the *American Medical Directory* or the *Directory of Medical Specialists.* Also, ask every friend, relative, or associate about their experiences with qualified doctors. If possible, ask others who have firsthand experience with qualified doctors. Also, you can readily contact family support groups through the local or state branches of such national associations as the National Alliance for the Mentally Ill and the Mental Health Association (see chapter 12).

Open to learning. It is important to realize from the outset that physicians, even board-certified psychiatrists, do not have all the answers to the great variety of problems in chronic mental illness. In fact, your own knowledge and that of your stricken family member or friend can be of enormous help in setting up the homecare treatment program. You are therefore looking for a physician who'll make the time and effort to learn from you and others as much as possible about the recovering individual, and who will work with you and others on a homecare plan.

Willing to participate. After you have located a potentially suitable doctor, schedule an appointment (with or without bringing the patient). At this meeting, present your expectations and discuss long-term care. Another useful procedure is to request that copies of the hospital record are forwarded to the doctor in advance of your meeting (see chapter 6). Regardless of how much information is available, it is important to involve the primary care physician as early as possible in order to obtain any contribution he/she can make toward homecare treatment planning (see chapter 4). You should indicate to the doctor that you are prepared to pay for this consultation, and that you do not necessarily consider the appointment a commitment on his/her part to partake in your household member's homecare. We believe that it is possible to come to agreement regarding long-term therapeutic involvement in a 30–60-minute interview, although some physicians might also like to spend additional time with the patient before reaching a decision.

Knowledgeable about treatment approach. During your meeting with the prospective primary care physician, it is crucial to establish satisfactorily that he/she would (a) be empathic to the patient's problems, (b) be technically competent to manage the recovering individual, as well as (c) be communicative with other members of the homecare team. Because most of the present treatment of chronic mental disorders is based on an understanding of its biological origins, try to discuss treatment philosophy by asking such simple questions as "What do you think causes schizophrenia (or depression, anxiety, drug abuse, etc.)?" Once it is clear that the doctor believes that these diseases may result from a malfunction of the brain, you might ask, "Do you believe that drugs can treat this?" (see chapter 7). The resulting conversation will quickly show whether the M.D. is conversant with present-day biological and psychosocial therapeutic approaches. He or she need not necessarily be an expert (even psychiatrists may not know all the details of these rapidly expanding treatments), but if they have heard of recent progress and are willing to contact colleagues or read some literature, they will be able to maintain and monitor the recovering household member on his/her (hospital-) prescribed drug treatment regimen.

Similar in values. A series of questions might be asked concerning a particular prominent or bothersome symptom of the patient. For instance, suppose he has a complaint about hearing voices accusing him of being homosexual because he lost his teaching job. Sample questions could be,

"What do you think can make him stop hearing voices?" then, "Should he go back to teaching?" Answers to these questions would reveal what the doctor thinks about the cause and treatment of the illness, and about homosexuality and the impact of public opinion on behavior. To find out whether values are shared may help determine what the fit between the patient and the doctor may be.

Respectful and flexible.   You must also ascertain whether the primary care physician is willing to accept suggestions for the recovering person's management from the individual him/herself, from other health professionals, or from you and other members of the homecare team, so that a home-care treatment plan (see chapter 5) may benefit from many different insights into the individual's behavior. In general, it is easy to find out during this first meeting whether the doctor is willing to listen to you and the patient as laypersons, or whether he/she expects that all that he/she says or prescribes will be accepted without much flexibility or explanation. In the latter case, the physician would not help you at all in expanding your own problem-solving skills.

Confidential where appropriate.   The next issue to settle during the initial meeting is how the primary care physician will handle the information provided him/her. Two considerations apply here. First, you should agree on how much of this information will be kept absolutely confidential. Second, you should find out how willing the M.D. will be to share information with other professional and nonprofessional helpers, relatives, or friends involved in homecare.

As to the first issue, you will have to be very explicit about matters that you don't want others than your doctor to know. Especially in chronic illness, where you often have to provide care in most, if not all, areas of your relative's or friend's life, it is hard over time to guard any aspect of the individual's life. In such cases, it is best that the patient and you decide who of your homecare team members should know, and for the rest trust the discretion of your primary physician. It often is not only impossible, but also not in the individual's best interest to have no one but the doctor know something that may significantly affect the individual's behavior.

> Debra, a 28-year-old female college graduate, has been struggling with a barbiturate addiction for the past 5 years. While employed as the secretary of a local M.D., she had over a period of time falsified his signature on many prescriptions and cleverly covered this up when a pharmacy called in. In the past year, her addiction had deteriorated to the point where she was unable to work and had gone into debt to purchase illegal barbiturates. She finally ended up losing her apartment and wandering in the streets. After an attempted suicide, she entered a detoxification program, and she has recovered enough to be able to confide fully in her parents and accept help from them.

> When preparing for homecare with the primary physician, the question of her criminal behavior came up in regard to possible employment. Debra and her parents agreed that if the doctor was to be involved in clearing her for a job, it would be left up to his discretion whether he would mention her past history of addiction involving illegal activities. There was also agreement that the doctor would inform Debra and her parents of any such information release.

This brings up the next issue: To what extent should you and the primary physician determine in advance what particular aspects of the recovering individual's prior history should be shared with which members of the homecare team (see chapter 5). The willingness to share information is greater with practitioners who already work in such a multidisciplinary setting as a mental health center or a rehabilitation agency. Put in other words, if you seek privacy, it certainly is preferable to deal with a private practitioner, whose secretary or nurse is likely to be the only one with access to office records. However, if you seek involvement of others to work as a team for the benefit of the recovering individual, you will have to make sure that the primary physician of your choice does not mind working as part of a team and will be able to communicate easily while remaining aware of who needs to know what.

Available.   A final consideration is the availability of the primary care physician in cases of crises and emergencies: Will you be able to reach the doctor? Help may be needed on weekends, holidays, or in the middle of the night. In many cases, an experienced physician can handle crises on the phone by communicating with other team members. In case of an emergency needing medical attention, however, the physician may either handle it personally or refer you to a hospital or crisis center. Again, the physician you choose must be willing to be involved on a daily basis if needed and must be experienced in communicating and establishing contact with community health facilities. You should ask about the primary care physician's feelings on this matter.

Mutually willing to cooperate.   It is almost impossible in one visit to find out whether the physician of your choice will be able to fulfill all these criteria in a satisfactory manner. Working with him/her is going to be the only way in which full mutual trust can be established over time. It is inevitable that at some time, errors of judgment or disappointments will occur on both sides. However, as long as you are willing to work to maintain positive relationships among the primary care physician, the recovering individual, and you, all will benefit in the long run. Make an effort to think about and write down what you discuss in your meetings with the doctor. Include specific questions that will allow you to find out in what direction and how fast you, the patient, and the doctor will be going.

Trustworthy and reliable.   Often, your questions will lead to more questions because your doctor may be able to foresee complications and to look farther into the future than you do. A doctor's task is to anticipate, and it is his/her technique of asking or answering that will put you at ease and will build trust. A psychiatrist is specially trained to perform this function, and, as emphasized previously, if you can find a suitable psychiatrist, work hard to involve him or her as the primary care physician. However, the psychiatric specialty is no guarantee for the ability to work with the chronic mental patient. Still seek to set up an initial meeting with any M.D. who comes recommended. Human relationships are personal and intuitive: If you like and trust the doctor, you should make up your mind there and then. But if you are not sure after the interview, allow yourself time to shop around for the best possible primary care physician, following the additional considerations provided in chapter 4.

WHAT ABOUT OTHER MEMBERS OF THE HOMECARE TEAM?

In addition to the primary care physician, you might need to engage others in the ongoing care of the recovering individual. A homecare team may be as small as the primary physician and the homecare coordinator. Or it may be so large as to include a hired homecare coordinator, other mental health professionals, family members, and friends. Nonphysician mental health professionals often have more time for continuing contact and for assessment of the functioning of the recovering person. Clinical psychologists, nurses, social workers, occupational therapists, rehabilitation counselors, teachers, the clergy, and others may be suitable for recruitment, especially if they have had prior exposure to working with the mentally ill. Their qualifications and roles are discussed in chapter 6; here, we review how you should determine whether they would fit into your homecare team.

All that was said previously about the personal qualifications of the doctor applies to homecare team members: They should (a) be empathic with the recovering individual, (b) have an interest in finding out about the particular mental illness, (c) be willing to work with the person as part of a team, (d) be able to make a long-term commitment to the team, and (e) (preferably) have experience with and be available to deal with crises and emergencies (see chapter 11). Just as it is unlikely that a physician can fulfill all of these criteria, so it is with the members of your team, but thinking and talking about these issues with your team members is a start.

THE MEDICAL ROLE OF A HOMECARE COORDINATOR

It is of course possible that no suitable psychiatrist, general physician, or other M.D. is available to act as a primary care physician. You may, in fact, have access only to an M.D. who will continue prescribing the medication with which the patient was discharged by the treating institution. In that case, you, as the homecare coordinator, may have to monitor the recovering person yourself. Or you may want to leave this to a mental health professional (nurse, social worker, clinical psychologist, or other professional) to be hired as homecare coordinator. He or she will have to undertake the responsibility for monitoring the individual's health and behavior and for guiding the homecare team. In such instances, you should make sure to have full agreement between yourself and the homecare coordinator regarding the cost of his/her services, the nature of the illness, and the agreed-upon treatment approach, record keeping, and confidentiality matters, as discussed in relation to physicians. In particular, you will have to discuss access to previous documentation (hospital and other medical records), as this pinpoints symptoms and describes reactions to treatment. This knowledge is especially important in times of crises and emergencies, and when there may be a need for change in medications or reason for hospitalization. In case you cannot obtain the records of previous treatments, try to have a physician give you a written summary and chronology (the exact time of occurrence in the patient's history) of the symptoms and their treatment.[1]

---

[1]Under the Freedom of Information Act, you may obtain any agency or institution records, but it is not always in the best interests of the patient to go this official route.

Again, as was the case with the primary physician, you should reach an agreement with the homecare coordinator as to what aspects of the individual's history and behavior should be kept confidential or shared with specific other members of the homecare team. The homecare coordinator should also be in charge of the schedule for any office or agency visiting appointments, including those for medication prescriptions, and he/she should be involved at all times when (medical) intervention would be needed. For your part, you should develop specific written instructions for action when you are unavailable. Details are provided in chapters 4 and 5.

4

THE ROLE OF THE PRIMARY CARE PHYSICIAN AND THE HOMECARE TEAM

John W. Lacey, III, M.D.

Into whatever houses I enter,
I will go into them for the benefit of the sick.

Hippocrates

When speaking of the primary care physician, we are most often referring to family practitioners and internists. Certainly, other categories of physicians may serve as primary care physicians, including, at times, psychiatrists themselves. However, for the purposes of this chapter, we assume that the primary care physician is not a psychiatrist. Also, we would like you to understand how a nonpsychiatrist primary care physician relates to the chronic mental patient and to those ill persons who may not yet have a clearly established diagnosis of mental illness.

The first part of this chapter examines how the primary care physician interacts with and affects the homecare team and the mentally ill person. The second part describes problems that may arise when both mental and physical illness occur concurrently.

PART 1: THE DOCTOR, THE HOMECARE TEAM, AND THE PATIENT

Physician's Attitudes and Aptitudes

As the homecare coordinator, you should be aware that physician attitudes toward the task of caring for the mentally ill person, as well as ability to provide this care, varies greatly from physician to physician. The physician's orientation toward mental illness is a direct reflection of his/her medical school's curriculum. Often, the emphasis in medical training is on defining a special biomedical disease process, as opposed to establishing the diagnosis of mental illness. While ancient medical practice was devoted to the relief of a person's symptoms, of his/her experience of ill health, modern medicine—with its burgeoning technology—is dedicated to the eradication of either the disease process or the disorder present in the individual organs and systems that give rise to ill health. Society generally encourages this approach, by favoring reimbursement and appreciation for testing and invasive activities, while giving relatively less reward for supportive treatment. Thus, the primary care physician can anticipate a greater reimbursement from third-party payors, such as Medicare or insurance companies, for cleaning out a patient's ear than for spending a greater amount of his/her time in counseling with a homecare team.

Communication between the primary care physician and the person with mental illness is another obstacle that doctors may perceive as limiting their ability to participate in the homecare team. This communication process may at times be adversely affected by (1) differences between the socio-economic, cultural, or religious background of the mentally ill person and the physician; (2) prejudice the primary care physician may harbor against mental illnesses as a result of previous experiences; and (3) the symptoms of the mental illness itself. An example of the third problem would be a patient with schizophrenia, whose thought disorder includes lack of attention, loose association, incoherence, and poverty of speech, thus directly short-circuiting information exchange with the physician.

Of all the potentially positive effects on the physician's attitude, you, as the homecare coordinator, may be the most important. Your ability—and indeed the ability of the entire homecare team—to influence the physician's approach should not be underestimated. By (a) demonstrating clear support for the mentally ill person; (b) willingly facilitating those aspects of the treatment program initiated by the primary care physician; (c) acting as an advocate for the recovering person when problems arise; and (d) demanding the best of care for him/her, in regard to both mental and physical illness, you and the rest of the homecare team can have a major positive influence on the partnership among the homecare team, the primary care physician, and the chronically mentally ill. The primary care physician will be most likely to respect and respond to any reasonable request for assistance from the homecare team when (a) you couch the request in terms that improve the partnership among those involved in the care of the mentally ill person and (b) you and the homecare team recognize the doctor's own limitations and potential frustrations.

Finding the Right Primary Care Physician

Knowing of some of the factors that may influence the primary care physician, you may now more effectively establish a relationship with the "right" (that is, best for your patient and your homecare team) primary care physician, as described in chapter 3. Most often, the primary care physician who has served as the family doctor and who has knowledge of the ill individual's medical history should be approached first. If a preexisting primary care physician relationship is not in place, then a physician must be sought to fill this role. As mentioned, information concerning physicians can be gathered from many sources, including friends, acquaintances, and other physicians.

When the list of possible candidates for primary care physician has been narrowed, make an appointment for the ill individual and you to meet with the most likely candidate. If possible, at the time of the appointment, bring the previous medical records to the physician, especially if the diagnosis of a chronic mental illness has been previously established. When such a diagnosis has been suspected but not established, be sure to express concerns, describe symptoms, and elucidate the history.

Though it is likely that the physician will interview the mentally ill person alone, you should request an audience with the physician at the time of this initial visit. In a busy practice, physicians allot very limited time for interviewing family or significant others, so prepare beforehand with a list of symptoms, concerns, and pertinent history.

At the time of the initial interview, it is appropriate to question the physician regarding his/her specific interest and training in the treatment of mental illness, thus giving an idea of the relationship that can be expected among the physician, the primary homecare givers, and the mentally ill person (see chapter 3). The physician may require a number of visits with the individual in order to assess further the nature of any present problems. At some point, it is imperative that the physician again counsel with you concerning findings, treatment plan, and other recommendations. If, at any time during the process, you or the other homecare team members do not feel comfortable with the situation or progress, express such concerns to the physician.

Again, keep in mind that each primary care physician has different interests and abilities in regard to diagnosing and treating mental illness. It may be that after the initial visit, the primary care physician will want to refer the mentally ill person to another physician with greater interest or expertise in this area or request that (additional) psychiatric consultation be obtained.

Other considerations in choosing a primary care physician include constraints, as might be seen in the case of a health insurance setting such as a health maintenance organization (HMO) or a private practice organization (PPO), wherein the choice of primary care physician and referral options by the primary care physician may be limited. You and the mentally ill individual must be prepared to reimburse the primary care physician appropriately for his/her time in working with you, just as you would expect for treatment of a physical illness.

Diagnosis—An Ongoing Process

General Survey and History

It is important for you to understand the process the primary care physician may use to evaluate the mentally ill person. The initial step in the physician's evaluation is usually to obtain an appropriate history. At present, historical information provides the foundation for diagnosing mental illness, although various technologies are expected to have increasing impact in this area in the future (see chapter 14, "A Look Toward the Future"). Aspects of the patient's history that the physician should review include the following:

1. The nature of onset of symptoms (Was the onset abrupt or gradual? Did the problem begin following a specific event, such as the death of a family member, or with a physical illness or after taking a medication or street drug?)

2. The evolution of symptoms (Has the patient had a similar episode of problems in the past?)

3. Family history of mental illness (Has major depression occurred elsewhere in your family? Have certain psychoactive drugs been used successfully to treat another ill family member?)

4. The quality of a patient's functional status at work and in the home

5. Positive signs and symptoms (such as hallucinations) at the time the patient is evaluated.

Following this general survey, a mental status examination is often the next step in the evaluation process.

Mental Status Examination

The mental status examination looks at different areas of brain functioning, including cognition, emotion, behavior, perception, and memory (discussed here next). The physician evaluates each area just as he/she would examine the heart, lungs, abdomen, and extremities during a physical examination.

Cognition involves thought processes, language, level of awareness, ability to pay attention, orientation, and insight into problems present. The physician asks questions that look at each aspect of cognition, especially orientation, attention, and memory.

Memory disturbances distort the processes by which the brain stores information for subsequent recall. When memory is impaired, the individual may try to fill the memory gaps by relating concocted stories in response to specific questions.

Emotion means feelings such as depression, joy, anger, or anxiety. The physician asks questions that may tend to bring forth emotions or show a lack of these feelings.

Behavior is assessed by observation and review of interpersonal activities.

Perception disorders include hallucinations and may involve any of the primary sensory modalities or a combination of these, such as visually hallucinating the presence of a deceased relative while hearing voices.

Differential Diagnosis

Once the mental status examination has been completed, the primary care physician combines this information with information obtained from history and from physical examination to begin to develop a differential diagnosis, or to fully understand the patient's current status. The differential diagnosis for mental illness has two basic cornerstones: (1) the need to rule out an underlying organic disease other than that of the brain itself (see chapter 1), and (2) consideration of possible different psychiatric diagnoses.

As noted previously, the basic training received by most physicians leads to an emphasis on a possible medical physical illness as the origin for symptoms, even when symptoms suggest a probable mental illness. Indeed, the more varied the complaints and problems presented, the more difficult it becomes for the physician to rule out an underlying systemic illness or successfully rule in a mental disorder as an explanation for all symptoms present.

Evaluation of Psychosomatic Symptoms

The diagnostic process is often confounded by the worldwide phenomenon called "somatization"—the mentally ill person seeks help for bodily complaints that are in actuality manifestations of the mental illness. Because about half of the patients seen by the primary care physician manifest some degree of somatization, the primary care physician needs to be able to uncover clues to the presence of this phenomenon

even in individuals who vehemently deny any mental disturbance.

From the standpoint of the primary care physician, at least
three categories of people might *present with* (that is, show, or
talk about or bring up for examination) psychosomatic
symptoms. First, a large number of persons may simply be
experiencing an acute episode of stress. Stress can increase
autonomic (i.e., involuntary nervous system) activity, causing
such symptoms as *tachycardia* (rapid heartbeat), *insomnia*
(sleeplessness), fatigue, anxiety, and loss of *libido* (interest or
enjoyment of sexuality). Persons suffering from acute stress
are generally treated by the primary care physician without
psychiatric referral.

A second category of ill persons may present with an acute
psychiatric illness but have no recognition of the nature of
their problem. These individuals may also have multiple
complaints, such as shortness of breath, insomnia or fatigue,
with the mental illness being masked by such complaints.

A third group of those looking for assistance may have
chronic psychiatric illness, with associated chronic somatization, which is used (a) to obtain secondary gain, such as
increased attention by others, (b) to manipulate the family,
(c) to avoid sex or intimacy, or (d) generally express their
dysphoria (unhappiness).

In addition, the ill person's expression of symptoms is
influenced by his/her culture, which in many cases, stigmatizes mental illness, thus resulting in denial or suppression of
psychiatric complaints. As the homecare coordinator, you
play a key role here in bringing forth history and pertinent
observation to help unmask or further clarify the status of the
mental illness. As the homecare coordinator, you can encourage the mentally ill person not to believe that it is inappropriate to complain of psychiatric symptoms to a family doctor.
Also, you can provide valuable information and additional
details to the physician in regard to the chronicity of problems and the evolution of symptoms, so that the physician can
reach appropriate conclusions as to the diagnosis and status
of the mental illness.

Is It Mental Illness or Physical Illness?

The physician's bias to rule out organic disease at the onset of the evaluation of psychiatric symptoms, while it may appear inefficient at times, is a potentially positive aspect of the role of the primary care physician. The physician is likely to view symptoms of mental illness as reflecting a dysfunction of the brain, which in turn is part of the body as a whole and influenced by the entire milieu of the body systems. This approach does appropriately acknowledge the fact that some individuals experience disruption of normal brain activity as a result of physical illness, which, if properly diagnosed and treated, may significantly improve the individual's mental functioning.

Organic brain disease shows clearly that the brain itself may be the cause of a number of problems, as when brain tumors, trauma, infections, drugs, and other toxins alter the brain functioning and result in symptoms like those attributed to functional psychoses (see chapter 1). In addition, illnesses in other parts of the body, or more diffuse and systemic illnesses, may also have profound effect on the function of the brain.

More than 100 such illnesses are presented in the physician's usual training, and they range from AIDS to zinc deficiency. Some such diseases are quite common, including hypertension and heart disease, thyroid dysfunction, various malignancies, nutritional deficiencies, cerebral vascular occlusive disease, altered carbohydrate metabolism (diabetes), anemia, and various infectious diseases such as encephalitis and meningitis. One stumbling block the primary care physician may encounter is that some of these diseases may present primarily with psychiatric symptoms, with little else in the way of symtomatology present. While in theory, this would allow for early diagnosis of such diseases, what may actually occur is that the ill person may be shunted directly to the mental health sector without adequate physiological testing to rule out the underlying medical illness. If the symptoms are then ameliorated (i.e., being made to lessen or decrease in intensity) by psychotherapy or psychopharmacology (see chapter 7), no further search may be undertaken for a systemic cause for the symptoms.

Medical Screening

As the advocate for the mentally ill person, you demand a thorough medical screening examination to rule out underlying medical illnesses as the cause for new or unexpected symptoms. Even when chronic psychiatric symptoms worsen, an evaluation should include a medical history, a mental status examination, and a general review of physiological systems. This will serve to ferret out such problems as changes in coordination, tremors, weakness, vision, memory, and alterations in sensation, as well as subtle seizure activity. Furthermore, appropriate laboratory screening, such as urinalysis, complete blood count (which looks at both red cell and white cell status), blood chemistries (which reflect kidney and liver function, as well as blood minerals and blood sugar), thyroid function tests, and measurement of certain vitamin levels, including serum B-12 folate determinations, should be considered as appropriate.

A more sophisticated examination using ever-evolving medical technologies may utilize an MRI (magnetic resonance imaging) scan or a CAT (computerized axial tomography) scan of the brain. Such tests are providing increasingly detailed ways of looking at the structure of the brain and even its functioning on a biochemical level (see chapter 14: "Looking toward the Future"). Various medical illnesses may be uncovered by this search, including those that may present as (a) *depression* (including hypothyroidism, Parkinson's disease, infectious mononucleosis, folic acid deficiency with anemia, and poisons with insecticides), or (b) *mania* or hyperactivity (including toxicity from amphetamine use, alcohol withdrawal, and hyperthyroidism).

Many illnesses may present with such *positive psychotic symptoms* as hallucinations and delusions, including amphetamine consumption, street drug use, temporal-lobe epilepsy, thyroid disorders, hypocalcemia, brain tumors, pernicious anemia, hypoglycemia, and medicine toxicities like that associated with the common medication cimetidine (Tagamet®, a drug used to treat peptic ulcers). Such conditions may alter brain function, resulting in psychiatric symptoms by a number of means: (a) a direct disabling effect on brain cells; (b) an alteration of sensory input to the brain; (c) a change in internal sensing mechanisms (thus resulting in distortion of body image); (d) a modification of the body's regulatory systems, which influence the brain's environment and nourishment; and (e) a change affecting the biochemical and electrical signals between brain cells.

Role of the Homecare Team

Your role in this process of ruling out physical causes for mental symptoms is to provide information to complete the medical history and review of systems. Often, you or other team members may give clues that the recovering individual may not notice or may be unable to express. Some clues might be changes in memory, in social interactions, and in physical symptoms such as coordination difficulty.

You and the other nonphysician members of the homecare team should become aware of symptoms of medical problems that may masquerade as *exacerbations* (i.e., worsening or intensification) of the mental illness. If no clear organic basis for psychiatric symptoms are found, then the psychiatric differential diagnosis must be considered. At that point, the primary care physician will attempt to place as clear a diagnostic label as possible on the problems present. As pointed out in chapter 1, an important step for both the physician and the patient in dealing with presenting problems is *diagnosis*, or establishing such a label.

Recognition of Nonorganic (Psychological) Causes for Somatic Complaints

Acceptance on the part of the individual of a nonorganic explanation for symptoms such as shortness of breath or fatigue is often difficult. In this situation, the challenge to both the primary care physician and you may be great because in this case, the mentally ill person may be angry, dependent, noncompliant, and demanding. Such attitudes may make the establishment of a homecare treatment program for symptoms difficult. It is imperative that such ill persons not feel abandoned by the primary care physician when symptoms are ascribed to mental illness rather than to physical illness. To prevent that, try to facilitate follow-up appointments with the primary care physician.

The physician's, the recovering individual's, and your ideas of mental illness should mesh as much as possible so that a treatment program can be formulated with a high likelihood of compliance on the part of the mentally ill person and with full enthusiasm on the part of you and the rest of the homecare team. It must be continuously reemphasized that psychosocial problems and reactions arising from a perceived illness must be noted and monitored by the homecare team, as well as by the primary care physician. The homecare team needs to learn approaches to the mentally ill person which allow for appropriate care to be given without the development of anger, rejection, or burnout.

To Refer or Not to Refer—This May Be a Question

In general, when the primary care physician manages psychiatric disorders, the modalities of treatment used include (1) psychotropic medications, (2) verbal therapy, and (3) referral for, and continuing interaction with, specialized mental health services. Once the diagnosis of mental illness has been established, the primary care physician may or may not choose the third treatment modality—to refer the mentally ill person to a psychiatrist. As indicated, referral may require continuing contacts and interactions with the other professionals involved. Primary care physicians tend to favor a single treatment modality. This relates in part to their need for treatment programs (a) that do not require large commitments of time and (b) that match their skill level in managing the problems of mental illness.

Drug therapy.   About 25% of all patients receiving any type of medication from a primary care physician are receiving a psychotropic drug. Typically, patients with mental illness receive 2–3 times more prescriptions than do those with only medical illnesses. In regard to the use of psychotropic medications (see also chapter 7), the primary care physician should ideally follow certain guidelines:

1. A comprehensive evaluation of symptoms is made, to rule out physical origin for problems present.

2. Medications are selected with specific therapeutic goals in mind and with specific symptoms targeted for monitoring progress.

3. Drug selection progress includes review of potential toxicities, drug interactions, and influences on the patient's overall functioning. (Medical tenet—first, do no harm!)

4. The drug and dosage are carefully explained to recovering person and to the coordinator.

5. Treatment contracts involving the ill person, the physician, and home coordinator are established, to help maintain compliance in regard to using the medication.

6. Follow-up is carried out by the physician in regard to the effects of the medication, both good and bad, and the needed adjustments in the treatment program as it progresses.

Verbal therapy.   The type of verbal therapy used most often by primary care physicians involves brief visits (rather than scheduled psychotherapy sessions), in which the therapy applied consists of supportive discussions, reassurance, and advice. Situations in which such brief or supportive types of verbal therapy might be of benefit include the ups and downs experienced during the course of chronic illness or when an active but not severe crisis occurs.

Referral.   While this approach of using medications and verbal therapy may be quite effective in some situations, in others, it may be less than adequate, so a psychiatric referral becomes necessary. Certainly for the more serious forms of mental illness with multifaceted problems, a referral for expert psychiatric guidance is desirable.

An Example of the Practice of Primary Care

Role of the Primary Care Physician

As an example of how treatment directed by a primary care physician may work, let's look at a particular illness, such as schizophrenia. The schizophrenias, as described in chapter 1, are a group of chronic psychiatric illnesses with symptoms that vary in intensity at any given time. Because there is no general cure, the physician's goal for this illness is to maintain the schizophrenic patient at the highest possible level of functioning. To achieve this goal, the primary care physician will probably establish periodic follow-up office visits in a consistent and safe environment where the recovering individual can discuss the events of his/her life and be offered support and advice, as needed. For example, the individual may be encouraged to discuss such symptoms as his/her delusions only in this setting rather than at work or other places where it will hinder his/her functioning.

The office visit can serve as a means of monitoring any antipsychotic medication being utilized—monitoring efficacy as well as possible side effects. Measurements of actual blood levels of certain medications, as well as other appropriate laboratory testing, may be desirable and may be obtained at the time of follow-up office visits. The efficacy of the medication can also be determined by monitoring particular target symptoms, such as hallucinations, agitation, and attention span, and by observing any impaired functioning, both in the work environment and in interpersonal relationships.

Side effects of the medication can be monitored by observing for the development of movement disorders (tardive dyskinesia, dystonia, or akinesia)[1] or excessive drowsiness. Furthermore, the office visits can serve as lookout posts for any decompensation of the chronic mental illness, which may show by deterioration of interpersonal relationships, increased agitation, or increased bizarre thought processes.

Role of the Homecare Coordinator

An increase in requests for office visits by the recovering person, an increase in visits for possible medical problems (suggesting somatization), or a failure to keep appointments may all signal possible worsening of the chronic schizophrenic illness. You should have a significant input throughout the treatment program in providing additional observation concerning illness and its treatment.

Role of a Psychiatric Referral

Furthermore, it is always appropriate for you to question the primary care physician about the possibility of psychiatric referral when observed problems are not resolved. Obviously, the process of psychiatric referral is affected by a number of factors, including the availability of clinical psychiatry, financial considerations (reimbursement of specialized psychiatric care by a particular insurance plan), and the biases of the recovering individual, as well as the rest of the homecare team, in regard to psychiatric referral.

The Partnership—Practical Aspects

As noted, the care of the mentally ill person must be looked upon as a partnership among several parties: the mentally ill

---

[1] *Tardive dyskinesia* involves twitches and other involuntary movements triggered by a disorder of the central nervous system. *Dystonia* refers to persistent focal inappropriate muscle tone. *Akinesia* is the lack of voluntary movements.

person, the primary care physician, the homecare coordinator, and the entire homecare team, along with any other specialized psychiatric caregivers. There must be free interchange of ideas among these partners, and each party must be interested in maintaining the partnership for it to be effective. Communication of facts and fears among those involved in a management process is essential. Therefore, as the homecare coordinator, you must ask questions and provide information as part of the overall management program.

Supervising the Medication

As the homecare coordinator, you should not only become familiar with medications being used, but also know of potential toxicity and expected side effects of these medications (see chapter 7 for details). Some of this information is contained in this book, but you may request additional information from the primary care physician. You may then receive copies from a compendium about medication, such as the *Physician's Desk Reference.* You may also obtain from local bookstores or from the local library a number of other sources of information concerning drugs used in treating mental and physical illnesses. This material can be read and digested, then you may direct any questions to the primary care physician concerning what you found. Again, it is your observations, or the observations by other team members, that may give clues as to the subtle effects or toxicity of medications, which could otherwise go unrecognized during brief office visits to the physician.

In this regard, the primary care physician may assign you certain responsibilities, as mentioned previously. Particularly, you often should be involved in the monitoring of compliance regarding medication.

From a physician's standpoint, monitoring blood levels of psychotropic medication will likely be necessary on a periodic basis, so it would be most helpful if you can provide the physician with an idea of just how compliant the patient has been with medication dosing, to help interpret the meaning of such blood drug levels. Further, noncompliance with appropriate use of medication may be a sign of exacerbation of the mental illness or may be the cause of such exacerbation.

To carry out this role, you may be responsible for daily laying out the medications and then observing that the medication is being taken, to further ensure compliance. For practical purposes, you may decide to use a plastic box with dividers (or other device) in which to put medications to be taken at various times during the day or night, and you may choose to require that such medications be taken in your presence or in the presence of other homecare team members whenever possible. **Compliance with the medication regimen is a major factor in treating any chronic illness, but particularly so in chronic mental disorders.** It has been observed that rehospitalization of the recovering individual is a result of failure to take medications properly in up to 80% of the cases.

Recording Medical Information

The homecare coordinator must keep a list of all medications taken by the recovering person—for both physical and mental illness. This list should be established in such a way that it can be taken to any physician (or dentist) providing treatment to the mentally ill person (as on a 3" X 5" note card such as shown in Figure 4.1). The card should also contain (a) names and telephone numbers of involved physicians and of you, the homecare coordinator; (b) major physical and psychiatric diagnoses; (c) allergies; and (d) any other medically important information.

A card such as this will help ensure that the appropriate medications and dosing prescribed by the primary physician are indeed being carried out. This list may also help prevent giving the recovering person medication that would have an adverse reaction when taken with the patient's other medications. Again, the card should be carried at all times by the patient and consulted when health care is provided. The listing of medical problems, as well as a psychiatric diagnosis,

(FRONT)

Name: _____

Address: _____

_____

Telephone Number: _____

Primary Care Physician: _____

Address and Telephone No.: _____

_____

Other Physicians Involved in Care: _____

_____

Homecare Coordinator: _____

Address and Telephone No.:_____

_____

(BACK)

Psychiatric Diagnosis: _____

Medical Diagnosis: _____

Allergies: _____

Medication   Dosage   Prescribing M.D.

1. _____

2. _____

3. _____

4. etc. _____

Figure 4.1. ID Card

will be of particular value if an emergency room visit is necessary. Here, records of the recovering person's medications and other details of history may not be readily available at a time when emergency treatment is needed. The primary care physician may also not be available, and the card carried by the recovering person may become the only source for accurate description for medications being taken, as well as for underlying medical problems. It should be noted that information contained in this list can be obtained from prescription bottles directly and reviewed and updated periodically by all the physicians involved in treating the individual at the time of follow-up office visits.

It is also desirable to complete a more detailed medical history. You may wish to do this in conjunction with the primary care physician, to list important aspects of medical history, such as previous surgeries, chronic medical illnesses, and previous adverse reactions to medications. This record should also contain a complete list of and location for all homecare team members, as well as step-by-step directions for the recovering person to follow in the event of any perceived urgent situations (see also chapter 11 on "Crisis Intervention"). This more detailed list of history, medications, and homecare team members should be carried by the recovering individual on all trips and at any time that he/she is to be seen by a new physician.

Another possibility is that the recovering person wear an ID bracelet or necklace alerting others of a medical emergency in case he/she becomes disoriented or starts hallucinating and the police become involved. This bracelet or necklace should have the name and telephone numbers of the homecare coordinator as well as of the physician. Again, all of this information may become invaluable at times of medical or other emergencies.

Speaking with the Physician

In addition to dealing with medications, an important aspect of the partnership among the ill person, the primary care physician, and you involves the need for the homecare team members to be alert and report perceived changes in the health status of the recovering individual. It is certainly true that in the office setting, the primary care physician has little time to read long letters and engage in long discussions with you or others on the spur of the moment. Therefore, you may deliver a brief note to the physician at the time of a scheduled office visit, stating in as clear terms as possible the concerns and observations of the team members. It may be necessary and indeed appropriate for you to set up an office appointment with the primary care physician for a brief discussion concerning such problems. Phone calls to the primary care physician may be an important source of help, but these should be kept to a minimum, to avoid frustrating the physician in this regard. The primary care physician bases his/her livelihood on the time he/she spends in the care of his/her patients, and reimbursement for time spent in discussions with homecare team members must be considered appropriate.

One aspect of the physician's obligation to the partnership is that of helping to introduce you and the rest of the treatment team to community resources that may help ease the burden of the home treatment program. The primary care physician should facilitate the educational processes required for all of you to become acquainted with the nature of the mental illness present and the treatment plan, as well as some basic knowledge of any medical illnesses present in the recovering individual. Do not hesitate to ask the primary care physician to help fulfill this part of the partnership obligation.

One of the axioms of clinical medicine suggests that if a physician will only listen to what the patient is saying, the patient will provide the physician with the proper diagnosis. In the case of mental illness, the physician should listen not only to the ill person but also to you and other members of the homecare team to facilitate diagnostic and treatment endeavors.

PART 2: PROBLEMS WHEN MENTAL AND PHYSICAL ILLNESS OCCUR SIMULTANEOUSLY

Unfortunately, a person may be afflicted with mental illness, and he/she may simultaneously experience any of the possible physical illnesses as well. Such physical illnesses are more likely to go unrecognized or misdiagnosed in mentally ill persons for the reasons discussed previously, including both somatization and difficulty in communication between the physician and the ill individual. Somatization may cause clues to medical illness, to be obscured and to go unheeded by the physician. Thus, like the boy who cried "wolf" too often, the patient with somatization may complain so often of chest pain that when more ominous chest pains actually reflecting underlying heart disease occur, she/he is ignored because the complaint has been voiced so many times in the past, without any true underlying physical basis. Also, many mental patients are less aware of such danger signals as pain or physical discomfort. Furthermore, side effects and toxicity of certain psychotropic medications may mask or alter organic symptoms so that these may be unrecognized as a separate underlying problem.

Considering these difficulties, you play a significant role in recognizing true organic disease in the person with chronic mental illness. Obviously, it is unfair to expect you to achieve expertise in diagnosis and management of the multiplicity of illnesses that could afflict the mentally ill person, but it should not be beyond your scope to appreciate the presence of certain symptoms and, because of your proximity to the ill individual, to serve as a valuable source of information concerning changes in symptoms reflecting physical condition, as well as mental status.

A review of the top disease killers in the United States, as designated by the National Center for Health Statistics, clearly demonstrates your important role in regard to physical illness of the mentally ill.

Coping with Chronic Killer Diseases

Cardiovascular disease. The number one killer in the U.S. is heart disease. The mentally ill person who has risk factors for developing heart disease (such as cigarette smoking, diabetes mellitus, hypertension, high cholesterol, and/or positive family history of heart disease), should be suspect when showing certain symptoms—particularly complaints of exertion-related chest pain. Some ill persons, especially schizophrenics, may not be sensitive to their bodies' sensations, and then they are unable to interpret the presence of chest pain or to express this to the primary care physician. Clearly, it would be invaluable if you were able to make pertinent observations, such as noting that the mentally ill person's activity level had changed (for example, she/he was becoming reluctant to walk or do other physical activities; the individual clutched his/her chest after walking up a set of stairs; or she/he had developed increasing difficulty breathing with exertion).

Once the diagnosis of *ischemic heart disease* (that is, caused by a deficiency in the blood supply) is established, you must ensure adequate compliance regarding medications used in treating the heart disease. If surgery is necessary to correct blockage of the coronary arteries, you can provide a valuable link between the patient and the medical personnel both before and after surgery. Upon returning home following discharge from the hospital, you may again play a major role in compliance with the treatment regimen.

You and the other team members should be aware that certain psychotropic drugs do have an effect on the cardiovascular system. An example would be the phenothiazines, an often-used family of antipsychotic drugs (see chapter 7). These drugs can affect pulse rate and blood pressure, most often causing lowering of the blood pressure, especially when the person stands up (postural hypotension). Furthermore, these medications can induce changes in the electrocardiogram (EKG) that may complicate this particular method of diagnosing and monitoring heart disease. Similar alterations can be caused by antidepressant medications known as tricyclic antidepressants, which may also be associated with various changes in heart rhythm and conduction, and even heart failure.

A person's preexisting cardiovascular disease may make him/her more sensitive to the cardiotoxicity of such medications. Also, medications such as tricyclic antidepressants can interact with certain other medications used to treat hypertension (such as inhibiting the hypotensive effect of the medication Clonidine resulting in an increase in blood pressure). Thus, it is imperative that you (and your team members) accurately report all medications being taken by the recovering person to the primary care physician, particularly when drugs used in treating mental illness may be prescribed by one physician, while cardiac medications may be prescribed by another. Neither of the physicians may be aware of the total drug regimen unless you provide this information. This shows the importance of the identification card to be carried by the recovering individual.

Cancer. Cancer ranks second on the list of major disease killers. Mental illness may complicate the diagnosis of malignancy either by masking symptoms that might give a clue, such as pain and mental status change, or by obscuring recognition of such symptoms as rectal bleeding, nipple discharge, or weight loss. Furthermore, mental illness may complicate the diagnosis by preventing the individual from following through with recommended cancer screens, such as routine mammography, regular Pap smears, and routine evaluation of the prostate gland, as well as regular evaluation of stools for occult blood. While these routine screens for cancer may be recommended to the mentally ill person, it may fall upon you to assure that the patient follows through with the screening process.

Cerebral vascular disease. The third most common cause of death is cerebral vascular disease. Some medications used

in the treatment of psychiatric disorders can cause disturbances of movement that could mimic certain strokes. And,
in contrast, certain personality changes accompanying some
types of strokes may be misconstrued as merely an effect of
the underlying mental illness.

Chronic lung disease. The fourth most frequent cause of
death, chronic lung disease, is often associated with long-
term cigarette use, but it may be associated with other disease
processes (asthma included). Here again, medications used
in treating the mental illness may have adverse effects on the
pulmonary disease, including suppression of respiration in
persons who tend to have difficulty in clearing carbon diox-
ide from their bodies and unwanted increases in *viscosity*
(stickiness) of pulmonary secretions. You may be the only
one to recognize a worsening of chronic lung disease by
observing changes in sputum (from coughing or spitting)
such as increased thickness or *purulence* (similarity to pus) of
the sputum; increased frequency or severity of coughing; or
increased difficulty in breathing, as manifested by increased
respiratory rate, and increased use of chest-wall muscles to
aid in breathing. Because the mentally ill patient may not
either notice or be able to interpret such changes, you may
have to report these problems to the physician. Similarly, you
need to ensure that the mentally ill patient obtains appropriate routine follow-up, including a yearly flu vaccination and
a once-in-a-lifetime vaccination against pneumococcal pneu-
monia where appropriate.

Diabetes and hyperglycemia. Another disease in the list of
top killers is diabetes. The diagnosis of diabetes may be
mimicked by certain psychotic behavior, such as increased
drinking of water. Medications such as phenothiazines,
which are used in treating mental illness, may have endocrine
and metabolic effects, including development of high (or
low) blood sugar and alteration of glucose tolerance curves.
Furthermore, drugs such as the tricyclic antidepressants may
alter gastric emptying and thus affect blood sugar levels,
complicating achievement of adequate blood sugar control.

In the mentally ill person with insulin-dependent diabetes, you may need to monitor not only the proper dosing of insulin and its administration but also the blood sugar levels. If so, you must become familiar with the use of Chemstrips® that allow blood sugar monitoring rather than urine sugar determination. You may also need to become familiar with simple home equipment such as *glucometers*, which facilitate blood sugar measurements. The use of such devices may aid in the process of accurately reporting blood sugar status to the primary care physician and thus facilitate therapy decisions.

As the homecare coordinator, you will also be responsible for ensuring that proper dietary restrictions are followed. In addition, become alert to the manifestations of low blood sugar (hypoglycemia), which include tremor, sweating, rapid heart action, and possible neurological manifestations such as confusion, bizarre behavior, seizure activity, or even coma (loss of consciousness). While low blood sugar during the night may often by asymptomatic, this may cause night sweats, difficulty in awakening, morning headache, or even nightmares. Low blood sugar can result from excessive dosing of medication (such as insulin or an oral hypoglycemic agent), and it may also occur due to a delay or omission of a meal or an unusual amount of physical activity.

High blood sugar or hyperglycemia on a persistent basis can result in classic symptoms of diabetes such as *polyuria* (frequent urination), *polydipsia* (frequent drinking), and weight loss. In addition to these symptoms, the progression of uncontrolled blood sugar may lead to *diabetic ketoacidosis*, with possible marked fatigue, nausea, vomiting, and finally mental stupor, which can also progress to coma.

Diabetic ketoacidosis may begin during an acute illness such as an infection or be associated with other illnesses, such as myocardial infarction, pancreatitis, stroke, surgery, or simply from inappropriate omission of insulin. Obviously, diabetic ketoacidosis requires vigorous medical treatment, but the best treatment is prevention, which means careful monitoring of the blood sugar during any illness and reporting of any persistent hyperglycemia to the primary care physician.

A second and less common form of hyperglycemia is *nonketotic hyperglycemic coma*, characterized by severe hyperglycemia in the absence of ketoacidosis. This problem may begin insidiously over days or weeks, shown only by weakness, polyuria, and polydipsia. The lack of toxic features as seen with ketoacidosis may retard recognition of this problem and delay appropriate therapy. The underlying precipitating factors may include reduced fluid intake due to inappropriate lack of thirst, to nausea, or to inaccessibility of fluid on the part of a frail or bedridden person. With this problem, lethargy and confusion develop, which may be misconstrued as an exacerbation of the underlying mental illness. The process may progress to convulsions and deep coma if not properly recognized and treated. Again, your observations and reporting may be critically vital in this situation. Become familiar with the symptoms reflecting significant alternations in blood sugar, and acquire skills and tools to monitor blood sugar status.

Chronic renal disease. The mentally ill person with this killer has to be as strict with dietary restrictions as does the diabetic. Here, achievement of a diet that contains a certain amount of protein and particular amounts of minerals, including sodium and potassium, may be required. Ensure that (a) such a diet is available and (b) the medication regimen gains compliance. This latter aspect may be particularly important because with altered kidney function, dosages of certain medications, including over-the-counter ones, may have to be reduced.

Liver disease. In the mentally ill person, liver disease also requires certain considerations in regard to medication used. It is known that psychotropic medications (especially phenothiazines) may cause liver toxicity. Furthermore, increased sensitivity of liver disease patients to the central nervous system effects of these medications should be considered.

Coping with Acute Medical Symptoms, Preventions, and Treatments

In addition to gaining familiarity with the mentally ill person's chronic medical illnesses, you can gather information concerning certain other symptoms. For example, abdominal pain may result from a myriad of underlying pathologies. Some simple observations by you may help clarify the origin of a particular pain for the primary care physician. Specifically, observations concerning the frequency of bowel movements, the character of stools, the incidence of nausea and vomiting, and the presence of blood in the stool may provide valuable insight for the primary care physician and may preserve information that would otherwise be unnoticed or lost. For example, peptic ulcer disease may present only with symptoms of weakness and may be difficult to diagnose without such observations by the homecare team, thus delaying institution of appropriate treatment.

Not only does mental illness make it more difficult for the primary care physician to diagnose physical illness, but also mental illness may actually predispose the patient to certain types of illness or injury. For example, psychiatric illness is present in a significant number of adult burn patients and can be an important factor predisposing a person to burn injuries. One study suggested that nearly 70% of patients with burn injuries had at least one psychiatric illness prior to the burn injury. Depression appeared in almost half of such patients, one third had a personality disorder, and approximately one fourth had a preexisting diagnosis of alcohol or other drug abuse. Because of alteration of perception, some mentally ill patients may be at increased risk for other types of accidents as well. Furthermore, medications used to treat mental illness may alter alertness, coordination, and response time, thus enhancing the possibility of accidental injury.

Other illnesses can be linked in part to altered perception and maladaptive behavior, which result in deterioration of personal hygiene habits, such as certain types of infectious problems that can be spread by improper hand-washing or other poor personal hygiene. Further, the chronic mentally ill person may not have the basic health knowledge and skills to maximize disease avoidance. For example, your patient may not know about the proper role of condoms in helping to prevent venereal disease or AIDS. Teach and review such skills and knowledge at follow-up appointments with the primary care physician. Furthermore, give the recovering individual the skills and tools (see chapter 5) to obtain help in medical emergencies. One important tool is a list of steps that he/she can follow for each of any anticipated urgent eventualities. Include in this list any appropriate actions, telephone numbers, or medications to be taken in the event of injury, sickness, or circumstances in which usual medications are misplaced or cannot be taken. Establishment of such a list is particularly helpful when chronic medical problems coexist with chronic mental illness.

In summary, mental illness may complicate the diagnosis and treatment of certain physical illnesses by the very nature of the illness itself, which both precludes accurate portrayal of symptoms by the patient and either masks symptoms or masquerades as another illness. Furthermore, while you cannot be expected to become an expert in all areas of medicine, you do need some expertise in regard to the particular organic disease process present in the mentally ill patient for whom you are responsible. All homecare team members would do well to know the medications being used to treat not only the mental illness, but also the physical illnesses present. Learn to monitor the organic illness and its symptoms, as well as the mental illness. Though you may be unable to interpret the significance of a symptom, you may be the only one with the opportunity to recognize either that a new problem has arisen or that changes have occurred in the character of old problems. You may be the only one with the opportunity to ensure that disease prevention activities (such as vaccinations, recommended cancer screening tests, and following of daily hygiene measures) are accomplished and, most important, that compliance with all prescribed treatment is realized.

PART TWO

BASIC PLANNING

5

PLANNING HOMECARE

A journey of one thousand miles begins with the first step.

Chinese proverb

THE CRUCIAL IMPORTANCE OF PLANNING

There is much to do and much to learn when a mentally ill person lives at home. The recovering person has to have the support of the family because the life of each family member will be affected. Further, the family must plan cohesive strategies to promote the well-being of *all* family members, not allowing the focus to center entirely on the ill family member. For example, if the family allows it, the disturbed person can create an environment of chaos. In addition to showing symptoms of the illness, the ill person can be rude, inconsiderate, irritating, and obnoxious. On the other hand, he/she can be warm, loving, considerate, and sensitive. The problem is, we don't know exactly when and to what degree these behaviors will occur. With willingness from the family to participate in and plan a recovery program, this chapter teaches you how to set up such a program. Planning for the unexpected as well as the expected will help resolve difficulties with the recovering individual.

When designing homecare treatment, consider the life styles of individual members of the family to ensure that the immediate stresses are not overwhelming. Different families and family members will respond to this situation in different ways. It is important to *plan* for adjustment. Take comfort in the idea that this transition is temporary, and that advance planning can ensure that the family, rather than the ill person, is in control of the household. Especially take heed if there are younger children in the family, who may feel embarrassed about their ill relative and may tend to change their own personalities (see chapter 6; also discuss this with others, see chapter 12). Encourage the children to continue to participate in school and related activities. Also, until a workable schedule is in force, all household members involved may have to readjust their day-to-day routines. Remember that things *will* calm down once the recovering person feels secure. To facilitate this sense of stability, these and other problems should be discussed in a family meeting.

STEP 1: MEET TO DISCUSS THE PROPOSED HOMECARE

The first step in planning the homecare psychiatric treatment program is to hold a team meeting. In the beginning, this may only involve the members of the family. If the ill person has been hospitalized for a period of time, the return home may not be a joyous occasion. Concerns of each team member should be voiced and considered, regardless of the fact that they may not have had a choice in whether to help to maintain the recovering household member at home. If there is no choice (because of numerous problems, such as money), all family members may just have to accept the fact that the recovering relative will be with them, and they may have to adjust accordingly. Nonetheless, many problems can be minimized by anticipating problems, communicating them, and creatively planning for their solutions. At this meeting, plan to discuss the following:

1. Consider ways to handle initial problems that may occur because the mentally ill individual may behave inappropriately in one or more ways:
    *   Continue to behave like an inpatient (e.g., passivity)
    *   Selfishly want his/her way
    *   Show little respect for the welfare of others
    *   Physically or verbally abuse other persons
    *   Act out sexually
    *   Disregard the effects of their actions on the activities of others (may have TV or stereo on loud while family members may be reading, eating, or sleeping)
    *   Disrespect the privacy of other family members
    *   Deviate from the routines of sleeping, eating, taking medication, or exercising
    *   Refuse to, or otherwise be unable to bathe, dress, and tend to personal grooming needs; do little of anything that is required of an individual in a family unit.

2. Anticipate the initial response, reactions, and possible bias of family members outside the immediate family, friends, neighbors, and other social or work contacts.
    *   Plan to let people know that the ill relative is coming home. What, when, and how will you tell others about your ill relative? Whom will you tell, and under what circumstances will you tell them?
    *   It is good to let close friends know what is happening. Denying or covering up or hiding the relative will only make matters worse.

- Encourage family members and others to learn about mental illness, and stress the fact that mental illness is an organic disease of the brain, much the same as cancer or diabetes is a disease of other parts of the body. Now that mental illness is out of the closet, the more family members accept the illness, the more it will encourage society to accept it as any other disease.

3. It is important that the family members, as well as the ill person, have time to themselves. Be sure to consider this in your planning (e.g., what type of action to have on weekends, holidays, and vacations). Call your local associations for ideas (see chapter 12). You may be able to locate a facility that offers respite care, or you could swap care times with another caregiving family, or you may want to hire someone to fill in. Additionally, plan for privacy when considering your household environment.

4. Plan ways to get life back on track. As with other illnesses, family members tend to overprotect the mentally ill person. Don't let this happen. The relative needs to recover from being hospitalized. The more quickly things are "normalized" the better.

5. Set goals for rehabilitating the ill family member, as well as the entire family. Once everyone is aware of the case of mental illness in the family, they must decide how to help the disabled individual.

For further planning of the transition from hospital to home, see chapter 6.

STEP 2: IF YOU HAVEN'T ALREADY DONE SO, CHOOSE YOUR HOMECARE COORDINATOR AND YOUR PRIMARY CARE PHYSICIAN

Actually, you may already have selected a homecare coordinator and your primary care physician prior to your first team meeting. But if not, please refer to chapter 3, regarding how to take this crucial step. Again, this book is written based on the assumption that you are the homecare coordinator, though all homecare team members may benefit from the information herein.

STEP 3: MAKE THE TRANSITION AND LOOK FOR ASSISTANCE IN THE COMMUNITY

If possible, bring the recovering person home to visit before the scheduled release time. This is discussed in chapter 6. Increase the visiting time from 1 to 2 hours to a weekend pass. This will enable the family and the ill person to visit with each other and to make plans for the complete move back home.

The homecare coordinator needs to check for every available resource in the community. This may be tough, but people are willing to help. The time before discharge is ideal to start forming a team (also see chapters 6 and 12) and to meet with each member to get input on homecare. Members of the homecare team include the primary care physician, the psychiatrist, social worker, local mental health worker (for definitions of these titles see chapter 6), teacher, employer, friends who are willing to sit with the ill relative, other relatives who will be active in helping, or anyone else who may be of service. Find out what roles each person will play in the rehabilitation of the recovering person. Check for part-time jobs (construction, yard work, car wash, etc.), day-care programs, school (public schools are required by law to educate all handicapped persons until the age of 21), or adult special education. Leave no stone unturned when seeking help and a future for the recovering person.

STEP 4: DEVELOP BEHAVIOR MANAGEMENT SKILLS IN THE HOMECARE TEAM

As mentioned earlier, this discussion assumes that you are the homecare coordinator. Nonetheless, all members of your homecare team would benefit from knowing how to use behavior management skills. If possible, invite all members of your team to work with you on developing these skills even *before* your ill family member returns home.

Positive Reinforcement

Before learning behavior management skills, take time to concentrate on the positive things (the good things) that the recovering mentally ill person can do. If you are inclined to say "Nothing," then dig a little deeper. What about dressing him/herself? Is that skill accomplished? What about saying "thank you" or "please"? Can she/he eat appropriately? Or even go to bed when asked? Most people focus on and remember only the bad or inappropriate things done by the ill member of their household. Our society tends to stress the inappropriate or undesirable because it deviates from what we expect or want. Notice this when you are speaking with someone in similar circumstances to yours. Bad things sell newspapers and television programs. But positive attitudes will help change a person's behavior.

When you see a person doing something good, quickly respond to the good behavior by saying something positive. This is called "positive reinforcement," or "catching a person doing something good." Saying "I like the way you picked up your clothes this morning" is far more meaningful than nagging because the clothes weren't picked up yesterday. People like to please, and people like to know that there is something good about them. Constant criticism will get you nowhere, and it will certainly not help the recovering person make any progress. If the individual completes only a portion of a task, reinforce that portion and ignore the rest. If you want a desired behavior to continue, then reinforce it with such comments as, "I'm so glad you're coming with us," "I really appreciate your waiting for me," "That's great," "I like that," "You look super," "You have nice manners," or "I'm proud of you."

Make sure you are sincere when applying reinforcement. A forced, dull or dry "that's wonderful" isn't very rewarding. A person's self-esteem is enhanced by making another person feel good, so let your "that's wonderful!" really mean something.

Further, positive reinforcement doesn't always have to be verbal; it can also be nonverbal. Nonverbal reinforcement includes smiling, winking, patting on the back, touching hands, kissing, hugging, rubbing hair, putting arms around the waist, or clapping hands. Nonverbal reinforcements can be the most effective, as well as the easiest to give.

Try always to reward good behavior, for many times only bad behavior receives attention (e.g., yelling about dirty clothes being on the floor, not noticing that the bed is made). This way, the recovering person has received attention for a bad behavior and the good behavior has been ignored. Watch these mistakes! Desirable and undesirable, all human behavior is learned; therefore, behaviors can be unlearned with the proper reinforcement. Just remember to positively reinforce desired behaviors, and, when possible, to ignore or otherwise discourage undesired behaviors.

Negative Responses

Of course life is not all positive, and there are times when you should use a negative response. If someone is in danger, yell "Stop, don't do that!" or if someone is about to harm another person, take immediate action. Another time to use a negative response is when something happens that is socially unacceptable (e.g., your mentally retarded child attempts to expose himself in a supermarket). At such times, you have to react quickly. A very negative "No, don't do that!" is bound to get the attention of the offender. When you have to be negative, don't feel guilty about it; you responded appropriately. Caution yourself, however, that you only use negative responses when it is absolutely necessary. Try also to note whether your negative response is increasing or decreasing the frequency and intensity of the behavior.

Negative Punishment

One way of giving a negative response is to withhold positive reinforcement. Parents often do this with children, such as revoking television privileges, phone privileges, or recreational privileges. Because this involves *not* doing something positive, it is called "negative." And because it is used as a punishment, it is called "negative punishment."

One very powerful form of negative punishment is a "time out from positive reinforcement" (usually shortened to simply "time out"). Generally, the positive reinforcement is considered to be social interactions with persons (e.g., family and friends) and experiences (e.g., playing games, talking) that the "offender" enjoys. Therefore, "time out" involves either removing the person from the situation (e.g., sending him/her to his/her room) or removing the experience from the person (e.g., turning off the television or not speaking to and not looking at the person). This type of punishment is most effective when used with younger children; however, it does work with older demented persons.

This example shows how time out works:

"Bill, you will *have* to spend 5 minutes in time out if you slam the door like that again." (**Note:** Start off using a small amount of time when beginning to use this procedure. You will get a better response if a small time limit is used. After your relative is used to this type of punishment, time may be increased, not to exceed 30 or 45 minutes.)

Procedure

1. Choose a place that does not offer extra stimuli—facing a wall somewhere. The time starts when the person is seated and is quiet.

2. Set a timer to the required amount of time (remind your relative that the time is up only when the timer goes off).

After the time is over, ask "Why did you have to sit in time out?" If you are given the wrong answer, reset the timer and say that you will ask again in 3 minutes.

(**Note:** You may have to coach for the right answer. This procedure puts the responsibility for the wrongdoing on the ill person and not on the caregiver!)

Positive Punishment

Occasionally, negative punishment may not suit the situation. For example, if the person isn't enjoying the situation, removal from it may not be a punishment. In these situations (or in life-threatening or otherwise dangerous situations), a more active, or "positive" form of punishment may be needed. The most commonly effective forms of "positive punishment" are showing disapproval and allowing the person to suffer the natural or logical unpleasant consequences of his/her actions.

Showing disapproval. This method includes frowning, scowling, or verbally scolding the ill person for doing something highly inappropriate or offensive. When the behavior happens, apply this punishment immediately! If you are in a public setting, go to a private setting before showing your disapproval.

Natural consequences. An example of letting a punishing natural consequence occur might be that a pet dog might bite a person if the person is teasing the dog. When things of this nature happen, be sure to put the blame where it belongs. In this instance, you could say, "Why did the dog bite you? Do you think the dog liked being teased? What do you think will happen if you tease the dog again? I think maybe you should leave the dog alone, or you may be bitten again." Clearly, this should not be allowed to occur if the consequences could be truly dangerous.

Another way to institute a behavior change is to use a contract. A contract is a special written plan designed to help a person accomplish a certain goal. This plan, which has to be negotiated and agreed upon by two or more persons, lists what must be done in order to reach that goal. The goal can be to change any kind of behavior. The key is to make the contract objectives clear and to the point.

When using a contract with a mentally handicapped person, talk to the individual about the behavior that is offensive. Let him/her help devise a way to alter the behavior. Decide on some type of reward to be given to help encourage the change. Choose rewards with care.

When designing a contract, start with changing something small, such as putting dirty clothes in the clothes hamper. Here is an example of how to devise a contract for putting dirty clothes in the hamper.

Goal: Put dirty clothes in clothes hamper.

Procedure: Write a contract as follows (you may either use the third person, using the person's name and "she/he," or you may direct the words to the recovering person, using "you.")

CONTRACT

When Jennifer puts her dirty clothes in the hamper, she will be allowed to watch television for ___ extra minutes.[1] If Jennifer does not put her clothes in the hamper, she will be escorted to her room and be instructed on how to put clothes in the hamper. She will then have to stay in her room for the amount of time set on the timer.[2]

When Jennifer has put her clothes in the hamper for 3 days in a row, she will get a special treat.[3]

Signed:

| _____ | _____ | _____ |
| Jennifer | Coordinator | Mom |

---

[1]Use any type of reinforcement that the person enjoys doing, such as bike riding, swimming, helping with meals, or smoking an extra cigarette.

[2]Start with small amounts of time, such as 1 minute, 2 minutes, 5 minutes. The contract will weaken if great amounts of time are requested in the beginning. Also, make sure the person knows why he/she is to sit in the room (or another place) for this period of time. Ask "Why did you have to sit here?" If the person doesn't seem to understand what is going on, have him/her repeat after you, "I did not put my clothes in the hamper." This may have to be repeated several times before it is understood.

When one behavior is effectively managed, start altering another behavior. If the contract doesn't work, change it. If you made a bad contract, you don't have to stick with it!

When using any type of behavior management, always follow these guidelines:

- Say the recovering person's name
- Establish eye contact (this is important whenever you are making any contact with the recovering person)
- Give clear instructions on what is to be done (start off with one-step commands, eventually adding other commands, one at a time)
- Have the recovering person repeat (acknowledge) what is expected.

STEP 5: DRAFT A SCHEDULE AND SOME SPECIAL INSTRUCTIONS

Perhaps the most important tool used in the homecare treatment plan is learning to make and use a schedule. The daily schedule gives needed direction to the recovering person and to the homecare team in leading their lives. The recovering individual needs direction and structure. Provide enough supervision to get the schedule into action without added frustrations. Again, if you can work with others to develop an appropriate schedule *before* your ill family member arrives home, you may be better prepared to help in her/his recovery.

Make a schedule by simply listing the activities included in

---

[3]The special treat can be a movie, a favorite meal, going someplace, or anything else that has a special meaning. Make sure the recovering person understands why the reward is being received: "Putting your clothes in the hamper regularly means you get to . . . . That's really good! Because now your favorite pair of jeans won't be lost either."

an average day. If the ill person is low functioning, list everything from brushing teeth to taking medicine. As the recovering person begins to establish a routine, the schedule can be changed or even done away with. However, the real importance of having a schedule is to get the mentally ill person into the habit of doing something. Because habits are hard to break, try to start to form good habits. Make the schedule to meet the needs of the home environment. Get the recovering person to help; ask what he/she wants to do in the household. You may be surprised at the answers! Be sure to include such things as home chores, meals, medication, recreation, trips to the doctor, feeding a pet, or any other special item that would give the recovering person a sense of responsibility.

When actually writing the schedule, make it in the form of a chart, as shown in Table 5.1. As the recovering person completes each item, he/she is required to check it on the chart. In the beginning, discuss the chart as each item is being checked. For example say, "Oh, I see that you have made your bed. That's very good; now we can put a check right here." You can be as elementary or as advanced as you need when devising a schedule or when discussing it.

There are two types of schedules—a *restricted schedule* (Table 5.1) which lists everything the recovering person is to do, and an *unrestricted schedule* (Table 5.2), which shows an overall view of what the individual is doing. When the recovering person starts working with the unrestricted schedule, a periodic check on certain things may have to be done.

Employers can use a schedule of this design while the recovering individual is at work. Just fill in what is to be done at the appropriate time. If the ill person becomes confused, don't start explaining or arguing, but refer to what the schedule says he/she should be doing. This uses the schedule to its best advantage. Post the schedule at first in a central place (kitchen,office); then when the recovering person is able to do the checking him/herself, let him/her carry it or move it to his/her room.

Table 5.1. **Restricted Schedule**

Time	S	M	T	W	Th	F	S
7:30—out of bed, turn off alarm							
7:35—make bed							
7:40—wash face, brush teeth, brush hair, use deodorant, dress for occasion (see chapter 9), put away bed clothes							
8:00—come to kitchen, eat breakfast, take medication							
8:30—do household chores or leave for school or work (*if doing household chores, list exactly what is to be done, e.g., water plants, water yard, sweep floor, put away dishes, etc., each on separate lines.*)							
10:00—morning snack break							
10:15—recreation: play a game, shoot basketball, read, jog, etc.							
11:15—relax, get ready for lunch, wash hands and face							
11:30—help with lunch							
12:00—eat lunch, take medicine, help clean up							
1:00—afternoon chores							
3:00—afternoon outing or recreation: work on hobby (building a model or needlepoint), work a puzzle, work on computer, take a music lesson, visit someone, etc.							
5:30—change work clothes, relax, wash hands and face, help put on dinner							
6:00—eat dinner, take medication							
7:00—evening activities: watch television, read, talk with family							
9:00—take shower or bath, *(see chapter 9)* use soap and washcloth, wash hair, dry hair, put away dirty clothes, brush teeth, take medicine, set alarm, private time							
9:30—go to bed							

Table 5.2.   Unrestricted Schedule

Time	S	M	T	W	Th	F	S
7:30—out of bed, shave, wash face, brush teeth and hair, use deodorant, eat breakfast, take medication							
8:30—morning activities *(recovering person is responsible)*							
12:00—lunch							
1:00—afternoon activities *(recovering person is responsible)*							
6:00—dinner							
9:00—get ready for bed, shower, put away dirty clothes							

What happens to the schedule when the recovering person is left with someone else for a period of time? The schedule should be followed as much as possible. However, if you are having a housesitter as well as a companion for your ill relative, you might want to leave your own version of the following list of instructions. If you have most of this ready in advance, it will be much easier to handle unexpected emergencies.

TO: *(Whomever is staying)*
CONCERNING: *(The recovering person)*
FROM: *(Name of family)*

MEDICATION:
With breakfast   —two Clozapine (yellow pills)
                 —one Sinequan (pink & white capsule)
                 —one Zantac (white pill)
After dinner   —Repeat the above dosages

NO CODEINE SHOULD BE GIVEN TO JERRY. HE HAS SEVERE REACTIONS TO IT!

Jerry has no other known allergies. He has never taken antibiotics by injection.

The foregoing information should be shown to any doctor or dentist who treats Jerry. Please note that his emergency card *(see chapter 4)* is in his wallet. There is also a copy on the table in the hallway. Show Jerry's Medicare card (also on hall table) in case he has to go to the doctor or hospital.

Our pharmacy is Comer Drugstore, on Alcoa Highway. The number is 555-4408. We have a charge account (ask for Mr. Comer). They deliver.

DRINKING BEHAVIOR:

Don't be alarmed if Jerry drinks small sips of water from the bottle in the refrigerator. He is doing this to avert a possible epileptic fit that could result from drinking too much water.

ACCIDENTS AND CLAIMS:

In case of theft, damage by fire, flood, windstorm, collision, or other cause of personal injury, notify both the local police and our insurance agents, Hill and Cross, 555-2543. In case of an auto accident, be sure to get all the information from the other driver (i.e., license, name, and address). Also include those of any witnesses, and notify the police immediately.

If any visitor to our home is injured by a nonautomobile accident, our homeowners policy will pay for the first $1,000 of medical expenses.

AUTOMOBILE INSTRUCTIONS:

You should use the Camaro. The Datsun may be used only when the Camaro is being repaired. For repair work, call Denney's Auto Repair Shop on Lebanon Road (555-1128). All necessary documents, a flashlight, and a flare are in the rear of the Camaro. Make sure you check the oil.

CARE OF THE HOUSE:

A list of contractors, etc., is in the drawer in the hall table. Follow the directions for the heat pump. Mr. Cagle (555-9341) will assist you.

MEDICAL PROBLEMS:

In case of a real medical emergency, call 555-9200 for an ambulance. Also try to reach Dr. James Ferguson (555-7866), who will send the appropriate specialist to U.T. Emergency Room to meet the ambulance. For nonemergency needs or concerns, call Dr. Copeland at 555-8600.

CARE OF TEETH:

Jerry's teeth should be brushed with toothpaste every morning and evening. His dentist is Dr. James Lockett (555-5749), on Concord Road.

BURGLAR AND FIRE ALARM SYSTEM:

If there is an intruder and the alarm doesn't go off, push simultaneously the two buttons behind the door in the master bedroom, and the police will arrive quickly.

Be sure to set the alarm if the house is left alone. If the alarm goes off mistakenly, either through error or malfunction, turn off the alarm with the key you use to turn it on, and stay in the house. The alarm company will call you and you should give your name and identification number (98765) and tell them it was an error. I have furnished your name and your identification number to the alarm company. If there seems to be a malfunction, call the alarm company for service (555-2341). Keep the cat confined to one room, as the cat can set off the alarm.

STEP 6: SET GOALS BASED ON A FUNCTIONAL ASSESSMENT

Setting goals is a top priority for any treatment programs. Ideally, this process begins before the patient is discharged— perhaps during an extended home visit. If you do not have this luxury, however, you may begin to set goals at any time during recovery.

Discuss appropriate goals in a family meeting with the ill relative participating. Of course, the main goal of all mentally ill persons is to live an independent and self-sufficient life; however, in order to do that, many other goals must be met first. Make a list of existing problems (based on the "Functional Assessment of the Recovering Person"), choose one of the problems as a goal, decide how that goal will be reached, and estimate how long it should take to reach the goal. This procedure could be written up as follows:

Goal: To teach Bill to use the city bus for transportation within a period of 2 weeks.

Procedure: Caregiver will show Bill how to do the following:

1. Get the right amount of money
2. Determine the time and place to meet the bus
3. Read a bus schedule
4. Wait for the bus

5. Get on the bus and deposit coins
6. Ask for a transfer
7. Sit on the bus
8. Signal the driver for getting off the bus
9. Get off the bus at your stop.

As you begin each step, briefly and simply state what is being done. You may also find it helpful to model the desired behavior. With the caregiver, the ill family member then completes one step at a time as he/she describes the action being taken. Eventually, the recovering person will be able to complete all steps without the assistance of the caregiver. Of course, the caregiver, as well as other family members, will apply the proper positive reinforcement. When the ill person has completed one goal, start on another. Soon you will be able to work on more than one goal at a time.

Occasionally, a goal or set of goals will be obvious, such as self-feeding or self-toileting. Often, however, you may be unsure as to what are appropriate goals. For this reason, the following functional assessment scale was devised as a tool to help the homecare team evaluate the progress or the lack of progress made by the recovering person. You should substitute, delete, or add to this tool, depending on which particular weaknesses or problems your team might want to monitor. Any time there is a change in the behavior of the ill person, you may refer to this assessment to pinpoint which areas of function are involved. You may also consult this scale before visiting the primary care physician. Also, if possible, consult with hospital staff to obtain a functional assessment, prior to discharge of your mentally ill family member. This may help your homecare team to set appropriate goals and to plan for their effective implementation.

Functional Assessment of the Recovering Person

1. Self-care

   a. Bathing (Does the recovering person . . .)
      * shower or bathe regularly?

- wash only when prodded?
- use soap & washcloth?
- wash all parts of body?
  (if not, which parts are unclean?)
- dry off with towel?
- keep the bathroom clean, or is it a disaster?

b. Grooming (Does the recovering person . . .)

- clean and cut fingernails?
- wash hair?
- brush hair?
- brush teeth?
- clean dentures?
- appear with hair or teeth dirty?
- shave only in spots or go unshaven?
- wear heavy or inappropriate makeup?
- refuse to wear normal makeup (whatever was her/his norm before onset of illness)?
- match own clothing?
- wear clothes appropriate for the occasion?
- need help with clothing?
- put away clothes in correct places?
- keep shoes clean?
- wear appropriate shoes for the rest of the clothing?

c. Toileting (Does the recovering person . . .)

- eliminate and void without any problem?
- wet the bed?
- soil clothes?
- clean self after toileting?
- flush toilet?
- wash hands after using the toilet and before going to eat?

d. Sleep habits (Does the recovering person . . .)

- pace the floor at night?
- sleep late?
- complain of a "radio" in head at night?

- have difficulties sleeping?
- sleep a lot more or a lot less than is normal?
- fall asleep during the day?

e. Eating habits (Does the recovering person . . .)
   - eat regularly (good balanced meals)?
   - eat alone or with group or family?
   - eat with fingers or with proper utensils?
   - use a napkin?
   - drink from own cup or glass?
   - eat at normal frequency (not too often or too irregularly)?
   - appear relaxed or frightened when eating?
   - tend to choke or gulp down large amounts?
   - eat regular amounts?
   - eat sparingly?
   - follow a prescribed diet (no caffeine, no sugar, etc.)?

2. Understanding and use of language
   a. Does the recovering person speak . . .
      - not at all or rarely?
      - only in a mumble?
      - by rambling?
      - only when prodded?
      - too slowly?
      - incessantly?
      - inappropriately?

   b. Does the recovering person talk or laugh to self . . .
      - not at all or rarely?
      - by seeming to respond to someone?
      - and admits to hearing voices?

   c. Does the recovering person demonstrate understanding and comprehension of spoken language by . . .

- appearing to listen to conversation (receptive)?
- responding to conversation (expressive)?
- actively engaging in conversation?
- communicating needs?

Or,

    d. Does the recovering person show problems by . . .

- repeating or echoing what is being said?
- talking in incomprehensible strings of words or syllables?
- talking about an unrelated subject?
- avoiding conversation?

    e. Does the recovering person demonstrate understanding and comprehension of written language by . . .

- responding to written words?
- talking about written words (book or letter reading)?
- rewriting what is written?
- writing about an unrelated subject when asked?

3. Cognitive functions (Is the recovering person . . .)

    a. oriented to time?

    b. oriented to place?

    c. oriented to person?

    d. able to use remote memory well?

    e. able to show recent recall well and reliably?

    f. able to concentrate (e.g., play cards, sports)?

    g. able to assume responsibilities (normal, little, none)?

4. Affective functions (Does the recovering person . . .)

    a. have interests?

    b. express emotions?

    c. make judgments?

    d. make independent decisions?

5. Mobility (Can the recovering person . . .)
   a. use phone to call a cab?
   b. use public transportation?
      • remembers change
      • knows how to wait
      • knows how to pay for ride
      • can get to where going
      • can return home
      • too disoriented for above

   c. ride in a car with someone?
   d. drive? (If so, does the recovering person . . .)
      • remember to get gas?
      • remember to have oil checked and changed?
      • know how to charge a battery?
      • know how to change a tire?
      • leave keys in the car?
      • leave windows down during the rain?
      • leave the the car unlocked?
      • leave valuable items in the car (golf clubs, etc.)?

6. Vocational skills (Does the recovering person . . .)

   a. work?
   b. want to work?
   c. seem willing to learn/train for job?
   d. have a job? (If so, does the recovering person . . .)
      • go to work when prodded?
      • go to work spontaneously?
      • go to work given a reminder?
      • complete half of a task?
      • complete all of a task?
      • put away supplies?
      • collect money for working?

7. Skills established before the illness (Does the recovering person retain . . .)

    a.   recreation skills?

    b.   educational skills?

    c.   work skills?

    d.   social skills?

8. Independent living skills (Is the recovering person able to . . .)

    a.   prepare a meal?

- barely
- enough to get by
- adequately
- well (e.g., with good choice of ingredients)

    b.   budget personal finances?

- write a check
- get money from the bank
- deposit money
- use a savings account
- pay bills

    c.   do laundry?

- separates light and dark clothes
- uses detergent properly
- allows time for drying
- folds clothing
- puts away clothing
- irons if needed

    d.   do housekeeping?

- washes dishes
- cleans floors
- dusts
- makes bed
- cleans windows
- cleans bathroom
- has a place for items

e. take care of clothing?
- knows items to be at cleaners
- hangs clothes in closet
- doesn't wear dirty clothing
- can replace worn clothing

f. do the shopping?
- grocery store
- restaurants
- drug stores
- department stores

g. Other (Can the recovering person . . .)
- keep scheduled appointments?
- answer the phone?
- make phone calls?
- take medications without supervision?
- socialize: initiated by others?
- socialize: self-initiated?
- attend church?
- follow a schedule?
- use a calendar?
- seem aware of outside temperatures and dresses accordingly?
- go to the dentist, doctor, etc.?
- go to lab and allow blood to be drawn?

9. Sexuality (Does the recovering person . . .)

a. show awareness of own sexuality, not express fear, guilt, or shame?

b. behave appropriately (discreet about sex life)?

c. use inappropriate sexual language?

d. masturbate in other than designated areas, such as bedroom, bathroom?

e. show other inappropriate activities, such as . . .

- exhibitionism (exposing genitals)?
- pederasty (attracted to children)?
- fetishism (desiring inanimate objects, such as lingerie, footwear, or objects made of specific materials, such as leather, rubber, etc.)?
- sadism or masochism (inflicting or enduring pain)?
- talk about rape (intercourse by force)?

f. use sex exploitatively?

g. display promiscuous sexual behavior?

10. Criteria that may alert to rehospitalization

   a. Does the recovering person show social isolation or withdrawal?

   b. Are too many environmental changes jeopardizing the person's success?

   c. Is the coordinator unable to maintain consistency and discipline required for at-home living?

   d. Is there a physical disorder that may undermine recovery?

   e. Do you fear a danger of physical, sexual, or emotional attack on the self or others in the present environment?

NOTE: For more information, see chapter 11 on crisis intervention. Good observation and quick action can sometimes stop a rehospitalization.

6

TRANSITION FROM HOSPITAL TO HOME

Seek to delight, that they may mend mankind,
And, while they captivate, inform the mind.

William Cowper, Hope, *I. 758*

Chapter 5 reviewed the planning needed for homecare psychiatric treatment, to show you a systematic way in which to handle the problems of a chronic mentally ill person. If it is at all possible, such planning should start from the moment that the individual is hospitalized. This chapter should help you prepare for the arrival home of the ill member of your household. First, we review how the hospital can and may help you in preparing for discharge. Then we list the different areas of life in which the recovering person may need the help of the homecare team members. Finally, we describe step-by-step procedures that help ease the transition from hospital to home.

PLANNING FOR DISCHARGE AND AFTERCARE SERVICES

We are accustomed to the idea that a hospital discharge is the end of the problems of illness, or at least a sign that the patient is on a certain path to recovery. However, in chronic mental illness, the problems often intensify in the household to which the recovering person returns. Planning for discharge is a transition period often filled with tension and anxiety, on the part of both the patient and the members of his/her household. Many institutionalized patients anticipate problems in the community, when the predictable routine of the hospital will be replaced with the changing demands of normal daily life. Most recovering individuals fear the feeling of being watched for abnormal behavior, and they become suspicious about the concerns shown for their illness. For this reason, as soon as possible during hospitalization, you may wish to start talking about what the patient can expect when she/he returns home. It is essential to anticipate that your ill family member will need help in all areas of daily living. Take nothing for granted about the functioning of a recovering seriously mentally ill person. Nonetheless, above all else, the individual will need fulfilling, satisfying work or other daily activities to restore his/her confidence and self-respect.

The staff of any decent hospital—that is, one accredited by the Joint Commission on Accreditation of Healthcare Organizations (JCAHO)—maintains standards pertaining to their function; and an important hospital standard is the provision of a discharge plan for all patients. This plan is part of the Comprehensive Treatment Plan, which is formulated within 11 days of admission and which should take into account any contribution you and the ill member of your household want to make to his/her treatment. It's essential that you ask the hospital treatment team to consider the possibility of homecare after discharge and to make plans accordingly.

Another standard of a JCAHO-approved hospital is the

provision of homecare services, either by its own staff or by written agreement with individual health care providers or agencies in the community. For instance, hospitals must provide aftercare services to educate and train individuals who cannot properly take care of the activities of daily living. Before discharge, the hospital staff can plan for a wide range of specific after-discharge support services. However, even in case your particular hospital is inadequate in the provision of some professional services, do not despair. You can bring your own homecare team to bear on problems the hospital could not take care of and still achieve results.

THE HOSPITAL TREATMENT TEAM

The ill member of your household is assigned to a hospital treatment team. Treatment team members represent an impressive array of professional mental health skills, which we would like to review at this time. As mentioned in chapter 5, many of these skills would be useful for your homecare team as well. Communicate any concern, question, plan, or procedure regarding the planning of the transition from hospital to home to hospital team members. A hospital treatment team will include the following members, though their titles may differ from institution to institution.

- The *psychiatrist* is a *physician* (which means that she/he possesses an M.D. degree and has the right to prescribe medication) with a specialty in psychiatry. As mentioned before, if possible, have the hospital psychiatrist serve as primary care physician for your homecare treatment team.

- The *psychiatric nurse* is a registered nurse (R.N.) with specialized expertise in the nursing of the mentally ill. In many cases, you may want to have a nurse on the homecare team, especially when there is a need to provide nursing services at home, such as the giving of injections and the execution of other special instructions from the M.D. for hygiene and dietary care.

- The *clinical psychologist* usually has a Ph.D. in psychology and special training in mental illness. If the recovering household member needs special psychological treatment, such as behavior modification or psychoeducation, the homecare team might want to engage a psychologist.

- The *psychiatric social worker* should have a Master's degree in Social Work (M.S.W.), with training in the provision of social services for the mentally ill. Especially in cases of long-term illness where the assistance (financial and otherwise) and networking of many different government agencies is required, the homecare team should include a social worker.

- The *rehabilitation counselor* guides the recovering individual on such issues as vocational evaluation, career orientation and training, job placement, and the use of available community assistance (mostly via the State Vocational Rehabilitation Offices). Especially for young adults who are chronically mentally ill, who have not had the opportunity to establish an employment record or are uncertain of their career, a specialist in psychiatric rehabilitation is a must for the homecare team.

- The *occupational therapist* and the *recreation therapist*, as part of the hospital team, are specialized in the evaluation of specific deficits, and they provide skill training to overcome these in the recovering person. There may be instances in which the homecare team will benefit from their participation, in particular when it is not so much the lack of employment, but the lack of daily living skills that troubles the individual.

- Often, other members of the hospital treatment team (such as the *licensed practical nurse*, the *mental health worker* [or mental health therapy aide], the *physical thera-*

pist, and the *special education teacher*) may provide services needed on the homecare team. Their involvement in treatment is understandable when we realize that, just as mental illness offers a great number of different problems, professionals in the mental health field have, over time, learned a great number of different problem-solving skills.

* In many larger hospitals, *treatment team leaders* may be assigned to coordinate the team, much as your function will be if you coordinate the homecare team. Treatment team leaders may belong to any of the aforementioned disciplines, and their assistance is crucial in planning for the transition from hospital to home.

SERVICES FOR THE MENTALLY ILL MEMBER OF YOUR HOUSEHOLD

Clearly, the better the preparation for the transition, the easier the adjustment of the recovering person to the community, with less stress experienced by you and the other members of your household. If at all possible, the discharge should be preceded by home visits of 1 or more days, to reintroduce the recovering member of the household into the home routine and to make everyone comfortable with the idea that he/she will be living there. In addition to becoming at ease with one another, you'll need to consider the details of many aspects of daily life, work, and recreation. Although support services are actually interrelated, it may be helpful to look separately at the three types of services needed in homecare: (1) basic services needed to keep the patient living at home; (2) services needed to occupy (or preferably employ) the patient during the daytime; and (3) services to fulfill the person's recreational and spiritual needs, especially after work hours and during weekends and holidays.

Basic Services to Enable the Recovering Individual to Live at Home

A review of basic services should be part of any treatment plan made to prepare for discharge. Obviously without assistance for psychiatric medication and supervision, health education, medical referral, or crisis intervention, you would be unable to take proper care of the recovering member of your household.

As mentioned in chapter 3, the choice of a primary care physician would be made more easy if the treating psychiatrist in the hospital would also make him/herself available for aftercare medication and continued supervision of the homecare plan of the mentally ill individual. But if you have to choose a primary care physician from those available in the community, he/she should be the one whom the hospital treatment team should contact prior to discharge. Also, upon discharge, the primary care physician should be forwarded a copy of the hospital record, or at least copies of the most important parts. The significant elements would include the intake/screening summary; the psychiatric, physical, social, nursing, and any other assessments; any consultations and laboratory findings; a list of medications given, with their dosages and effects; and the discharge summary. You should ask the hospital administration for any procedures and fees connected with this service and have the patient sign information releases. A hospital may not share, without formal approval by the patient, any of its medical records with nonhospital health care professionals.

In case the hospital provides homecare services for the patient, JCAHO standards state that a copy of the record pertaining to these activities will be forwarded at least once in 60 days to the person you have identified as the primary care physician.

For any physical ailments of the patient (as described in chapter 4), your family doctor should be involved, whether or not he/she is to be the primary care physician. If the patient does not have complicating medical illnesses such as diabetes, no special contact is needed prior to discharge between the hospital and your family doctor. When your family doctor will also be the primary care doctor, he/she will be receiving all the aforementioned records pertaining to the patient. However, when the primary care physician is a psychiatrist, both the psychiatrist and the family doctor should know about any physical problems before discharge. In that case, the easiest way is to ask hospital staff to forward copies of the physical assessment, any consultations or laboratory findings, and the discharge summary to both the family doctor and the psychiatrist (and primary care physician). It is also possible to have your psychiatrist (as primary care physician) either forward copies from the hospital records he/she received, or discuss the findings directly with your family doctor. In that case, prepare to have the patient sign a release form for the primary care physician as well.

A final problem may be the provision of specialized medical services for the recovering mentally ill person. It is often extremely difficult to locate a dentist or a physical rehabilitation specialist who is willing to take the extra time and make the special effort to work with the mentally ill. You must make a special effort to find the suitable, compassionate professional (as was described in chapter 3 regarding the primary care physician).

Services Needed to Occupy or Employ the Recovering Person

Apart from medication as part of the continuing psychiatric and medical treatment of the recovering individual, nothing is as important as his/her involvement in ongoing activity, especially employment. Work is an excellent treatment for the adult mentally ill, and homecare team members should stress its importance. Because of the prevailing work ethic in our society, it may be considered the most important aspect of treatment if we are to return full self-esteem to the recovering individual. For adolescents and young adults, employment may be replaced by or combined with continuing study programs or school. Remember never to give in to the inactivity seen in many recovering mentally ill persons (and encourage the members of your homecare team to do likewise).

It is true that in many cases after a serious mental illness, the discharged person cannot find employment or resume a previous job immediately. In such cases, there are several possible approaches to meaningful daily activities. If there is a rehabilitation counselor on the hospital treatment team, this person should be involved in the choice of alternatives.

A sheltered workshop offers entry level work for the lowest functioning persons. The workshop provides an atmosphere of gainful employment under minimal wage conditions for persons unable to hold competitive jobs. Because staff in such workshops offer work evaluation and training, as well as individual and group counseling, it is often possible for the individual gradually to gain sufficient work habits and incentive to be able to leave for employment elsewhere. However, for some recovering persons a sheltered workshop may be the only way to remain in the community and not burden the household during work hours.

Other approaches are transitional, such as continued day treatment programs provided either by the hospital or by an agency. These time-limited programs expect the recovering person to participate in learning activities pertaining to different areas of daily living, such as money management, shopping and food preparation, or application for employment. It is clear that successful completion of such a program will give the individual basic skills for independent living.

Another possibility is to have the recovering person enroll with the local or state Office of Vocational Rehabilitation in your community. This office will help the individual explore career opportunities and offer training courses in case he/she does not already have a specific skill or can no longer pursue a career begun before the illness.

Finally, you can look for an agency specialized in the rehabilitation of the chronic mentally ill. Such agencies often offer the range of services covered in continued day programs and have collaborative agreements with Offices of Vocational Rehabilitation to provide for employment opportunities. If you have difficulties motivating the recovering member of your household to look for employment, enrollment in a rehabilitation agency is a good option because it offers all job-related incentives, including prevocational work programs, transitional employment, and job placement. Further details of homecare planning to help develop skills for living in the community are discussed in chapters 5, 8, and 12.

If the discharged person is willing and able to work, even if it is initially only part time or on a volunteer basis, this is something to be strongly supported. The recovering individual sometimes wants to resume studies or decides to prepare for a different career. Any wish to explore the future is important and must be encouraged. Again, chronic mental illness typically robs a person of self-esteem and future expectations, so please use any interest that the person expresses to its fullest extent!

Often, a job or an apprentice position must be carefully chosen, with a view toward finding a milieu in which some understanding of chronic mental illness exists and you can count on some tolerance for the recovering individual. If you or members of your homecare team know of people in a position to arrange for such a job, spend time on cultivating this possibility. For the recovering person's future, this may be as important as finding a primary care physician!

As was the case with Debra in chapter 3, you must address confidentiality issues regarding possibly problematic aspects of the recovering person's behavior when trying to find or keep employment, apprentice, or volunteer positions. This needs much preparation and preferably the full understanding and cooperation of the recovering individual. It would be unrealistic to count on achieving an individualized employment plan as part of your homecare treatment program before discharge. But gainful employment and any preparation for it is as important as proper medication if you want to restore self-esteem to your loved one and offer him/her a chance for a satisfactory future. Constantly bear in mind ways in which to promote and encourage success in this area.

Services for the Individual's Recreational and Spiritual Life

After the provision of a roof over the head, basic health services, and regular daily productive activities, the recovering person will need opportunities for social, cultural, and religious life. Some of the mental health agencies, especially comprehensive rehabilitation agencies (discussed in chapter 12), offer the services of a social club and occasionally even provide linkages to local churches, synagogues, or mosques. In most cases, it will be up to members of the homecare team to encourage and guide the individual in developing relationships after hours.

Any chronic mental disease brings about disruption of previous social contacts, and, given the still existing fear of mental illness, the individual may feel truly shunned after discharge from the hospital. This is often further aggravated by the recovering person's tendency to withdraw. For the schizophrenic patient, this may be because of lingering feelings of suspicion or even positive symptoms of a delusional or a hallucinatory nature. In addition, such negative symptoms as lack of concentration and loss of initiative not only plague recovering schizophrenics and those suffering from anxiety or mood disorders, but also occur in many afflicted with organic brain syndromes, and even personality and substance abuse disorders. Stigma, shame, and fear aggravate the tendency to withdraw, thereby creating a vicious cycle of social isolation. Carefully plan for the ill person's social life when thinking about homecare.

To begin with, provide the recovering individual with the

means to communicate freely and, if you can afford it, provide opportunities for privacy by arranging for a separate phone extension or even an individual phone number. Encourage socialization by including the person in as many communal household activities as possible. Activity pace and frequency should not, however, be allowed to overload or frighten the individual. Try also to keep a record of any reactions, beginning with those that occur during home visits prior to discharge. After discharge, however, if agreed upon by the primary care physician, homecare members should involve the recovering person in shopping trips, visits to the movies, concerts, museums and events in the community for social stimulation (see more about this in chapter 10).

The next step is to guide the mentally ill individual to use any community resources that afford an opportunity to socialize. Possibilities include the local library, hobby clubs, and volunteer organizations. Volunteer organizations are especially well suited for recovering persons because not only do they involve social activities, but also they make demands for caring and giving to come from your mentally ill family member. And as is so often the case, she/he may be most helped by helping others! Initially you, or members of the homecare team, may have to accompany the patient to community activities, as was the case with William in chapter 2. Pay special attention to socializing with members of the opposite sex (as discussed in chapter 9).

We make special mention of religious activities because these have a personal spiritual dimension beyond the social and cultural advantages gained from participation in the life of the congregation. If the recovering individual or any member of the homecare team belongs to or has access to prominent members or leaders of any local church, synagogue, mosque, or meetinghouse, pursue the connection vigorously. Although there are still many barriers to the mentally ill in religious congregations, as there are in other aspects of public life, there have been recent efforts by organized religious organizations to minister to the mentally ill, both by training their leaders to help mentally ill individuals and by encouraging their congregations to make their suffering members feel welcome.

STEPS TO FOLLOW PRIOR TO DISCHARGE

Be sure to discuss all of your plans for discharge with your hospital treatment team. Tell them of your questions and concerns, as well as your hopes. Work to get all parties involved to agree when planning for discharge and for the implementation of the aftercare activities by the homecare team. For instance, as was shown in the case of Carlos in chapter 2, unless everyone has the same perspective on the need for medication and the avoidance of certain activities, rehospitalization may soon be needed. However, any of the aforementioned suggestions to meet the recovering person's needs in the areas of health, daily activities, and social and spiritual life may bring about conflict unless everyone, including the person him/herself, knows what the homecare team's expectations are.

When the hospital and you agree on how to accomplish the discharge goals and objectives, it is time to see if the recovering individual is ready for the transition from hospital to home. Here are some considerations when preparing for discharge:

1. *Is the recovering individual ready and able to live in a normal household?* The best way to find out is by trying repeated home visits. As with anything involving treatment and care of the recovering person, good planning is essential to make the home visit a positive learning experience. Be mindful of the fact that the transition period can produce tension and anxiety for the individual, your household, and everyone else involved. Think of what problems you can anticipate, and prepare for them. On the part of your household, discuss every member's expectations, decide who will manage prob-

lems, what methods will be used to handle them, and what your plan of activities for the day (or the weekend, etc.) will be. Make sure that your recovering household member understands the expectations of the family, agrees to the rules of conduct in problem areas, and generally accepts that there has to be structure and predictability to the home visit.

Most recovering persons are so eager to leave the hospital, even if it is just for a few hours, that they may ignore anything you tell them regarding the expectations for the home visit. You may experience difficulties communicating with the person if your statements are vague and offer too many options. Initially, please try to talk about things calmly and simply, never giving the individual more than two choices. And after the home visit, if need be, calmly go over one or two things that went wrong. Do not get excited when the recovering person does not act as controlled at home as he/she did in the hospital. The chronic mentally ill do not adjust easily to environmental changes, as they have difficulty *generalizing* (applying what they learn from one situation to another situation). Let's look at an example:

Vera, a 23-year-old office worker, had been hospitalized for schizophrenia for the second time in 2 years. The hospital treatment team decided that she was to prepare for discharge. She was to return to live with her widowed working mother and 25-year-old unemployed brother, a would-be drummer and aspiring rock musician. Her second home visit was planned to be for a weekend. The main purpose of this home visit was to determine whether Vera would be able to spend time with others outside her family.

The plan was that she would leave the hospital Friday after hours, spend the Saturday helping around the house in the morning, and visit friends in the afternoon. Sunday, she was to attend church services, including a congregational brunch. After an afternoon by herself, she was to return to the hospital in the evening. Choice of what to do on Friday and Saturday evening had been left up to Vera. Because she felt somewhat anxious about her first overnight visit, she opted to stay home both evenings.

The mother, upon returning her to the hospital early Sunday afternoon, reported that everything went well until late Saturday evening. At that time, Vera became increasingly restless and complained about the loud music her brother played until the early morning hours, as he practiced with his friends in the basement. By Sunday morning, Vera did not want to get up, and then she proved irritable, absent-minded, and withdrawn. Because is was important to keep her home visit schedule, the mother took her to church, but during the service, Vera became so distracted that she had to go outside. During the after-service social, she could not follow the conversation, and when she became loud and argumentative, her mother decided to take her home. At home, Vera accused her brother of playing rock music containing threats against her. When he ridiculed this notion, the argument escalated, and it soon became clear that the home visit had to be cut short.

During the week, the psychiatrist called the mother to explain that Vera had experienced a setback, most likely caused by environmental overstimulation. Vera needed more psychotropic medication because she showed more signs of being psychotic, especially in her complaints of hearing voices and feeling persecuted. In a subsequent analysis of the home visit, all agreed that the loud rock band practice had been the straw that broke the camel's back. It was decided that she would be protected in the future by either having the band practice elsewhere or by using earplugs. In addition, it was agreed by all that for a while Vera would be exposed to less sensory stimulation. This can be achieved by such precautions as using radio and television less often, avoiding bright lights in the rooms, giving her wraparound sunglasses for outside wear, asking her whether she feels up to social events before going, cutting off interaction as soon as she becomes irritable, and so on. Also, it was important to make her brother understand the nature of her vulnerability to overstimulation so that he could become more solicitous to her need for privacy.

Looking at Vera's home visit, we notice her own fears of being overstimulated in her choice of spending both evenings at home. We also notice (as with Bernard in chapter 2) that a sibling's sensitivity is needed to avoid a setback. The value of repeated home visits lies in learning how to deal with the recovering person's vulnerabilities and how to take precautions in the social environment.

2. *How is the person going to spend the working hours? And what help, if any, is to be provided at times when no member of the household is home?* Arranging for a daily activity program or employment is best, and, depending on the condition of the individual, it may be necessary to provide for supervision of the house at all times. The need for constant supervision depends on what the hospital team suggests and your own expectations of what potential problems may arise if the recovering person is alone at home. In many cases, during home visits, you may be able to observe whether the individual is able to take care of him/herself at home. During home visits or after discharge, the homecare team can try using a schedule to help guide the person in what to do when he/she is home alone. In other cases, however, (as for Zena, discussed in chapter 2), a schedule of 24-hour around-the-clock home coverage must be developed.

3. *What preparation must be made for the reaction of others not connected with the homecare treatment team, such as neighbors or children in the household?* Any close acquaintance of the mentally ill individual may feel guilt or anger: *guilt,* because they wonder whether they contributed to the illness or failed to be aware of the early warnings that something was wrong, and they did not help to prevent it; *anger,* because they may resent either the loss of a companion, or the obligation to take on more responsibility. Anger may also result from frustration due to a sense of helplessness in the face of what is happening to the ill person. Very often, acquaintances feel embarrassed or humiliated when someone from the same social circle is perceived as "different" because he or she behaves in unusual ways. Siblings or close friends often ask themselves, "What will others think of me when they know of my relative/friend?"

Address any of these feelings before the recovering person comes home. First, discuss problems privately with the siblings, neighbors, relatives, or friends. Later you might want to go over the important points of such conversations again, with others or the ill member of your household present if need be. Tact, patience, and love must guide such discussions.

Naturally, when discussing mental illness with young children, do so at their level of understanding. If necessary, involve someone else on the homecare team who knows how to communicate with youngsters about mental illness. In this way, everyone involved (even children) can view mental illness (and their own relationships with the ill family member) from their own perspectives.

Difficult as it may be, you must discuss the attitudes of members of your household and the homecare treatment team toward such issues as work, recreation, sexuality (see chapter 9), religion, and so on. Do not forget to talk about any emotions that may adversely influence the homecoming member of your household. This avoids a negative atmosphere in the household or disagreements among prospective members of your homecare team. The dangers of expressed or hidden negative emotions, and the lack of a consistent perspective for the treatment of the recovering person, have been discussed in chapter 2.

A FINAL WORD ON TRANSITION FROM HOSPITAL TO HOME

If you live in a town, region, or state where there are inadequate community support services, or if you are discouraged by the minimal support for discharge from your hospital, do not give up! As we mention throughout this book, homecare as an alternative to psychiatric hospitalization is not accepted universally. But if you and your homecare team focus on the recovering person's problems, one by one, you may be amazed at how much a homecare team can accomplish. Every small step forward is actually a major achievement. Further, each member of your team can then personally testify to homecare's success in assisting the chronic mentally ill to become self-sufficient. Household advocacy is a powerful lever in moving legislators and in formulating programs for change and progress. It also helps to speak about mental illness in an increasingly objective and open manner helping to eliminate the stigma. Thus, the difficulties associated with the release of the recovering person from the hospital will lead to the opening of our own minds.

7

MEDICATION

[Medicine] bitter to the taste,
restores health to the soul.

Ancient Dutch saying

The medical treatment of psychiatric illness, especially the use of psychotherapeutic (psychotropic) drugs or psychopharmacology, has become a specialty in itself. We do not intend to give a complete overview of psychopharmacology, but we discuss the most important drug therapies for the types of chronic mental illness mentioned in chapter 1.

For the functional psychoses—the schizophrenias and the mood disorders—remember two essential points: (1) Medication is often the *only treatment* that can keep the patient out of the hospital, and (2) medication is effective when it makes it *possible* for the patient to lead an *active* life, especially if it keeps him/her employed. In other words, medication for these disorders is mostly given long-term, not necessarily because it cures the illness—as a matter of fact, most of the time, we are happy if it just controls the positive symptoms—

but because it keeps the patient in the community, and, best of all, in a condition to engage in productive activities.

For the anxiety disorders, the organic brain disorders, and the personality and substance abuse disorders, medications are usually not given long-term. Instead, they are given periodically for specific symptoms and whenever there is a crisis. Some of the indications for medication with these disorders are discussed after we have had a chance to look at the uses and problems of long-term medication.

LONG-TERM MEDICATION: CAUTIONS AND PRECAUTIONS

The greater part of this review applies to the use of medication in the treatment of schizophrenias because almost all of the psychotropic drugs may be used in treating these illnesses at one time or another. First, we suggest some overall strategies and cautions for implementing drug therapy. Next, we suggest some factors to consider when planning for long-term maintenance drug therapy. Following that, we review the different types of drugs in use. Finally, we warn about some of the potential problems of long-term therapies.

As noted in previous chapters, the homecare coordinator should pay attention to the following:

1. **Information.** Try to keep yourself, as well as the recovering individual, educated about the effects and side effects of the particular medication(s) prescribed. As chapter 4 described, this will prepare you for what you might observe. Please ask the prescribing physician for what you might expect and also keep a reference guide such as the *Physician's Desk Reference* at hand.

2. **Advice.** Ask for advice about what to do when there are undesirable side effects. When in doubt, call your primary care physician or whoever is assigned to cover. Psychotropic drugs are quite safe to use and many

alarming side effects are not dangerous (described later in this chapter).

3. **Update.** Keep any M.D. or dentist abreast of all medications the recovering individual is taking. The easiest way to do this is to keep the psychiatric/medical identification card updated, as mentioned in chapter 4.

4. **Other Drugs.** See to it that the recovering individual does not drink alcohol, smoke marijuana, or use other street drugs. As described in chapters 1 and 2, chronic mentally ill persons often cannot tolerate these substances to begin with. Also, alcohol interacts with psychotropic drugs, and this may lead to serious side effects. If the individual wants to drink socially, keep to non-alcohol-containing substitutes or sodas (if possible without caffeine; see next point).

   If the ill person appears to be under the influence, don't panic. Being drunk may often safely be slept off. If there is an increase or change in symptoms, call the primary care physician or treat it as an emergency (see chapter 11). If habitual drinking jeopardizes continuing recovery, treat it as a warning signal for possible rehospitalization. Look for ways to decrease stress, consult your primary care physician (medication adjustment may help), or consider a self-help group such as Alcoholics Anonymous (see chapter 12).

5. **Nicotine and Caffeine.** Try to have the recovering individual avoid cigarettes (and pipes and cigars), coffee, and caffeine-containing drinks. It has been suggested that nicotine and caffeine interfere with the blood levels of medication and this would mean that prescription drugs would be less effective in helping the patient. In addition, caffeine tends to make a person nervous or jittery. If smoking and coffee drinking are useful in helping the recovering individual adjust, and team members would like to use coffee or cigarette breaks as reinforcement for good behavior,

try to substitute sweets for cigarettes and use decaffeinated coffee as much as possible.

6. **Logbook.** Monitor all medications used by entering the date and time of day in a logbook. Also monitor when the individual has had laboratory tests, and be sure to return on the dates prescribed for any repeat tests.

   Because it is in everyone's best interest to give no more medication than needed, monitoring of blood levels has been suggested. Although not all drugs can easily and inexpensively be detected in the blood, the technology is improving. Medication blood levels can be used to determine whether the person is actually taking the medication (compliance) and whether sufficient medication is being absorbed to provide an effective blood level. The latter is a check on whether the amount of the drug prescribed falls within a "therapeutic window." This window consists of two values: a minimum blood level below which the drug would be ineffective, and a maximum, beyond which medication is not needed or could become undesirable. Consult with your primary care physician if the medication prescribed for the recovering individual should be monitored in this manner.

7. **Frequency.** When it is at all possible, have the M.D. prescribe the medications on a once-a-day basis, preferably evenings, and note when medications have to be taken (such as after meals, before bedtime, etc.). Some psychotropic drugs may be given as a long-term injection (once a week or once a month), which makes compliance easy.

8. **Dietary Restrictions.** Make a list of all foods and beverages to avoid, and remind the recovering individual regularly to check it.

9. **Restricted Activities.** Remind yourself and the recovering individual regularly of any activities he/she is to

avoid when taking certain medications. Especially
during a crisis, medications that impair certain skills
may have to be prescribed. For instance, avoid driving
when heavily medicated, especially with antianxiety
drugs.

Maintenance Medication Therapy: What to Consider

Patients with a chronic mental illness need to maintain, often
for an indefinite time, the medication that helped them
during the acute phase. Often, much less of the medication
required when the patient was in a psychotic phase with many
positive symptoms, will be prescribed on a long-term basis.
But the great majority of studies has shown that uninter-
rupted medication is needed to keep positive symptoms
suppressed and to give patients the best chance to lead an
active life and thereby overcome their negative symptoms.
Therefore, (a) give maintenance drug therapy top priority in
the homecare plan, and (b) do everything you can to make
sure that the number of possible errors stays as low as possible.

First and foremost *keep a complete record* of any medication
the patient received and his/her reactions. It is best to keep
this record chronological, starting with the first medication
given when the patient showed symptoms but you were far
from thinking that his/her condition might become chronic.
Often you will have to go back to the record of the M.D. or
hospital to refresh your memory. Try to make a note of (a) the
name (trade or generic; see later), (b) the dosage, (c) the
time of day or night it was given, (d) the length of time for
which it was prescribed (with possible changes in dosage),
and (e) the effects noted at different times and with different
dosages during the illness. When tracing hospital records,
also pay attention to medications prescribed temporarily in
times of crises, for instance when the patient was violent, or
could not sleep. The p.r.n. medications (from the Latin *pro re*

nata, or "according to the circumstances"), if helpful at the time, certainly should be considered for use during times of homecare crises as well.

The next issue is to determine whether the patient can be trusted to take the medication by him/herself (i.e., *self-regulation*). Some chronic patients can be taught to be sensitive to their own symptoms and to be in charge of when and how much medication they need to take. It would be ideal if all patients could be so sensitive to their own needs and able to administer correct dosages as, for instance, many diabetics are in terms of keeping a diet and administering insulin or other antidiabetic drugs. And indeed, there are patients who will tell you of an increase in their symptoms and who are willing to change their medications accordingly.

However, in the great majority of cases, the very existence of such symptoms as inattentiveness and lack of motivation in schizophrenia make it necessary that recovering persons are under some sort of supervision. In addition, it is known that most chronic mental patients do not like to take medication. One reason is simple: If the drug makes them feel better and causes them to have fewer symptoms, the result is that they feel good and "back to normal." And, so they reason (and unfortunately, many outsiders tend to agree; see the case of Carlos in chapter 2), "Why continue taking it?" Another frequently cited reason for a recovering individual stopping medication is the fear of side effects, which often can be annoying and sometimes become debilitating (see later).

As a consequence, many studies have shown that the greatest single cause for rehospitalization is "medication noncompliance." In up to two thirds of repeat admissions, it has been found that the patient stopped taking medication months, weeks, or sometimes days before returning to the hospital. (Another frequent reason that most of the time leads to the stopping of medication is the patient's [ab]use of alcohol, marijuana, or street drugs.) Therefore, although as a rule all patients should be involved in understanding the effects, side effects, and need for their medication, a recovering person should not be entrusted lightly with self-medication, and only in exceptional cases should you trust an individual's self-regulation of medication.

A third consideration is the *attentiveness to medication on the part of homecare team members.* As mentioned in previous chapters, we think it is essential that all team members, without exception, be made aware of the patient's need for psychotropic medication. Further, each homecare team member should know which drugs are being taken, at what dosages, and on what schedule. When a team member is averse to medication, or in disagreement with the need for it, that attitude may be picked up by the recovering individual. Combined with the mentally ill person's own powerful feelings arguing for discontinuation, negative feeling within the team would sooner or later lead to undermining the effort of keeping the patient on maintenance medication.

But the awareness of medication needs has to go beyond full understanding of and support for the taking of particular drugs. All team members, as well as the patient him/herself, should look out for the return of symptoms that would indicate a relapse and may necessitate rehospitalization. Some of the most frequently found symptoms are that the recovering individual (a) feels tense and nervous, (b) has trouble sleeping or concentrating, (c) feels depressed, or (d) becomes suspicious of others. Others in the immediate environment of the person most often see such signs as him/her (e) becoming restless, (f) not being able to remember or show an interest in things, and (g) starting to laugh or talk to him/herself. If a functional assessment has been completed on the person (see chapter 5), this can be used to compare with previous behavior. Further description of danger signs and symptoms that should lead to quick intervention is provided in chapter 11.

Often, it is possible to make a *list of signs and symptoms* that could lead to a relapse. Each patient may show specific problems when (a) not taking medications, (b) being under stress, and otherwise (c) relapsing into illness.

Fay is a 30-year-old unmarried female who had to drop out of theological seminary 5 years ago because of diagnosed paranoid type schizophrenia. She's been living at home and working as a legal secretary for the past 3 years after her second hospitalization, while being maintained on the same medication. This recovering individual has come to know a sure symptom of deterioration: When she becomes hostile and argumentative, she will talk to the family about it and call her primary care physician for advice. Family and friends know that when she isolates herself and becomes engrossed in religious matters, this is an equally important sign that needs attention. These symptoms and signs have shown themselves to be easily corrected with an increase of, or temporary addition to, her medication.

A list of her danger symptoms and signs might therefore read: being argumentative, hostile, irritable, socially withdrawn, and/ or excessively religious.

Knowledge of specific signs and symptoms for a particular patient may be used for a quick check-up with the primary care physician or, if the patient refuses a doctor's visit, a request to the public health nurse to administer extra medication at home. If need be, and your community provides this facility, use a crisis residence as one of the strategies to prevent rehospitalization (see chapter 12).

There are other considerations in long-term medication maintenance: what to do when an accident, physical disorder, or pregnancy occurs. In the case of pregnancy, medication adjustments have to be made with caution (consider that no medication at all should be prescribed during pregnancy, certainly not in the first 3 months), and they should involve consultation between the psychiatrist and other medical specialists. In chapter 4, some of the problems arising when there is a need to treat both physical and mental illness have been discussed. The interaction between simultaneously prescribed drugs are complex and many. We want to point out that when in doubt, you should always discontinue the medication and see the primary care physician as soon as possible, or if the situation seems alarming, do not hesitate to take the individual to a hospital emergency room.

Another important consideration you might want to discuss with the primary care physician may be the question of *cost*. Apart from shopping around for the least expensive pharmacy and trying to buy medications in the largest size and quantity possible, we suggest three ways to economize. These range from easy to difficult and therefore will increase the time that your physician must spend on decision-making.

1. Most medications may be given in once-a-day dosage (long-term injectables can be given once a week or once a month), and that will be a saving because, in general, unit cost decreases with higher dosage. Although some doctors may be reluctant to prescribe all medications to be given at one time, it has been shown that an evening dosage in the majority of instances is well tolerated and is just as effective as taking medications two or three times a day. It can do no harm to try this easy method of cost saving to see if the patient agrees with it—an incidental benefit is that any side effects of the medication would occur during sleep when it is least annoying.

2. Another saving would be to have the doctor prescribe the medication under its generic rather than its trade or brand name. Most drugs are less expensive and of the same quality when provided by pharmaceutical companies other than the original producer. However, there may be some slight differences, and the doctor might want to consult the literature or a psychiatrist with experience in this matter before going along with this suggestion.

3. Finally, it is possible to experiment by switching the originally prescribed medication to one of its less expensive equivalents (discussed in the next section). However, this is rarely done before the patient has achieved a consistent stable level of functioning and thus can afford to experiment. On the part of the doctor, it requires research into current equivalency findings and price differentials (you might do well if you know a knowledgeable pharmacist!). Not many doctors are willing to spend the effort, but if your patient has been receiving an expensive psychotropic drug while in the hospital, it might be worth your trying to change it for routine long-term medication.

MAINTENANCE THERAPY: PSYCHOTROPIC DRUGS

All drugs with a psychotherapeutic effect on mental function or behavior are called "psychotropic." The drugs most used in maintenance therapy are of five types: (1) antipsychotics, (2) antidepressants, (3) anxiolytics or antianxiety drugs, (4) anticholinergics and other drugs against side effects, and (5) lithium and other miscellaneous drugs.

For the functional psychoses, the main drugs are *antipsychotics,* which also have been called "major tranquilizers" or "neuroleptics." Originally, it was thought that they made the mind more tranquil and therefore the patient more easy to work with. However, they do not always produce tranquilization, and other drugs that do quiet patients down are not able to influence psychotic symptoms, so the name *tranquilizer* has become confusing. However, their designation as antipsychotics is correct because they do control the positive symptoms of severe mental illness. They do not as such cure the illness, and it is best to compare them to the kind of drugs that control the symptoms of diabetes, which cannot be cured either.

The main classes of antipsychotics and the most representative drugs in each group are provided in Table 7.1 (the oldest antipsychotic is chlorpromazine, known as Thorazine® in the U.S., discovered and named Largactil® in France, 1952). The last column in these drug tables shows the equivalent dosage—that is, the amount of the drug to be given in order to match approximately the effects of one of the first discovered and most established drugs in the group. A daily dosage most likely to be effective is also shown. We emphasize that these figures only provide guidelines and that doctors differ in their equivalency estimates. In addition, needless to say, many patients will do well with much less of the drug, or may need much more to experience positive results. If the particular drug can be detected in the blood (e.g., Haldol®, Serentil®), determination of its blood level and adhering to

Table 7.1. Types and Equivalent Doses of Antipsychotic Drugs

Family	Trade name	Generic name	Equivalent dose[a] (baseline Thorazine daily dose of 300 mg, divided by . . .)
Phenothiazines	Thorazine (Largactil, etc.)	chlorpromazine	—
	Mellaril	thioridazine	2
	Serentil	mesordazine	4
	Vesprin	triflupromazine	6
	Trilafon	perphenazine	12
	Stelazine	trifluoperazine	15
	Prolixin (Permitil)	fluphenazine	30
Butyrophenones	Haldol	haloperidol	30
Thioxanthines	Navane	thiothixene	15
	Taractan	chlorprothixene	4
Dihydroindolones	Moban	molindone	10
Dibenzoxazepines	Loxitane	loxapine	10

[a]The equivalency figures are only approximate and apply to drugs given by mouth. The calculation is as follows:For any 300 mg of Thorazine, you may consider substituting, e.g., 24 mg of Trilafon or 10 mg of Prolixin. Cells with dashes are already equivalent.

144

the "therapeutic window" is the best way to settle this question.

For use in depression, panic disorders, or phobias (morbid fears connected with specific objects or circumstances), and many of the substance abuse disorders there are *antidepressants*. These medications are very effective in treating symptoms of depression—hence the name. But some of these therapeutic drugs have also been used in preventing severe anxiety attacks and the craving for addictive substances, especially cocaine. Additionally, in some cases of depression occurring in schizophrenic patients, or in a mixture of mood disorder and schizophrenia, the so-called schizo–affective disorder, antidepressants may be prescribed. There are two major classes of antidepressants: the monoamine oxidase inhibitors (MAOIs) and the tricyclic-like antidepressant drugs (TCAs). The TCAs are most commonly used, and in many cases, their blood level may be taken to determine whether it is within the "therapeutic window" mentioned earlier.

The MAOIs have the disadvantage of severe restrictions with their use. For instance, with certain foods, "hypertensive crises" may occur—that is, a sudden increase in blood pressure, which may lead to serious consequences. That is why in the great majority of cases, TCAs are prescribed. There are depressive syndromes for which some doctors would prescribe MAOIs, and at times the combined use of an MAOI and a TCA might be considered, but this should be done with great caution. The most common antidepressants are shown in Table 7.2, which provides the generic name as well as the trade name and the therapeutic equivalent dosage.

Anxiolytics are the most commonly prescribed drugs for use in states of excitement, (muscle) tension, or anxiety. In the past, drugs from the class of sedatives–hypnotics (e.g., chloral hydrate or such barbiturates as Luminal® and Nembutal®) were used,[1] but because anxiolytics, especially many of the

---

[1] Barbiturates are generally only used in hospital practice and for seizure disorders. Because of their side effects, they should not be used to calm one down or as a sleeping pill.

Table 7.2. Types and Equivalent Doses of Antidepressant Drugs

Family	Trade name	Generic name	Equivalent dose[a] (baseline Elavil daily dose 150 mg)
TCA and like	Elavil (Endep)	amitriptyline	—
	Aventyl (Pamelor)	nortriptyline	divide by 2
	Vivactyl	protriptyline	divide by 4
	Tofranil (Janimine)	imipramine	—
	Norpramin (Pertofrane)	desipramine	—
	Sinequan (Adapin)	doxepin	—
	Asendin	amoxapine	multiply by 2
	Ludiomil	maprotiline	—
	Desyrel	trazodone	multiply by 2
MAO inhibitors	Nardil	phenelzine	divide by 4
	Marplan	isocarboxazid	divide by 8
	Parnate	tranylcypromine	divide by 8

[a]See Table 7.1 for explanation. Cells with dashes are already equivalent.

benzodiazepines, are much safer and do not make one sleepy, they are preferred today. For this reason, they are also called minor tranquilizers, because they calm the patient without putting him/her to sleep. Nevertheless, such drugs should be given sparingly and generally for short periods only. One of the important disadvantages of prolonged use is that one can develop a tolerance for their effects. More important, because they provide easy relief and relaxation, abuse and addiction are common. There are three classes of anxiolytics: the glycerol derivatives, the benzodiazepines, and the azaspirodecanediones. Table 7.3 describes their characteristics.

Among the *miscellaneous drugs* used for psychotic and nonpsychotic mental disorders, the following have come to be generally accepted (for a discussion of miscellaneous new medications and some other medical treatments, see chapter 14, "A Look Toward the Future"):

Lithium is one of the most useful drugs (it is actually a salt, which is one of the reasons it took a long time to get established in psychiatric treatment because no drug company wanted to develop it for the market). It was first used for the treatment and prevention of mania and manic-depressive psychoses, but then it showed its usefulness in periodic depression, schizophrenia, alcoholism, and other disorders with mood disturbances, including schizo–affective disorder.

Carbamezapine (Tegretol®) was introduced as an antiseizure medication, but it has become useful as a replacement for lithium, for patients who responded but experienced serious side effects. Carbamezapine may also be used in certain forms of schizophrenia; in such cases, it is often prescribed together with an antipsychotic. Unfortunately, Tegretol® has its own serious side effects, and users therefore must be carefully monitored.

Clonazepam (Clonopin®) is a benzodiazepine and as such also used against seizures. However, like Tegretol®, it can serve as a replacement for lithium, and it is used as temporary support during withdrawal of drug addictions as well. An-

Table 7.3. Types and Equivalent Doses of Anxiolytic Drugs

Family	Trade name	Generic name	Equivalent dose[a] (baseline Miltown daily dose 800 mg divided by . . .)
Glycerol derivatives	Miltown (Equanil)	meprobamate	—
	Solacen (Tybatran)	tybamate	2
Benzodiazepines	Librium	chlordiazepoxide	80
	Valium	diazepam	150
	Tranxene	clorazepate	30
	Dalmane[b]	flurazepam	30
	Ativan	lorazepam	400
	Serax	oxazepam	50
	Xanax	alprazolam	800
	Clonopin[c]	clonazepam	400
Azaspirodecanediones	Buspar	buspirone	30

[a]See Table 7.1 for explanation. Cells with dashes are already equivalent.
[b]Used primarily in the evening and for sleep.
[c]Used in drug withdrawal and to prevent seizures.

other well-known drug is *methadone,* used as replacement therapy in patients addicted to heroin or other opiates.

For all these drugs, a therapeutic window exists, and blood levels should be checked regularly.

LONG-TERM MEDICATION: POTENTIAL PROBLEMS

The main problem, and the one that is responsible for most of the resistance against the taking of drugs both in patients and in the public at large is undesirable side effects. Although all drugs, even such widely used and accepted ones as aspirin, may cause side effects, those caused by drugs used to combat mental illness seem the most unpopular. This is not because psychotropic drugs are a danger to physical health or life. On the contrary, drugs used against the functional psychoses belong to the *safest and least addictive drugs* in medical use. Psychotropic drugs are often looked upon negatively because (1) especially initially, they often cause noticeable, bothersome, and often frightening mental and neurological side effects, even while they are effective against symptoms of mental disorder, and (2) they may cause lasting and possibly irreversible side effects (such as tardive dyskinesia) when used long term.

We cannot possibly discuss all side effects of the categories of drugs used for the maintenance therapy of the chronic mental patient. However, we try to give an overview of the most common problems encountered in long-term administration of medication. There are positives in this difficult therapy maintenance: For instance, once the medication has been taken for a while, the chance of any new type of side effect appearing is minimal. Also, many of the initial side effects have either spontaneously disappeared or have been brought under control by other medications. All in all, during maintenance drug therapy, the number of annoying or debilitating side effects is limited, and any remaining potential danger associated with taking the medication is minuscule.

Yet, as is the case with any side effect to any drugs used in medicine, their appearance and seriousness cannot be predicted in advance with any accuracy, but we do know which ones are often or rarely seen, and much literature is available about their frequency. Both the drug package insert and the *Physicians Desk Reference* list the possible side effects. Here, we briefly review the most memorable types of side-effects: (1) Those that are common, perhaps annoying, but generally nonserious (these can, less frequently, become more serious and even—in very rare instances—become dangerous to life); and (2) those that are seldom seen, but alarming, as well as the rare toxic conditions that are life-endangering. Finally, we will briefly review tardive dyskinesia.

Common, Relatively Safe Side Effects

Patients complain of many side effects when they first use a drug. These usually diminish or disappear completely after the first few weeks of use. In the case of neuroleptic drugs, many side effects are not alarming (such as feeling drowsy, weak, and dizzy—as remarked earlier, this is one of the good reasons to take medication in one dose before bedtime!).

Other nonserious side effects are frightening or annoying—such as the so-called dystonic reaction, which is the least serious of the so-called extrapyramidal symptoms (EPS). In the dystonic reaction, certain muscles become stiff and begin to spasm, especially those of the neck, face, or eyes. These reactions are unpleasant and alarming both for the patient and for the onlooker. Luckily, they can be quickly reversed by giving an anticholinergic or benzodiazepine drug. Other EPS's are not generally confined to the beginning of medication, but they become part of ongoing use, especially with higher doses of the medication. The most important are *akathisia* (a feeling of extreme restlessness, also described as "restless legs"), and Parkinsonism. The latter name comes from the resemblance to a neurological disorder, Parkinson's disease, but it is not the same. The main components of Parkinsonism are *akinesia* (a slowness and poverty of voluntary movement); tremor and rigidity of muscles, especially fingers; and a tendency to shuffle when walking and automatic movements (*dyskinesia*).

Because many of the antipsychotic drugs produce these unpleasant side effects, several drugs have been used either to prevent or to decrease these reactions. The most widely used are the so-called *anticholinergics*, which are useful against the EPS's involving muscles and movement. Some other drugs for long-term use are also mentioned in Table 7.4, which provides a summary of the most important names and uses. However, the widely used anticholinergics of Table 7.4, while decreasing EPS side effects, may themselves cause anticholinergic side effects: dry mouth, blurred vision, rapid heart beat, constipation, and so on. Unfortunately, such anticholinergic side effects are also commonly seen at the outset of medication with many antipsychotic or antidepressant drugs; they often disappear after continued usage. However, when anticholinergic drugs are used against EPS caused by antipsychotic drugs, the annoying anticholinergic side effects may return or become permanent.

Moreover, because of possible *synergism* (that is, a working together of different substances whereby their effects are increased) between antipsychotic–antidepressant and anticholinergic drugs, such rare and very serious anticholinergic side effects as paralysis of the intestines or urinary retention may occur. Also, we may observe such toxic anticholinergic side effects as impairment of memory, disorientation, and even visual hallucinations. In other words, although this does not often happen, if combinations of medications are not carefully watched, they can induce life-threatening and even psychosis-like symptoms because of an increase in the anticholinergic side effects! This is the main reason why some practitioners do not like to use anticholinergics on a regular

Table 7.4. Names of Drugs Used against EPS and Other Side Effects

Family	Trade name	Generic name	Used for		
			EPS[a]	Parkinsonism	Spasms, seizures
Anticholinergics	Benadryl (Sominex, etc.)	diphenhydramine	Yes	—	—
	Cogentin	benztropine	Yes	—	—
	Artane	trihexyphenidol	Yes	—	—
	Akineton	biperiden	Yes	—	—
	Kemadrin	procyclidine	Yes	—	—
Dopamine agonist	Symmetrel	amantidine	—	Yes	—
Benzodiazepines	Ativan	lorazepam	—	—	Yes
	Valium	diazepam	—	—	Yes

[a]EPS-extra-pyramidal symptoms.

basis. Instead, they either (a) try to decrease the antipsychotic medication to see if the positive symptoms can be controlled on a lower dosage without causing EPS for which anticholinergics are needed or (b) choose from the other two families of anti-EPS drugs mentioned in Table 7.4. Another reason for such conservative practice is that some patients get to like the "high" (elated feeling) caused by the toxic anticholinergic effect and learn to abuse such drugs as Cogentin® and Artane®.

Other less common but long-term side effects are orthostatic hypotension (a sudden drop in blood pressure when standing up from a sitting or prone position, which may cause fainting) and weight gain. An overview of these side effects for the anticholinergics and the other drugs discussed is given in Tables 7.5 and 7.6.

Rare, Serious Side Effects

Among the less frequently seen but often embarrassing side effects are those of hormonal nature: menstrual changes, discharges from the breasts, and such sexual problems as impotence. One may also see skin reactions: *photosensitivity* (sensitivity to sunlight; especially when receiving chlorpromazine, stay out of sunlight!) and allergic reactions, fever, rashes, and so on. Then there are the extremely rare but serious problems, primarily associated with the blood-forming organs, with the liver, and with the retina of the eye. Another side effect to watch for, especially in summer, is heat stroke. Needless to say, any of these more serious reactions may have to lead to complete discontinuation of the medication. We can only repeat at this point that these reactions are almost never seen in long-term medication, especially if it is carefully monitored by a knowledgeable physician. We have stated this as the foremost consideration in homecare!

An embarrassing syndrome associated with long-term medication, which sometimes is a real handicap to the

Table 7.5. Common and Not Serious or Dangerous Side Effects[a]

Class of drug	General[b]	EPS			Anticholinergic[c]
		Dystonic	Akathisia	Parkinsonism	
Antipsychotic	++	+	+	++	++
Antidepressant	+				++
Anxiolytic	++				
Lithium	+ nausea & tremor				
Carbamazepine	+				
Anti-EPS:					
Anticholinergic					+++
Other	+				

[a]Empty cells indicate the absence or rarity of this symptom.
[b]Drowsiness, weakness, and feeling dizzy.
[c]Dry mouth, blurred vision, rapid heartbeat, constipation.

Table 7.6. Long-term, Less Common, or Rare but Serious Side Effects[a]

Class of drug	General[b]	EPS		Anticholinergic	
		Akathisia	Parkinsonism	Physical[c]	CNS[d]
Antipsychotics	+	++	++	+	
Antidepressants	+			+	+
Anticholinergics				++ synergism	++

[a]Empty cells indicate the absence or rarity of the symptom.
[b]Weight gain, fainting.
[c]Such as intestinal paralysis, urinary retention.
[d]Such as confusion, hallucinations.

patient's functioning, is *tardive dyskinesia*, which involves *stereotyped* (that is, repeated and involuntary) movements of the mouth and face, also of the head and neck, less often of the limbs, and sometimes of the torso as well. Most noticeable are chewing, sucking, or tongue-licking movements; blinking of the eyes; or grimacing. Hands or feet (or arms and legs) may tremble or move slowly, and the patient is often not aware of such movements. Often, these symptoms increase when the individual experiences stress. These symptoms may appear when medication is given long term, or they may first show when long-term medication is discontinued. The reason for tardive dyskinesia is unclear, and there is no generally accepted way to prevent or treat it, although there are some new drugs that either do not cause or seem to decrease the symptoms of this disorder (see chapter 14).

A FINAL WORD OF CAUTION

Much can be said about the dangers of psychotropic drugs used in combination with other medications or in certain physical diseases or environmental conditions (extremely hot weather was mentioned earlier). We do not discuss the potential problems here. They are not to be handled by a layperson, and you should call the primary care physician at any time when homecare team members of the recovering individual notice something unusual. If you cannot reach the doctor, you should stop giving any medication, and if needed take the patient to the nearest hospital emergency room.

> Notice how important it is to have remembered to keep the psychiatric and medical identification card carried by the recovering person up to date, as described in chapter 4.

You may like to know that interruption of long-term medication for period of up to a few days is not harmful. In long-term medication maintenance practice, it even has become usual to allow "drug holidays."

As long as you and the recovering individual remain focused on the fact that medication is most important and should be thought of first when something unusual occurs, you'll keep your loved one safe. The fact that there are many possible interactions among drugs (including among different types of psychotropic drugs, as shown earlier), is the most important reason to leave all medication decisions in the hands of your competent primary care physician and to keep looking for good cooperation among the different medical specialists who may be involved in homecare treatment.

PART THREE

INDIVIDUAL PROBLEMS

8

THE RECOVERING PERSON

Masking sober thoughts, concealed
  behind a Mona Lisa smile.
Tasting Bitter Words congealed,
  beneath a safely honeyed guile,
Keeping Gypsy Laughter sealed,
  within a valentine of lies,
A silent stranger shares my world
  and mocks it with my eyes.

Charlotte Pais, The Censor

NORMALIZATION

It is usually not the way a person looks that says, "I'm mentally ill"; it's the way the person acts that tells the truth. The "silent stranger" tries to rob the mentally ill person of any concept of normality. In order to counteract this situation, the individual must try to reach a degree of normalization. This chapter is designed to help reach this goal of recovery.

Normalization means having a normal routine of living—

that is, getting up every morning; getting dressed, going to work or school; enjoying recreation; celebrating birthdays and holidays; experiencing and receiving love; and taking care of the self (physical, emotional, and spiritual). Normalization also involves imitating the behaviors of other members of society. Most of society's required behaviors for being normal are not very complex. They are behaviors that are taken for granted; for instance, a man walking down the street, wearing an expensive suit, is considered normal, and his behavior is taken for granted. However, if this same man were carrying a metal lunchbox, his behavior would be considered abnormal or different. Abnormal appearance or behavior stigmatizes and ostracizes the mentally ill. Therefore, the recovering person has a better chance of acceptance and overcoming stigma by appearing to be normal. It is important to discuss these issues repeatedly until the individual is fully aware of their importance.

For instance, staying up late and sleeping in the daytime may be normal for the mentally ill person. However, getting up in the middle of the night and wandering the streets may draw the attention of the police. It is not uncommon that a recovering person is addressed by police in the streets and then panics. This may also lead to being arrested and either booked at the police station or taken to the emergency room of the local hospital. Sometimes, it can lead to (unnecessary) hospitalization. Not only is this seen in persons recovering from a functional psychosis, but also, as mentioned previously, in older demented persons, who often have a different "psychic clock," getting up at odd hours and wanting to leave the home. For such individuals, it is imperative to have identifying data on the person at all times. This can be done using an identification bracelet or necklace, as discussed in chapter 4.

SELF-CARE SKILLS

Specific skills are needed to make the recovering person feel sufficiently in control and looking as if he/she belonged. Self-care skills are a key part of the process of appearing normal. In fact, most people never think twice about bathing, brushing their teeth or hair, cutting or cleaning their nails, or even dressing appropriately. However, one of the first signs of mental illness is lack of concern for personal appearance and personal hygiene. A person may have to relearn all the steps necessary for self-care. For this purpose, we have taken certain skills and broken them down into small steps appropriate for relearning. Items needed to complete each skill are also listed.

Skill:	Taking a bath or shower
Items needed:	wash cloth
	towel
	soap
	nail brush
	shampoo if washing hair
	cream rinse or conditioner if washing hair
	deodorant
What to do:	Undress
	Put dirty clothes in hamper
	Hang up other clothes
	Run water until warm
	Get in shower or tub
	Shampoo hair first
	Rinse hair
	Put cream rinse or conditioner on hair
	Rinse hair again
	Wet wash cloth and put soap on
	Wash and rinse face
	Wash all other body parts
	Rinse body
	Use nail brush and clean nails
	Stand up and use towel to towel dry hair
	Let tub water drain
	Dry body
	Put on deodorant

Return soap, shampoo, rinse to proper
place
Hang towel and wash cloth
Dress

Skill:	Brushing teeth
Items needed:	toothbrush
	toothpaste
	glass of water
	mouthwash
What to do:	Put toothpaste on toothbrush
	Brush teeth, using up-and-down strokes
	Rinse mouth with water
	Rinse with mouthwash
	Rinse toothbrush
	Put items away

Skill:	Hair care
Items needed:	towel
	hair dryer
	comb
	plastic bristle brush
	(rollers or styling instrument for females)
What to do:	After shampooing, use brush to remove tangles
	Towel-dry hair
	Complete drying with hair dryer
	Brush hair into place
	Use styling instrument or rollers to hold in place
	Recommended: a body wave for females

Skill:	Cutting fingernails and toenails
Items needed:	curved nail scissors or nail clippers
	waste basket
	emory board
What to do:	Holding scissors, trim nails
	Use emory board to shape nails
	Trim toenails

Put clippings from nails into wastebasket
Put items away

Skill:	Shaving face (men)
Items needed:	electric shaver
	mirror with good light
	soap to wash face
	after-shave lotion
What to do:	Wash face
	Turn on shaver
	Shave each side of face
	Shave upper and lower lip
	Shave throat
	Put on after-shave lotion
	Note: Men who have trouble shaving will look much better with a trimmed beard and moustache. A once-a-month trip to the barber for a haircut and trim might save frustration.

Skill:	Shaving legs and underarms (women, if desired)
Items needed:	electric shaver
	soap for washing legs or underarms
What to do:	(It is best to shave right after a bath or shower)
	Wash legs and underarms
	Turn on shaver
	Shave underarms
	Shave legs
	Put items away

Skill:	Feminine hygiene (women only)
Items needed:	Self-sticking sanitary napkins
	Clean underpanties
What to do:	Put on panties
	Pull off paper strip from bottom of sanitary napkin
	Stick napkin on inside of panties

Throw away paper strips
Wrap dirty napkin in tissue paper, and put
   in designated garbage container

Skill:	Using makeup (women only)
	Note: This section is only for women who prefer to wear makeup or for caregivers teaching the use of makeup. The applying and wearing of makeup can sometimes be difficult for a demented person. It is much more important to have a clean face than to wear makeup inappropriately.
Items needed:	moisturizer
	flesh-colored foundation makeup and powder
	cheek blush (use a nice soft color)
	eye shadow (color of eyes)
	mascara (dark brown or black)
	lipstick (same color as blush)
What to do:	Start with a clean face
	With fingertips, apply moisturizer onto face
	Apply makeup lightly on face
	Use brush to apply powder over all of face
	Apply a little blush on cheeks
	Lightly apply shadow on upper eyelids
	Use mascara on upper and lower lashes
	Finish with lipstick applied on lips
	Note: Wash off makeup at the end of the day, before going to bed.
Skill:	Eating and drinking
Items needed:	food and drink
	napkin
	knife, fork, spoon
	plate
	glass
What to do:	Put small amounts of food on plate

Put a drink in glass
Sit at table
Put napkin on lap
Cut meat with fork and knife
When finished with knife, lay it across the
   back of the plate
Eat with fork
Put other hand in lap
Use napkin and spoon as necessary
Drink from glass when necessary
When finished, place knife, fork, and
   spoon across plate
Wipe mouth, and place napkin back on
   table

These charts can be copied and posted so that the recovering person will be able to see them as each task is being completed. Completed tasks can be recorded on a chart of accomplishments (Figure 8.1). We strongly recommend that a routine be established when developing self-care skills. If the listed steps are particularly difficult, feel free to break them down into even smaller steps. If needed, and if the recovering person is too young or just doesn't remember how to care for his/her body, show the correct way—reading from your chart as you teach the skills. Remember that your

Skill ✔ (check when completed)							Date						
Take a Bath	S	M	T	W	Th	F	S	S	M	T	W	Th	F	S
1. (items) ___													
2. ___													
3. ___													
4. ___													
5. ___													

Figure 8.1.   Chart of Accomplishments

relative will respond better if he/she is rewarded with positive reinforcement, such as, "You smell so nice when you've taken a bath." If the individual is having trouble doing anything toward self-care, reinforce the first tiny positive thing accomplished, such as, "You did well by putting soap on your wash cloth!" (The chart of accomplishments is a simplified version of the schedules shown in chapter 5.)

WARDROBE PLANNING

When planning a wardrobe (see Table 8.1), stick with the basics and put a name inside each garment. We also recommend a color analysis for both male and female. This will help avoid dull, drab clothing that does nothing for the recovering individual.

Other items that both male and female need are sleep clothing; robe (summer and winter); at-home leisure wear; exercise and sports clothing; old clothing for working outside; swimsuits, shoes (for dress, casual, sport, and house), and sandals; gloves and hats; and intimate apparel (under-

Table 8.1. Basic Wardrobe*

Women	*Men*
Warm basic dress coat	Warm basic dress overcoat
Rain jacket	Rain jacket
Heavy sweater or jacket	Heavy sweater or jacket
Everyday coat	Everyday coat
Basic suit (gray or blue)	Basic dark blue or gray suit
1 for winter and 1 for summer	(wool blend)
2 Basic dresses (for dress)	Dress pants (two)
Everyday dresses (2)	Everyday pants (jeans for casual
4–5 Other casual skirts	or work, other for golf or
and pants	meeting with family & friends)
4–5 Casual tops	4 or 5 casual shirts, 3 casual
Dress and casual handbags	t-shirts, 3 dress shirts, 3 ties

*This is intended to be a basic wardrobe only. Clearly, more or less could be included.

wear, socks, hose). Also on this list should be a watch and other jewelry the recovering person feels would make him/her look or feel better.

These clothes are arranged in the closet and in drawers, according to where they should be worn. Reevaluate clothing each season, and decide what needs to be replaced. Check the person's shopping skills when something has to be bought, as explained in chapter 10.

PLANNING FOR BEHAVIORAL PROGRESS

Will the Recovering Person Continue to Progress?

Yes, progression will continue if the treatment regimen is followed and the caregivers are willing to help. At times, this progression will seem to level off, but it will pick up again after a period of consolidation. Please remember that attempting to achieve too much progress too soon is unrealistic and can be counterproductive. In your eagerness to help, you may be planning for accomplishments that the recovering individual is not ready to achieve. Studies in normal people have shown that too much change at one time can be stressful and cause harm. For instance, starting a new job while either moving to another place to live or socializing with heretofore unknown people may stress the recovering person so much that psychotic symptoms return. Therefore, please plan to go slowly, especially during other transitions, such as hospitalization or a new treatment.

Starting the recovering person at his/her own functional level is highly important. If the person is 22 years old and functions as a 3-year-old, you must act as though you are working with a 3-year-old. It is not degrading to the recovering person to do this. If a person can't read, you would not give her/him thick novels to read; you would begin by teaching the person to read simple words, then you'd expand the reading vocabulary. The same thing goes for mentally ill people. They may have read complex or technical literature before their psychotic break, but when recovering, they may not be able to read at that level. You will need to check with your own functional assessment (discussed in chapter 5) when you suspect problems.

Will There Ever Be Setbacks?

It would be nice to say that there would not be any setbacks; however, that is not the case. Things can be moving smoothly without a problem in sight, then something will happen that will call a halt to progression. This halt can be caused by an environmental, physical, or medication problem. Results can be regression in behavior. Here again, refer back to the functional assessment (in chapter 5) to get an idea of what is happening. You may have to let up for a while and assess the situation; things may clear up. If they don't, report your evaluation of the situation to the doctor or let the team decide what needs to be done.

Can You Expect Smooth Sailing with Only Minor Setbacks?

Yes and no—at times, everything will be smooth. At other times, there may be violent outbursts; inappropriate manners; distrustful behavior; withdrawal; excessive smoking; a refusal to get out of bed, take medication, bathe, change clothes, or speak when spoken to; or running away.

What Can Be Done About These Inappropriate Behaviors If They Happen?

Because the behaviors are different, you may have to manage each one differently. Here are some examples to help you.

- **Violent outbursts.** First, get a safe distance away from the ill person. Yell, "STOP!" once. Don't repeat the yelling and arguing, as it will only make matters worse. If your effort at getting attention works, keep your distance and calmly talk to the person; ask what has upset him/her. If the person doesn't talk, try to figure out what might have caused the outburst. Was a routine changed? Was the person unsuccessful at performing a task? Was the person in a social or crowded situation that was overwhelming? Did a movie or television show precede the event? Is there undue stress among members of the household?

When you can't reason with the ill person, you may have to call for outside help—maybe even involving the police. An assault is an act of violence, and police will answer when this act is taking place. There will be no time on the phone to explain; just give your address and say that there has been an assault. (Also see chapter 11.)

- **Inappropriate manners.**   Ignore as much as possible. Try using positive reinforcement for the behaviors done correctly, or start a conversation about something the recovering person enjoys.

- **Distrustful behavior.**   Try to discover why the ill person is acting distrustful. Make sure you are not whispering in his/her presence. Avoid being tricky in order to get things accomplished, especially if the individual is aware of what you are doing!

- **Social withdrawal.**   Stay with the recovering individual so that you reassure him/her of your love. Use simple, nonthreatening language. Comment positively about the way the person looks or something he/she did that was successful.

- **Excessive smoking.**   Have certain rules on where a person can smoke. In the beginning, it is not advisable to let the recovering individual smoke in the bedroom (especially the severely ill person) unless this activity is under control. This means that you may have to write a schedule or make a contract to ensure that the individual knows when and where smoking is allowed, how to use ashtrays, how to make sure that nothing is left burning when there is an interruption, etc. Cigarettes can be used as rewards; this will help moderate how often and how many the individual smokes.

- **Refusal to**
  - *Get out of bed.* Check with the schedule, saying, "This schedule says that the time to get up is 8 o'clock. Are you up yet?" (You can't give a check mark if the task is not completed). Find out if the individual is physically ill. Ask if you should call a doctor.
  - *Bathe.* Refer to and read the schedule with the individual; always ask questions; don't make demands. Reinforce anything done toward bathing.
  - *Change clothes.* Check with the schedule again. Give the individual clean clothing, saying "I'll be happy to wash the favorite clothes you have on if you will give them to me. I know that you like the feel and smell of your favorite clothes being clean." Another approach might be, "As soon as you put on these clothes, we will go out."
  - *Speak when spoken to.* Sometimes, the recovering person just doesn't have anything to say about what has been asked, or maybe the statements were misunderstood. If it is not important for the recovering person to answer you, just wait until later to talk.
  - *Take medication.* Make sure you have specific instructions from the physician about how much, and when medication should be administered. Follow the advice given in chapter 7, and learn how the drug works, how long it takes to work, and its side effects. If the individual is handed the medication and a glass of water, he/she will usually respond without any question. If it is refused, ask how the recovering person prefers to take the medication. Let the recovering person discuss the medication with the doctor and ask for a different way of taking it. Knowing the feelings behind the person's negative reaction will

help in solving the problem. Compare the ill person's medication to a person having to take medication because of another illness. Let the facts be known about why the ill person has to take medication. If you need to, buy a pillbox that has separate compartments for daily use of the medication, as described in chapter 4. This may help the recovering person remember to take it.

- *Go to the dentist.* List this trip on the daily schedule for that day. Ask the ill person to read what is on the schedule for the day (you read the schedule if the individual can't read). Don't ask questions or make any comments unless you have to; then just go. The dentist is part of your team and will know how best to serve your relative.

- *Have blood drawn.* This is something that has to be done, especially if the individual is on medication. But this is also something that a mentally ill person (like many others) does not like to do. Include the lab technician trip on the schedule for that day. Just say, "Today is the day we go to visit the lab technician." This has been done before, so the recovering person is aware of what this means. The lab tech should know the ill relative and be part of the team.

- **Running away (or wandering away).** This is one of the saddest events that can occur. Sometimes, the ill person believes the voices are saying to go somewhere else. The response to the voices can be devastating. Follow the advice given in chapter 4, and make sure that the ill person has his/her vital information in his/her possession. A medic alert necklace or bracelet should be worn at all times—complete with name, address, phone number, and medication used. Name tags and phone numbers should be on all articles of clothing. Discuss with the individual a place where "mad money" ($20 bill) is kept (e.g., in a special section of the wallet, taped in the top of a favorite hat, or taped into the side of the shoes that the ill relative wears). Practice what to do in case the ill person ever becomes lost.

- Look for a person in a uniform and show the officer the medic alert necklace or bracelet
- Ask for a phone
- Call home
- Stay in the place (or outside the door) where the phone call was made (stress the importance of doing this)

Other problems that can arise are situational, such as deciding whether to (and how) to handle family meals, and to travel with the ill person.

- **Leaving the ill person alone.**　Sometimes, this is a touchy situation, especially when the individual may not be entirely trustworthy. For example, she/he may turn on the stove and leave it, or leave the refrigerator door open, or leave open all the outside doors and windows, or bring complete strangers into the house, or eat raw meat, or spill food and drink on furniture, etc. If this is the case, it is best to determine whether the person should ever be left alone. If you must leave her/him alone at times, start off leaving the person for very short intervals, then slightly longer intervals, then gradually stay away for longer lengths of time. Just tell the recovering person where you will be, when you'll return, and your expectations of him/her. You can also start teaching some basic house rules if your relative is guilty of the aforementioned.

- **Safety-proofing the house.**　According to the severity of the illness of the recovering person, you may have to take a careful and thorough look around your house to see what kinds of dangers may exist. Try not to be embarrassed or upset if you find that you have to lock certain rooms, stoves and ovens, cabinets that contain medications, chemicals or other toxic materials, and even the cars. A little extra caution may save someone's life. If you are in doubt about what might happen when your ill relative lives with you, keep all dangerous things locked until you are sure you know what might happen. Valuables should be locked also. By the way, you keep the key!

- **Family meals.**   Do not insist that the ill person eat with the family or share in conversation at first if this is not the chosen activity. Invite the person to join you, but don't make a big deal out of it if you are refused. You must, however, tell the recovering person where he/she can eat. Remember that you are in charge of the household.

- **Traveling with a mentally ill family member.**   This can be hard on everyone concerned, but the key is in the planning. Plan what you will do and when you will do it. Allow for several stops if you're traveling by car. If you are traveling by airplane, take a short trip with the individual to test out the situation before you attempt a longer trip. Make sure you take along reading material about something the person enjoys doing (e.g., a book on football if he/she enjoys the game). Also include some writing or art material.

CONCERNS OF THE RECOVERING PERSON

Here are some suggestions about responses you can make when the ill individual asks for answers to common concerns. These answers are phrased as if you were reading them to your mentally ill relative. However, only you can know exactly how to communicate with your ill relative in a way that she/ he can understand. Do not take these as a literal monologue.

How Can I Handle the Need to Talk to People?

Lots of times, people don't want to be bothered, so if they appear busy (reading, writing, looking out the window, etc.), don't try to start a conversation. However, if the person is sitting with hands folded, or is aimlessly looking around, say "hello." This will usually start a conversation. The weather, the transportation you're taking, a trip you've taken, a sport you're interested in, and so on, are always good openers. (Check chapter 10 on behavior in public for more on this.)

Should I Drive a Car?

You can drive a car only if you pass the driver's test given in each state. If you are supposed to take medication, you need to make sure you are taking it and that you report that fact. Most states require that the medication (as well as glasses) be listed on your license. Don't ever get behind the driver's wheel if you are not sticking to your recovery routine.

Most people with a mental illness can still drive a car unless the person

1. Is heavily medicated
2. Is not in control of his/her body or mind
3. Has been advised not to drive by the physician, the health worker, or the caregiver.

If you are given these reasons for not being able to or permitted to operate a car, be sure to ask for other transportation alternatives.

How Can I Build a Social Life?

If you have lots of spare time, choose a sport that you enjoy, and start taking lessons to learn what to do. Tennis, golf, bowling, or dancing are good choices. Call the Chamber of Commerce in your area for information. Once you learn the basics, you can join an athletic group or a league. This will put you in touch with other people who have an interest like yours.

The local mental health organization or the local affiliate of the National Alliance for the Mentally Ill can give you advice on joining support groups where people help each other with everyday living problems. Planning to do things outside the meetings will extend your social life. A church group for individuals your age is another way to meet people and participate in social gatherings. Church attendance itself will give you other opportunities.

Don't underestimate the value of spending time with your family. Going out to eat, visiting a park, or going to a movie can be a nice sharing time.

How Can I Handle Not Getting Along Very Well with My Family?

First, you must understand that your family wants only the best for you. The illness you have puzzles them as much as it puzzles you. In the healthiest of families, there are always conflicts. You'll just have to work together, and you'll have to abide by the household rules. You give and they'll give. If you can't, you may have to find other living arrangements. After all, if you live in your parent's home, they have a right to expect your cooperation.

9

SEXUALITY

You may drive out Nature with a pitchfork,
yet she still will hurry back.

Horace, 23 B.C.

Sexuality is an important aspect of everyone's life, including those with mental illness. However, the subject of sexuality has often been ignored and dealt with as a deep-seated mystery that should not be discussed openly. In our society, sexual matters are often presented with immoral or obscene connotations. This has resulted in a widespread adherence to sexual myths, ignorance, and uncertainty.

Realistically, people are sexual and have sexual lives. The more that is known about sexuality, the greater the likelihood that the sexual behaviors exhibited by the mentally disturbed person will be understood. This chapter is aimed toward helping you to teach the mentally disturbed person about sexuality rather than to dismiss or try to ignore the sexual acting out.

Like hunger and thirst, sex is a biological drive—a part of

nature. A drive is a basic urge, instinct, or motivation. For example, the hunger drive motivates a person or animal to find and ingest food that is necessary to maintain life. Prolonged failure to satisfy certain natural drives can result in death, impaired health, disease, frustrations, and abnormal behaviors—nature's way of trying to restore itself. Although sexual activity is necessary and responsible for the continuation of humankind, it is not essential to keeping a person alive. But denial of the sex drive creates frustrations and abnormal behaviors—especially in the mentally ill person. While there are few restrictive guides for other basic biological drives, society limits an individual's sexual behavior. Because of this, awareness of the sex urge is greater and more persistent and insistent than that of other drives. Sex is one of the most powerful forces influencing human behavior. When sexual feelings are thought to be separated or different from other kinds of feelings, there are problems.

Because mental illness affects the individual's ability to interact normally—that is, affects his/her interpersonal relationships—sexual difficulties are amplified in the recovering person. This situation may cause the ill person to feel powerless or inferior in a relationship. Furthermore, someone with mental illness may have much greater difficulty in achieving sexual satisfaction than other persons would. The mental illness frustrates and complicates sexual fulfillment. If this predicament is not resolved in a nonthreatening way, the mentally disturbed person will find other means of gratifying the sexual urge. This usually manifests itself in abnormal sexual acting out.

RECOGNIZING A SEXUAL PROBLEM

Sexual desires are not under our voluntary control—they originate in the brain under the control of the autonomic (or involuntary) nervous system. Though these desires are dormant during childhood, they are activated when a male or female reaches puberty. At this time, we begin to notice sexual desires and to search for a way to bring pleasure and relief from sexual tensions.

As stated earlier, these feelings are normal, natural, healthful, and pleasurable. But when mentally ill persons try to express themselves sexually, problems can arise, such as

- *Inappropriate sexual language* (such as asking a stranger or a child to have sex, or constantly talking about sex in the presence of anyone.) (One mentally ill person used to ask the priest how his sex life was.)

- *Being prey to sexual abuse* (that is, persons may force the mentally ill to perform degrading or abnormal sexual acts, such as having sex with animals, touching someone because of having been told to do so, homosexual advances, wearing clothes of the opposite sex just to be made fun of, and other deviations at the expense of the ill person.)

- *Inappropriate touching* (such as touching people on the breasts, in the crotch area, or on the buttocks.) (A family reported that when they took their mentally ill son out to eat, he would attempt to touch the waitress on the breast. This created much distress and embarrassment for the family, who attempted to ignore the behavior.)

- *Indiscrete masturbation* (such as in inappropriate settings [e.g., in front of family and children] and at inappropriate times.) (A 20-year-old man was reported to be masturbating on a downtown city street.)

- *Promiscuous behavior* (that is, having intercourse with anyone and anywhere.) (Patients in mental hospitals may have sex in locations without privacy.)

WHAT TO DO ABOUT THESE PROBLEMS

It is not fair to household members to have to tolerate an atmosphere of sexual intimidation and embarrassment from their mentally ill relative. The homecare team must be straightforward and positive in taking the necessary steps to reduce the undesired behaviors. There are no quick or easy answers in dealing effectively with sexual problems. It is, however, important to design a workable plan that will allow mutual respect from both the caregivers and the ill person. This plan should have a step-by-step procedure to allow the recovering individual to understand fully what is and is not expected.

Before trying to help your relative or friend, first examine your own sexuality. Calling sexual acts "dirty," "bad," "disgusting," or "repulsive" are reflections of your own beliefs. These judgmental perceptions can induce feelings of fear, guilt, or poor self-esteem. If you approach management of sexual desires with these kinds of feelings, you will lose perspective on what you are trying to achieve. You'll need to change your attitudes or get professional help about these attitudes before you can help your ill relative understand what changes to make. You may also want to engage a sex therapist to help your loved one (see case study in this chapter), but if funds are not available, the following suggestions are made to help you in setting limits on undesired sexual behaviors:

1. Sometimes, sexual acting out can be a cry for attention (e.g., "Care for me, too"). As much as, and even more than others, mentally ill persons need love and attention.

2. Don't expose the recovering person to movies and television shows that rely on sex and violence to entertain their audiences. When watching shows of this type, some ill persons can't generalize or discriminate as to what is appropriate, the circumstances under which it is appropriate, and what is inappropriate.

3. When beginning treatment, praise appropriate behaviors. Sometimes you may do this even before the desired behavior happens (e.g., "Thank you for not discussing sex with the guests").

4. Use kindness and patience when correcting sexual problems—remember that each person must learn at his/her own speed.

5. Let the mentally ill person know that sexuality is a private matter and that his/her illness does not excuse inappropriate sexual behaviors.

6. Be open, frank, and honest about the existing problem (inappropriate talking or touching, or sexually acting out). State directly and specifically why the problem has created so much concern.

7. Provide alternatives.
   - Offer a time and a place for sexual talk, but intersperse it with other subjects with which the recovering person is familiar.
   - Encourage appropriate nonsexual touching (such as a handshake with an acquaintance, or a hug with family and friends. Stress that each person is the owner of his/her own body. Therefore, it is that person's right to decide if and when touching is allowed, and the recovering person has no right to violate someone else's rights.

8. Talk about masturbation, what it is, why a person has these urges, why it is helpful, and why it is to be done privately (more on masturbation later in this chapter). Show the recovering person where the appropriate places to masturbate are located (his/her bedroom, bathroom, or shower). When this particular behavior is about to occur, kindly escort the person to one of the designated areas and say, "This place is private and you won't offend anyone by masturbating in here."

9. If the recovering person has difficulty complying with the request that he/she masturbate in his/her own room, encourage the use of fantasies or pictures in that area only. Stress that any erotic magazines or

pictures are also personal and should be kept in private areas.

10. If the recovering individual is still sexually soliciting persons in public, a time to masturbate can be included on the daily schedule. This will help cut down his/her sexual drive.

11. Naturally, if the recovering person can develop a relationship with someone who takes the individual's limitations into account, this may be the best way to solve sexual problems.

12. If the homecare team can't respond openly to sexual matters, it may be good to work with another caregiver and a sex therapist as one family did in the following case history.

USING A SEX THERAPIST TO HELP CONTROL PATIENT SEXUALITY

Perhaps the best treatment for inappropriate sexual behavior is in realizing that the mentally ill person is acting out of sexual frustration and is seeking relief. As previously noted, there must be a great deal of openness and frankness about sexuality between the homecare team and the recovering person.

This account, based on the sexual problems and treatment of an actual mentally ill person, shows how a compassionate and knowledgeable doctor helped the recovering person understand and appropriately deal with his own sexuality.

Joe, a 25-year-old chronic schizophrenic, was referred by Dr. Nathan Kline to a leading New York sex therapist, Dr. Helen Singer Kaplan. The problems presented were inappropriate touching, inappropriate sexual language, and a preoccupation with sexual ideas, gestures, and thoughts. Joe lived at home with his parents, along with a brother and a sister. His sexual gestures caused great embarrassment and humiliation within the family unit. Resorting to isolation, the family began to refrain from inviting friends and other family members into their home. Because of Joe's inappropriate sexual expressions, not wanting to risk further distress, and possible legal jeopardy, the family did not allow Joe on family outings to public places (restaurants, ball games, grocery stores, etc.).

When Dr. Kaplan first talked to Joe about his sexual desires, he was reluctant and embarrassed, but he finally spoke about his sexual tendencies. He stated that he had masturbated while he was growing and even had intercourse with a few women—before his illness—but had not recently attempted it. He was very attracted to the opposite sex, and he was concerned about having relations, but he didn't know how to find a partner.

Joe was first taught appropriate sexual behaviors, including the expression of his desires by masturbating in the privacy of his room. He was told that his feelings were natural and normal and that everyone basically had the same desires. To help stimulate and bring relief from sexual tension, he was encouraged to use extra stimuli (pictures, music, smells, fantasies) to enhance the pleasure of his masturbation activity.

Eventually, Joe's sexual health program included a sexual partner. She was a considerate, pleasant young woman, who taught Joe how to interact appropriately with other people. He learned how to ask for a date, how to enjoy a woman's presence, and how to make love to a woman.

These changes didn't happen overnight, but with reinforcement of proper behaviors, his improvement was remarkable. He learned not to discuss sex in public or within the family unit (he was allowed to discuss sex with Dr. Kaplan, the homecare team, his friends, and his partner); he was taught to keep all erotic pictures and books in his room; he learned that instead of touching a woman he met in public, he could go to a bathroom and masturbate; and he learned to meet his own sexual needs without shame and humiliation. Dr. Kaplan took extra steps in making sure that Joe liked himself and that he took pride in the fact that there were things that he could achieve.

Although there were a few setbacks in Joe's sexual behavior, his progress helped to create a home environment in which Joe could once again fully participate.

CONCERNS AND QUESTIONS ABOUT SEXUALITY

Can you explain the moral issues of masturbation, and is it harmful in any way? Condemnation of masturbation by religious authority resulted because of misinterpretation of Onan's behavior in the Old Testament (Genesis 38:9). Onan, not wanting to have a child by his brother's widow, Tamar, had begun sexual intercourse, but he withdrew his penis from her and spilled his seed (sperm) on the ground. This act was not masturbation.

In the eighteenth century, Tissot, a leading French physician, stated that masturbation caused most illnesses. This idea was soon taken up by other doctors. In *Gunn's Family Physician* (1857), the following passage is typical of the moral tone of that time:

> This single pernicious habit of Self pollution [masturbation], by the youth of our country, is the direct cause of more physical and mental debility, the destruction of more constitutions, the ruin of more minds, and the source of more wretchedness and misery, than any other one cause. It tends directly to weaken and destroy the force and energy of the physical system, and to impair the intellect, weaken the memory, and debase the mind; resulting often in early decrepitude, permanent nervous affections, weak eyes, blindness, emaciation, and insanity.

With all this false information handed down through the ages, no wonder people suffer from sexual hang-ups! This book even blames masturbation on the parents, "Parents are often more to blame than children for the ruin which this dreadful vice entails." It seems that parents have been blamed for everything!

Today, we know that the foregoing misinformation is not true and that masturbation is not known to cause an illness, but it may in fact help relieve tensions that could cause symptoms of an illness (headaches, stress, etc.).

When does a person start to masturbate? Masturbation

serves as the training ground in which most males and females are introduced to their own sexuality and to their own response technique. Boys tend to experience masturbation before adolescence, whereas females usually don't experiment with masturbation until after they've had intercourse with a partner. If the recovering person was sexually active before the illness struck, this could cause some of the inappropriate sexual behaviors subsequently exhibited. The individual might be trying to relieve sexual frustrations as before, without thinking of the circumstances.

Is it necessary to put limits on a female's sexual behavior?   By all means, like the male, the female's sexual desires are not under completely voluntary control. Also, women who act seductively in an inappropriate manner may be both victimized and abused. The same steps apply for males and females in controlling undesirable sexual behaviors.

Should both male and female experience sexual intercourse in order to be relieved of sexual tensions?   No, masturbation is equally effective in both sexes. A male's sexual tension is relieved by masturbating his penis. In the female, the clitoris (not the vagina) is the source of the female orgasm.

What about birth control?   The main function of our sexual organs is to reproduce. In order to achieve this, nature made the sexual experience pleasurable and exciting. Whereas the idea of having a baby may highly interest a mentally ill person, the realities of caring for and raising a child may not be compatible with this wish. Therefore, the mentally ill person should be protected against reproducing.[1]

---

[1]If you'd like help in dealing with these issues, call Planned Parenthood. These professionals provide counseling and/or make referrals for birth control, pregnancy, sexually transmitted diseases, abortion, sterilization for men and women, menopause, sickle cell anemia, and vaginal infections. The cost is based on what you can afford to pay.

It is wise to have the mentally ill person use some form of birth control in case the unpredictable occurs. This precaution should be considered even though the ill person may not be sexually active. Be sure to consult your doctor before deciding which form of birth control is best suited for the recovering person. Some popular forms of birth control are

- *Birth control pills.* Taken orally daily (there are many different types); these are up to 99% effective.
- *IUD, or intrauterine device* (e.g., coil, loop, and shield). These devices are semipermanently placed inside the uterus by a doctor and must be removed by a doctor; they are up to 98% effective.
- *Diaphragm and spermicidal jelly or cream.* Made of soft rubber in the shape of a shallow cup that fits snugly over the cervix, it must always be used with spermicidal cream or jelly and is 90% to 98% effective.
- *Condom.* A man places over his penis this thin rubber bag (found in most drugstores and supermarkets).

Less effective forms of birth control are

- *Foam or aerosol vaginal spermicide.* Foam and aerosol spermicide cream has the consistency of shaving cream. It supposedly blocks and kills the sperm before they enter the cervix.
- *Withdrawal* (coitus interruptus). The male removes his penis just before ejaculation.
- *Rhythm method.* The partners have intercourse on all but the 4 or 5 days when ovulation is likely to occur during a woman's menstrual cycle.

Although all of these methods have their risks, the condom is probably the safest.

What about sterilization? Sterilization is an operation that makes a male or female incapable of reproduction, and it is

100% effective. This is the surest way to prevent a pregnancy. The female can undergo a *tubal ligation*, which does not affect her hormone secretions, ovaries, uterus, or vagina. Her menstrual cycle continues, and her sexual response is not lessened at all. On the other hand, sterilization by a *hysterectomy* involves removal of the uterus, with cessation of menstrual cycles.

A *vasectomy*, (sterilization for the male) is simply a cutting and tying of the tubes that carry sperm from the testes to the penis. It prevents sperm from being carried by the semen when ejaculation occurs. The operation takes about half an hour and leaves the man's genital system basically unchanged. It does not harm the man's sexual desires or his sexual performance.

If sterilization is being considered, the recovering person must give his/her consent and be fully aware of the consequences.

What about venereal diseases?   Condoms should be used in sexual intercourse when the health status of the partner is unknown. Beyond that precaution, the reality of AIDS has curtailed much of the sexual freedom of the recent past. The use of erotic pictures and movies while masturbating has been recommended as the safest means of satisfying sexual needs while avoiding venereal disease.

Can AIDS be a problem to mentally ill individuals?   Contracting AIDS is a problem for any individual, mentally ill or otherwise. AIDS does not discriminate according to gender or age. Striking mostly intravenous drug abusers, the sexual partners of such individuals, and homosexual men, AIDS is now a leading cause of death in this country.

The authors do not recommend sexual contact with unknown partners. If the recovering person insists on any of the aforementioned high-risk persons as sexual partners, urge her/him to take strict precautions. These include (but are not limited to) using condoms, avoiding deep "French kissing," avoiding contact with the blood of another person (e.g., use separate toothbrushes, etc.), and never sharing needles.

Can AIDS be diagnosed in mental illness?   For the question of diagnosis, refer back to chapter 1, in the section about organic brain disorders. It has been shown that AIDS can initially manifest itself in being forgetful, undergoing personality changes, having trouble concentrating, or showing impaired judgment.

What are sexual deviations?   Some of the most arbitrary definitions imaginable are listed as sexual deviations. Many forms of sexual behavior are considered "deviant" because they deviate from what society believes to be normal sexual behavior. What may be perfectly acceptable in one society may be considered a sexual deviation in another. For example, in some countries, homosexuality (the most common sexual deviation) is considered a crime; in other countries, it is not.

Persons apprehended for deviant sex practices (such as exhibitionism, rape, *pedophilia* [liking for children], or *pederasty* [sexual contact with a child]) are penalized legally. It is important that the recovering person be educated about the nature and consequences of imposing his or her sexual desires upon other persons. If a harmful deviation cannot be controlled, it is not safe for the mentally ill person to live within a community setting.

10

BEHAVIOR IN PUBLIC PLACES

The man who removes a mountain
begins by carrying away small stones.

Chinese proverb

Integrating the mentally ill person into public activities doesn't have to be especially difficult. The key is to start small. In other words, go to small, nonthreatening, quiet places where appropriate behavior and manners can be reinforced before going to larger and busier places. In this way, you protect the recovering person from the stress and anxiety of a potentially overwhelming situation, and you help prevent acting out behavior. Starting with outings that avoid crowds will also give you the chance to set up a less stressful teaching model from which the recovering person can learn or relearn basic social functioning.

The first thing to instill into the individual is not to draw attention to him/herself in public, as was discussed in chapter 8. Convince the individual that it is important to follow social conventions. Even simple behaviors like blowing your nose (not in your hand; always learn to carry a handkerchief), or urinating (always in a bathroom and not outside, even in your own garden, where neighbors might take offense), and cleaning your ears (do this at home or in a bathroom), should be done *deliberately* (that is, by thinking before doing).

RESTAURANTS: A MODEL FOR LEARNING SOCIAL SKILLS

How Does Teaching Guide the Individual Back into Social Functioning?

Let us first consider eating away from home. To teach the ill person how to function at a restaurant, start by deciding how much money you want to spend on eating out; then determine the type of restaurant desired. Though fast-food restaurants may be quick and desirable for members of the homecare team, they are not the most appropriate for the recovering individual. Eating at small restaurants with a relaxed atmosphere will give the experience of being seated by a hostess, reading a menu, selecting which foods to eat, placing an order, leaving a tip, and paying a check. With you as the model, the ill person will soon learn how to accomplish eating out by him/herself.

After selecting a small restaurant that will meet the aforementioned needs, decide on the type of transportation you will take to get to your destination. Next, decide on the type of clothing that should be worn to the particular restaurant.

Talk through the expected sequence with the recovering person. Tell him/her what you are going to do and why you are doing it. For example, when you arrive at the restaurant, you could say, "Jane, because there are four of us, we will ask the hostess for a table for four." After the menus have been distributed, discuss the amount of money each person should spend and the names of the main dishes within that price category. This sounds very elementary, but to a person learning or relearning how to eat out, it is best to start with these very basic concepts. Try not to spend a long time at the restaurant because the recovering person is nervous anyway, and making an evening or day out of eating out can only add to the stress.

After the meal is finished, speak to the other members present and decide how much money should be left for a tip. This method helps teach the recovering person how to arrive at the usual 15%.

What Does the Process of Social Guidance Accomplish?

This process sets up a model for the ill person to practice. The model consists of decision-making skills (where to go, kind of transportation, amount of money to spend, what to order, how much to tip); reading skills (reading the menu); social skills (asking for a table, interacting with the hostess and waiter, being with more than one person, going out to a public place); money management skills; and personal grooming skills.

Each time you practice this model, give the recovering person the chance to make a choice on where to go and what to do. Don't worry if you don't get a response in the beginning; just be pleasant and go ahead with the decision making. Eventually, you will get a response, and that will fill you with joy.

SHOPPING

What About Shopping for Food, Gifts, Clothing, or Personal Goods?

Shopping doesn't have to be a problem if you set up a practice model. The model should include a shopping list, an amount of money to spend, a mode of transportation, and a place to shop.

Shopping list.   When developing a shopping list—whether it be for personal supplies, food, gifts, or clothing—write down what is needed. After the ill person learns how to purchase needed items, he/she can be taught how to buy ahead of time if items are on sale.

Money.   The recovering person should have some earned money that he/she intends to spend. This money can be earned in any way that the schedule determines—preferably from a regular job outside the home or from doing chores around the house. An important feeling of accomplishment is derived from earning and spending one's own money (this doesn't mean that tips can't be given for extra-special effort). Decide the amount of money that can be spent for the desired items. If the ill person doesn't have enough money, help the ill person to decide which items are needed the most, and purchase those. The other items can be bought on another trip when more money has been earned.

Transportation.   The means of transportation will help determine the character of the shopping trip. For example, if public transportation is being used, this may limit how much can be carried. Use of a cab, or having someone else drive may affect what can be carried. If the recovering individual uses his/her own car, find out if there is adequate gas. The amount of money needed to reach the shopping destination can greatly influence the amount of money being spent once you get there!

Where to shop.   As stated earlier, start small. Go to a small variety store. The prices may be higher, but this is a learning experience, and it is worth the extra cents you might have to spend. Show the ill person how to locate everything on the list. A small calculator is very beneficial in keeping track of how much is being bought/spent. Avoid crowds no matter where you go. If the small stores are crowded, treat your ill family member to an ice cream or yogurt while you wait until it is less crowded.

RECREATION

What About Theaters, Concerts, or Ball Games?

When beginning to go to public functions, you must again refrain from being in crowded situations. If the ill person enjoyed certain types of activities in the past, chances are that he/she will still enjoy them. You might start by going to a small musical with one or two acts. Seek out one with lively music thus giving you an opportunity to evaluate the actions and responses of the individual. A good musical will help increase the recovering individual's attention span if he/she enjoys it.

Try to avoid symphonies and loud concerts until the ill person has improved. Though symphonies may be soft and placid, possible anguish at having to sit quietly for a long time may be more than can be handled at first.

If the ill person likes sports and ball games, go to small local high school or college games before going to the larger university or professional games. Get there before the crowd arrives, and leave before the game is over in order to avoid the crowd.

A word of caution: If the recovering individual smokes, make sure the "No Smoking" signs are observed. Reviewing this rule before you arrive at an event will help ameliorate any problems you may have while in attendance.

PUBLIC TRANSPORTATION

How Do I Teach the Use of Public Transportation?

First, decide what your mentally ill family member needs to know in order to get from one place to another. If the person is going to ride the local bus, subway, or train system, gather information about each. This information should include the routes, time schedules, cost (the ill person may get the reduced rates for handicapped persons), ticket purchasing, and where to get on and off.

One of the biggest problems in using the public transit system is in waiting. While the mentally ill person can be taught the mechanics of using public transportation with great success, learning the skill of waiting, however, is another thing. It is during such waiting that ill persons may lose patience, hallucinate, and bother other waiting people. If this becomes a problem, the individual needs to have something to do while he/she is waiting. Such activity might involve reading a book, reading the transportation schedule, or maybe even eating a snack. Go with the ill person until he/she learns the route and the skill of waiting. On the way, point out landmarks that can serve as familiar grounds. These marks can always assure the ill person that the point of destination is near. Don't forget to demonstrate, demonstrate, demonstrate; practice, practice, practice; observe, observe, observe until the ill person has learned well enough to go alone. It is also important to remember that some ill persons will accomplish these skills faster than others—be patient.

What About Longer Trips?

These need to be handled in much the same way as less extensive trips, except that attention needs to be given to practicing how to sit, buckle up, eat, and even go to the bathroom on board an airplane, bus, or train. Role-playing (pretending) is a good way to practice. Make sure the "fasten seat belts" and "no smoking" signs are understood. If the ill person smokes, and the airplane trip lasts fewer than 2 hours, talk in advance about what to do in case of the urge to smoke (chewing gum usually works best), and it may help with ear sensitivity, which can upset an ill person).

When it is time for the ill person to travel alone, make sure he/she takes along something to do. This can be reading material, magazines, cards, crossword puzzles, or something that needs to be accomplished (for instance, reading and writing about a certain assignment or completing a sheet of math). This will occupy the individual's time and give much satisfaction in the meantime. (Don't forget to make sure that the traveling person carries the data sheet listing steps to be taken in an emergency, as well as the list of medications discussed in chapter 4).

While Traveling, What About Conversation with Other People?

Guide the ill person into developing interest in some major social topics. This includes what to say about the subject, some possible responses, and how to respond to what the other person says. The weather is always good to talk about, and a favorite sport, hobby, subject, or person are also good topics. Teach several different things that might come up in a conversation. Role-playing as in a possible conversation (and reversing the roles between you and the ill person), could go like this:

Ill person:	"It's a nice day today."
Stranger:	"Yes, it certainly is."
Ill person:	"I'd love to be able to be in the sun all day."
Stranger:	"So would I."
Ill person:	"You have a good day."

It is also good to guide the ill person into saying positive things about people. People like to hear good things about themselves. Many mentally ill persons tend to say such negative things as "You are an ugly person," and negative statements may bring about instant rejection. Guide the recovering individual into acting congenially toward others because they will be more accepting.

PANHANDLING (BEGGING)

What About Panhandling for Money in Public?

Some mentally ill persons deal with their lack of money, (or their want of more money) by begging for it. This can be an embarrassing situation for the families of the ill person. The best way to handle this is to ask the ill person exactly what it is he/she wants and then help him/her figure out how to get it. This is when you can use extra tips for jobs well done. Work out a contract, and proceed from there. If the ill person refuses the contract and continues the panhandling, we suggest that you start buying things from the ill person. For example, personally owned items such as a radio, TV, or stereo can be taken in return for a certain amount of money. For example, you can say "Mike, here is $5.00 for your stereo. I will continue to buy your things until you learn to stop begging." This is a form of bribery, but if all other reasoning fails to stop the panhandling, this may work.

Similarly, do not tolerate stealing or walking off with items without having paid for them. If you strongly believe that something has been stolen, try to become certain before taking action. If it was stolen, have the ill person go with you to return the item. Try to negotiate with the recovering person to determine appropriate ways to obtain things he/she desires. This behavior, if unchecked, will have serious consequences, which, at a minimum, may lead to rehospitalization. If a contract or some other form of behavior modification does not produce results, you may need to get specialized help to consult with your homecare team.

SEXUALITY

What About Sexual Behavior in Public?

Stop any public sexual behavior. Explaining that this is a legal matter and might involve the police will help end inappropriate behavior. It will be helpful also to explain to the recovering person how this type of behavior makes other people feel and react. For details about how to deal with sexuality, see chapter 9.

SOME ADDITIONAL TIPS

- Go to small hotels, not large ones.
- Don't get on crowded elevators; wait for another one or use the steps.
- Stay close to the recovering person at all times, unless you are in that stage of your guidance that you want to observe how he/she is doing by him/herself.

In closing this chapter, the most important thing to remember when trying to integrate someone into public places is to take one step at a time. If you are disappointed, wait, then try again later, or break the one step into a few smaller steps. You can avoid uncomfortable situations if you practice this. If something does happen when you are in a public setting, leave immediately, and, in a controlled voice, explain why you had to do so.

11

CRISIS INTERVENTION

The ability to be calm, confident, and decisive in crisis is not an inherited characteristic, but is the direct result of how well the individual has prepared himself for the battle.

Richard Milhous Nixon

Webster's Ninth New Collegiate Dictionary defines a "crisis" as "an emotionally significant event or radical change in status in a person's life ... an unstable time or crucial time ... with the distinct possibility of a highly undesirable outcome." Indeed, in the routine of daily living, all of us are constantly faced with unstable times. Anything that disrupts what is deemed to be normal functioning for a person is considered a crisis. A crisis can range in severity from a child not being home on time, to a death or divorce. Many of us are equipped with the ability to handle a crisis without experiencing a great deal of stress or anxiety. But some of us need help in working through a crisis. This chapter is aimed primarily at offering help when a crisis arises that involves the mentally ill person, whether the crisis originates in the lives of the caregivers or in the activities and behaviors of the mentally ill person.

A CRISIS IN THE LIFE OF A CAREGIVER

What Happens when the Homecare Coordinator Has a Crisis?

The homecare coordinator should not do everything. It is impossible to be everything to everyone. So don't even try it. Delegate to other team members and plan for personal, alone, "I don't want to do anything" time for yourself. Crises will happen; but if there's a plan, and another team member designated to assume the coordinator's role, the crises won't necessarily mean disasters.

What Kinds of Crises Could the Coordinator Have?

You and the other members of your homecare team will doubtless experience many of the normal everyday problems that none of us plan for. These include physical illness of self or other family member, stress, anxiety, death or injury of self or other family member, divorce, automobile wreck, sudden hospitalization, and so on. The important thing to do is to learn to identify potentially troublesome situations of extraordinary stress. Once a stressful situation is identified, decide how you and others can either avoid or intervene and control an impending crisis, or even "burnout" (an extreme form of exhaustion due to prolonged periods of extreme stress).

If any of the following danger signals are familiar to you, you may have to rearrange priorities, become engaged in something enjoyable like a sport or a hobby, or take a vacation. To avoid burnout, recognize the following warning signs, and take immediate action to relieve some of your stress.

- Prolonged headaches
- Stomach problems
- High blood pressure
- General irritability or restlessness

- Insomnia or waking too early
- Weight gain or loss
- Obsessional symptoms
- Crying spells or feeling miserable and sad
- Loss of interest in former hobbies and friends
- Exhaustion or lethargy for no reason
- Nightmares
- Change in bowel habits
- Forgetfulness
- Inconsistency of mood or behavior
- Dizziness or weakness

Clearly, the more signs you see, the more alarming is the warning. Giving care to a mentally ill person can be extremely demanding, even under the best of circumstances. What's more, the mentally ill person is highly vulnerable to crises of her/his own.

A CRISIS IN THE BEHAVIOR OR ACTIVITIES OF THE MENTALLY ILL PERSON

The ill person's readjustment to family and community living can sometimes be quite an ordeal. If the ill person has been in the hospital or is accustomed to managing his or her own household, he/she may rebel at any change of situation or environment. This rebellion can take the form of deviant behavior, withdrawal, refusal to take medication, self-mutilation, assault, threatening homicide or suicide, substance abuse, or running away, etc. Because the recovering person is acting out because of his/her inner experiences, these crises must be handled in a timely manner. Failure to act immediately could contribute to the deterioration of the functioning level of the individual, could result in the rehospitalization of the individual, or could pose a danger to members of the homecare team or the community at large.

How Can I Recognize a Crisis?

When the recovering person begins to deviate from a normal routine, suspect that a crisis may occur. Because of the ongoing contact between the homecare team members and the ill person, they may be able to determine when a deviation might occur. It is worth the effort on the part of the homecare team to learn to recognize the signs of distress. Some signs are changes in the following: daily grooming routine, eating or sleeping habits, as well as signs of agitation, depression, or apathy (refer to functional assessment, chapter 5, if you're not sure about these changes). In particular, team members should pay attention if there is an increase or change in the nature of any "command" hallucinations. When the ill person mentions that voices tell him/her to do something dangerous, illegal, or irresponsible, please take the time to find out precisely what is involved, and consult your primary care physician if in doubt.

Whom Do I Contact when There Is a Crisis?

Because rapid intervention is the key, try to solve the crisis immediately yourself. If the homecare coordinator is a person outside your household, contact her/him. Next, contact other appropriate persons on the homecare team, such as the primary care physician. If this is an emergency, call the police or an ambulance (keep these numbers by the phone). If this is a case of behavioral acting out, remember to keep a safe distance away from the individual.

What Should Happen when There Is a Crisis?

Table 11.1 lists some potential crises, along with some possible interventions that have been tried with success. As each mentally ill person is unique, it is difficult to arrive at interventions that would be suitable for each situation. However, these suggestions may help you plan what to do in case a crisis happens.

Table 11.1   Handling Specific Crises

Crisis	Intervention
Suicide threats	1. Regard these as a desperate cry for help.
	2. Remove all guns; sharp instruments such as knives, scissors, razors, glass, etc.; anything that can be used as a hanging device; poisons; and hypnotic or sedative drugs must be kept away from the ill person.
	3. Assess the suicidal potential; in other words, has the individual threatened or made attempts at suicide before? What happened? At the time of the threat, what was different in the ill person's life? Was the threat used to arouse sympathy from family or friends?
	4. It doesn't matter how you feel about the situation, just don't dismiss the threat as merely an attention-getting factor.
	5. Talk to the individual about suicide, what it means, and the finality of it all. (Lending a helping hand and offering companionship will sometimes pull a person through a tough situation.)
	6. Alert the physician or hospital if any of the following has taken place: voices have told the ill person to kill him-/herself, the ill person has attempted suicide before, or the ill person has planned how the suicide will take place.
Attempted suicide	1. Call emergency services immediately!
Threatened homicide	1. Keep an approach distance.
	2. When the ill person is responding to a voice or a hallucination, he or she must be hospitalized immediately.
	3. If a lethal object (knife, gun, etc.) is used while the threat is being made, make an emergency notification to the authorities and physician.

(continued)

Table 11.1 (continued)

Crisis	Intervention
Threatened homicide *(continued)*	4. When the threat has just been verbalized, talk to the recovering person and find out (a) what the problems are (refer to the functional assessment scale in chapter 5 for comparison with past circumstances), (b) how you can help restore lost faith, or (c) how to soothe the anger felt toward the threatened person. Find out the who, when, how, and why.
	5. Make sure you follow up with any concerns or suggestions that were made during this conversation. Discuss this with the appropriate team member.
	6. Notify the potential victim.
Attempted homicide	1. By law, you have to notify the police immediately.
Assaultive behavior	1. Protect yourself; keep a safe approach distance.
	2. You may have to call the police and report the assault.
	3. Don't try physically to touch the ill person; wait until he/she has calmed down. You can then offer loving reassurance.
	4. Find out what is wrong; is the individual responding to hallucinations or delusions? Was something said that was misinterpreted? An ill person will react physically to a situation that was similar to an act that had created some pain in the past.
	5. When you are in a position like this, be a person with few words. Overreacting will sometimes make matters worse.
	6. Calmly talk about what happened and the consequences that could occur (such as both persons or several persons being hurt; loss of respect and trust; and possible police intervention, etc.).

Table 11.1 (continued)

Crisis	Intervention
Assaults in public	1. This is more of a practice of prevention rather than intervention. Refer back to chapter 10 on "Behavior in Public Places." Most important, stay away from overcrowded places.
Total withdrawal	1. Realize that the mentally ill person is using this as a protective maneuver.
	2. Reassure this person that he/she is loved.
	3. Sit quietly and hold the person's hand, or touch in another way if necessary.
	4. Using simple words, initiate a conversation in which the recovering person can give brief responses. Build on the individual's strengths (e.g., talk about an activity that brought success, a favorite sport, etc.).
	5. Don't be disappointed if this is a one-way conversation!
	6. Don't demand responses.
	7. Don't leave the ill person.
	8. Start some plan of action (e.g., do jumping jacks, run in place), and ask to be joined.
	9. Repeat the preceding steps.
	10. Call physician if necessary.
Self-mutilation	1. Call for help!
	2. Preserve your own safety by keeping a safe distance.
	3. Yell "Stop!" then use a calm tone of voice to talk to the ill person.
	4. According to the age and strength of the ill person, you may be able to restrain her/him by holding the wrists or using a small chain as a protector, but remember to guard your safety until help arrives.

(continued)

Table 11.1 (continued)

Crisis	Intervention
Exhibitionism	1. Yell "Stop!"
	2. Leave the place where you are, and go to a private area.
	3. Explain the importance of not doing this is simple terms (e.g., a police matter, other people viewing the recovering person as being different).
	4. A severely mentally ill person usually will not do this unless it is a reaction to a sexual problem (see chapter 9).
Inappropriate language	1. Ignore this as much as possible.
	2. Stay calm and neutral.
	3. Move away and give the recovering person physical as well as emotional space.
	4. Don't make sudden approaches.
	5. Respond only to appropriate language (e.g., "Thank you for speaking those words, I like to hear you use correct language.")
	6. If this happens in a public place, tell the ill person that the behavior is inappropriate, and the right to return to the place will have to be earned.
Getting lost or running away	1. The recovering person and the homecare team should have a prepared a plan of action.
	2. Call family or friends to make them aware of the missing person.
	3. Call familiar places that the ill person attends.
	4. Within a period of time, if the ill person has not returned home, call the authorities.
	5. Give the police a full description of the missing person (clothes worn, physical features, etc.).
	6. Stay by the phone in case the police or others with information should call.

Table 11.1 (continued)

Crisis	Intervention
Getting lost or running away *(continued)*	7. If the ill person returns, be sure to call the authorities and thank them for their help and concern.
Drunk driving	1. Take the car keys.
	2. Calmly explain the seriousness of this crime, in that it could take the lives of innocent men, women, and children.
	3. Tell the ill relative that he/she will have to use other means of transportation until responsibility can be shown.
	4. When the ill person begins to show some responsibility, allow him/her to drive *only* with another licensed driver in the car.
	5. If alcoholism continues to be a problem, seek the advice of the physician for possible treatment or hospitalization. Drunk driving should not be taken lightly.
Drug overdose	1. Take to the hospital emergency room immediately.
Physical illness	1. Call the primary care doctor, and follow the advice given.
Rape	1. Rape causes further mental and physical damage (both to males and females). The best way to try to avoid a possible rape is to teach the ill relative some prevention techniques.
	2. Some homosexual men will take advantage of mentally ill males; mentally ill women always seem to be at a disadvantage when they are unprotected. Call the rape crisis center in your area for advice. Some things to teach:
	• Don't open the door for strangers.
	• Avoid being out alone after dark.
	• If you find yourself alone, go to where there is light and people.
	• Scream if assaulted.

(continued)

Table 11.1 (continued)

Crisis	Intervention
Refusal to take medication	1. Though the recovering person has a right to refuse medication, living at home should be contingent upon following prescribed treatment. This needs to be understood and written in a contract.
	2. If you think the ill person is forgetting the medication, ask whether the schedule was followed and the medicine was taken.
	3. If the medication was not taken, ask why.
	4. When the ill person reports that the medicine is poison, or gives some other absurd tale, consult the primary care physician and others on the homecare team.
	5. If it is concluded that the medicine is okay and doesn't need changing, you may have to resort to other means for noncompliance.
	• Have other people ask whether the medicine has been taken.
	• Give the medication yourself to the ill person with a glass of water.
	• Point out that the medication keeps the ill person from having strange feelings.
	• Talk about other people who have to take daily medication in order to survive, (heart patients, diabetics, etc.).
	• Tell the ill person that as soon as the medicine is taken, he/she may have a cigarette (or anything else that brings enjoyment, such as juice, candy, bubble gum, etc.).
	• Remind the ill person of the contract.
	6. Don't make threats you can't (or won't) follow through with carrying out.
	7. Be consistent—if you say you will do something, do it.
Fire	1. Teach the appropriate action to take in case this crisis happens.

Table 11.1 (continued)

Crisis	Intervention
Fire *(continued)*	• Have a portable fire extinguisher in each room.
	• Know how it is used, and show how it is used.
	• Show how to put out a small fire.
	• Know how to call the fire department.
	• Learn an alternate route for getting out of the house.
	2. Practice fire prevention
	• Don't allow smoking in bed (it is better to designate a smoking area).
	• Make sure the ill person can use the stove before allowing its use (post a cooking class schedule if the relative insists on cooking).
	• Don't allow the making of fires in a fireplace unless the family is together.
	• Add other precautions as the need arises.

After the crisis has been identified and a course of action has been decided upon, timing is of utmost importance. Appropriate intervention may help prevent the situation from becoming uncontrollable.

MIGHT HOSPITALIZATION REOCCUR?

Despite all your efforts there may be times when the troubled person will have to be rehospitalized. Whether in connection with one of the discussed crises or coming after a decision by the ill person and the homecare team, admission to a hospital may be needed to meet urgent needs of the patient. As with all other illnesses, there can be a relapse in mental illness. Families will need to notice any "warning" signs that something is happening (refer to the case of Fay in chapter 7). Recovering individuals may differ in showing signs of relapse.

Please consult the functional assessment scale of chapter 5 to evaluate changes in behavior.

Seek medical advice when you notice negative changes in behavior. Adjustment of medication may help, or the doctor can help you determine if there is added stress in the patient's life. Sometimes, a patient will show a change in behavior if someone new has joined the household or if someone is missing from the household. Determine any change in schedule that may be causing a reaction from the patient.

What Are the Legal Issues Concerning Psychiatric Hospitalization?

Every state has its own laws pertaining to psychiatric hospitalization. You should check with your state authorities concerning these laws. Basically, however, there are four types of admissions.

1. **Voluntary admission.** Any person over the age of 16 years may request admission. State facilities usually screen for possible admission, leaving the final decision to admit to the attending physician.

2. **Emergency admission.** In order to qualify for this type of involuntary hospitalization, a person must prove to be a danger to him/herself or others, or to have placed others in fear because of violent behavior, or to be unable to care for him/herself because of the illness. This type of admission requires an examination by an experienced and licensed physician acting for the city or county authority (in some places, this may be a licensed psychologist). This examiner must render a statement saying that the individual is a danger to him/herself or others before the involuntary commitment takes place. A court hearing on this procedure is usually held within 5 working days, to determine whether longer hospitalization may be needed.

3. **Judicial commitment.** Often called a "Two Physicians' Certificate" because of the requirement that two M.D.'s

must attest to mental illness, this type of involuntary hospitalization is sanctioned by the court system. Court commitments are usually ordered when the person is a danger to him/herself and others, yet is unwilling or unable to admit to his/her being ill. A relative or hospital superintendent may file a petition in order to mandate a psychiatric evaluation of the ill person by two physicians. If the ill person refuses, the police will have to accompany him/her to a hospital for the evaluation. After the evaluation, the court decides what is best for the ill person. After hospitalization, it is up to the attending physician to discharge the person to outpatient care when the mental condition has improved.

4. **Criminal court commitment.**   This happens when the ill person has been accused of a crime and the court feels that he/she is not competent to stand trial. A psychiatric evaluation is ordered, and the results are reported to the criminal court. The length of stay and other measures are determined by the court.

What Are the Legal Rights of the Mentally Ill?

A mentally ill person who is not posing an emergency because of danger to him/herself or others has the same basic human, civil, constitutional, and statutory rights as any other human being. Legally, these persons have rights to

- Treatment
- Refusal of treatment
- Maintenance of confidentiality
- Protection of privacy
- Informed consent
- Communication and information regarding the following:
  - Other treatment plans
  - Risks and side effects of medication
  - Right to refuse medication

- Right to refuse treatment procedures
- Right to refuse to participate in research
- Transfer inside or outside the facility
- Discharge plans
- Other issues.

The family will need to consult a lawyer on any legal responsibility for their mentally ill relative (such as who's responsible should the ill person cause bodily damage to someone else, or charges on a credit card other than his/her own). It may be that a family will have to emancipate themselves, or have him/her declared legally incompetent, in order to cope with or manage the behaviors of the ill person.

PART FOUR

SOCIETY AND THE RECOVERING PERSON

12

SUPPORT FROM THE COMMUNITY

Inasmuch as ye have done it unto one of
the least of these my brethren, ye have done it unto me.

Matthew 25:40

In a society that places a great value on a single, appropriate, normal way of doing things, having a mentally ill relative can cause many psychological problems for the family members and the larger community. As discussed earlier, these problems may manifest themselves as stress, depression, shame, ambivalence, withdrawal, and loss of self-esteem, which may affect a family member's ability to function at work, as well as at home. For most families, having a family member with an ongoing chronic mental illness is harder to accept than the death of a loved one. Family relationships become uncomfortable and strained as members try to seek answers to their unresolved conflicts. As a result, many families split up. Divorce or separation may occur as marriage partners begin to accuse each other. Underneath all this commotion is the haunting concern that mental illness may strike oneself or another family member.

In order to quell this turbulence and implement a more healing relationship with the troubled person, the family must actively strive to preserve itself and to function in a unified manner. It has been proven that living in servitude to someone else is not physically or emotionally healthy for anyone. Directing the life of a mentally ill person is a job not to be undertaken alone, no matter how dedicated, strong, or skilled the caregiver might be. This responsibility can drain one's time, feelings, patience, and endurance—life itself.

STRATEGIES FOR HELPING THE HELPERS

How Do You Get Control of Your Household?

Regain control of the household by deciding that the mentally ill person will not be in charge of what and when something happens within the family unit. Not only has the family had to adjust to the shock of having a mentally ill relative, but they also most likely have been living in a climate of fear and uncertainty: fear because they were not sure what would happen next, uncertainty because they weren't sure when something would happen. Family members may have strong feelings and opinions, especially when their own needs are set aside while everyone focuses on the ill person.

Begin this new regimen by literally joining the family into a team. This may require a great deal of insight and change, but it especially requires a unified idea of goals for all. Family members can then make decisions about what to do. As there are no quick and easy answers in regaining control, refer back to chapter 5 on goal setting and scheduling. The recovering person needs to assume some responsibilities as part of a family unit. Being mentally ill does not doom an individual to a useless or unproductive life. Start off with minor changes where success is assured (for example, use positive reinforcement one time; if it works, do it again; if it doesn't work after a few attempts, try a different approach). Don't give up, keep trying until a workable approach is found. Make changes slowly. Suddenly initiating dramatic changes in the home could split everything apart.

What About Setting Goals?

Setting goals for improvement and experiencing new ideas does not cease when a person is identified as being mentally ill. Though the goals may be different than they were before the illness, don't abandon goal setting. Concentrate on setting realistic goals, goals that can be reached, and, most of all, goals that all agree to. It is detrimental to the ill person and to the family when goals or expectations are set too high. Go slowly. For example, you cannot confront the recovering person with the immediate goal of living independently. That would be a long-term goal, as reviewed in chapter 13. Immediate goals should allow us to reach the long term goal. Look at this guide:

Long-term goal: To lead an independent life.
Steps:
1. Have necessary grooming and self-care skills
2. Know how to get food to eat
3. Be able to get public transportation
4. Be able to get medical assistance
5. Be able to handle money
6. Find a place to live away from homecare team

Procedure: Implement goals relating to Step 1...

Short-term goal: Is able to groom and bathe self
Steps:
1. (Follow guidelines in chapter 8 for grooming)

Do the same thing for all of the other goals. Discuss each step with everyone, and make each one simple. If that is too hard, break each skill down into even smaller steps. Picking up the laundry or even a toothbrush could be a step. Make sure the proper reinforcement is applied by all.

At some time, begin to strive for more than one goal at a

time. Just write down the goals separately and keep track of the directions you're taking. As one step is completed, move on to the next. Share this with the recovering person. Discuss it at get-togethers or at family meals. Be positive about what is being accomplished. After you have established goals for behavior at home, make sure to work on goals for being able to follow the conventions of the community. In this way, the recovering person will begin to use available public resources without problems. For behavior in public places, see chapter 10.

When implementing this type of program, consistency is of utmost importance. For example, if you don't want eating or smoking in the bedroom, don't allow it sometimes and disallow it at other times. This would be confusing to a mentally ill person—to any person. Be consistent in the changes you want. It may take time to make the changes, but changes can be made.

The family as a team will need to be consistent also. Teamwork does not mean that each family member has separate decision-making power; it means that goals are set as a team, with the best interests of all concerned in mind. And these goals are to take care of problems that have been solved together. However, the family may not be able to provide for their loved one without outside help.

HELPERS FOR THE HELPERS

Who Will Help?

Ask for it; create a team of helpers. Families need assistance in planning a course of action when working with recovering persons. Mental health professionals, dentists, lab technicians, mental health organizations and advocacy groups, volunteer services, members of religious congregations, friends, neighbors, and extended family members—all of these can aid in psychiatric homecare.

Mental health professionals. As you begin a homecare program, solicit the help of physicians, nurses, social workers, psychiatric nurses, rehabilitation counselors, or psychologists. Consultations with these people can help you decide on what type of plan you will have in your home or community. They will also be available to advise you on what to do when altering the program or when you need professional advice. To reiterate, the recommendations for choosing a psychiatrist or a primary care physician apply to the choice of other mental health professionals, as every profession has better and worse practitioners. Make sure that (a) they understand what it is like to work with a chronic mentally ill person in a community setting; (b) they understand some of the problems the families of the mentally ill endure; (c) they are willing to work with you, the family, and the ill person; and (d) they realize that they are working on long-term problems requiring a long-term commitment to help. Equally important is that the mental health professional is someone you trust and someone who listens to you and treats you with understanding and respect. The mental health professionals must also realize that they are working in a team with others.

Dentists. Everyone needs to go to the dentist. The homecare coordinator must approach the dentist about the ill person and explain the illness. The dentist in turn will have to spend more time than usual and not rush the individual. A lot of dentists may want to refer a mentally ill person to someone else, who may refer the individual on to yet another colleague. As you can see, it is best to be candid from the beginning so that neither person is short-changed. Dr. James Lockett of Knoxville, Tennessee, said in a telephone interview, "We need more dentists who care more about people than about the number of people they see."

Laboratory technicians and nurses. Get compassionate and competent persons to help in these capacities. If the ill individual is taking medication, the blood will have to be checked. Again, explain the illness. Have the technician establish rapport with the mentally ill person right from the beginning. It will save the homecare coordinator a lot of grief.

Occupational therapists. The occupational therapy evaluation is needed to show how much the ill person is able to do. The therapist will devise ways to help the person become and remain as independent as possible. Contact your state rehabilitation office or hospital for information about this service.

What Can You Expect in the Community?

Federal assistance. The federal government is trying to support the creation of community resources for the severely mentally ill. This is the outcome of many studies that had shown that the mentally ill need to feel embedded in a social network, because their general coping skills (within the family, at work, etc.) are strengthened by greater social participation. This improvement has to do with the ill person learning different skills from different people, as well as the experience of the appreciation for proper behavior in many different settings. However, as we mentioned before, the pace of introduction to new situations and new people must be unhurried and deliberately geared to any increase in social skills experienced by the recovering individual. When social pressures are expanded too fast, anxiety, low self-esteem, and suspiciousness may (re)appear. The Community Support Programs (CSP) are designed to make possible the gradual adaptation of the severely mentally ill to the pressures of the community. Most often, they are funded through existing mental health facilities in the community.

Community-based mental health services. Many counties have an accredited community mental health center (CMHC) staffed by professionals who are trained to diagnose and treat mentally ill persons. These mental health centers are supported by governmental and/or private funds, and they are supposed to assist the effort of servicing chronic mentally ill people in the community. Unfortunately, not many CMHCs are prepared to deal with the severely mentally ill. A fee (based on the family's ability to pay) will be charged, even though you may have to teach these professionals about living with a mentally ill person first. Sometimes, it is hard for people to conceive the reality of daily living with a mentally ill person unless they've had first-hand experience. Be patient in your dealings with the center. But also make sure you tell exactly what is happening at home so that you may receive the best possible assistance. Their help is often quite good because in some communities, the CSP will have good consultation and education services, which can help families, friends, employers, and others who are in frequent contact with a mentally ill person, to deal with the experienced stress. Sometimes, even a respite center may allow the recovering person to spend a few days (crisis homes) or a few nights (crisis residences) to give primary caregivers some free time, to avoid burnout. In rare cases, some communities take even better care of the chronic mentally ill, with outreach programs (e.g., The Bridge in Chicago) or clubhouses (the best-known being Fountain House in New York City), which include rehabilitation services.

Mental health association and advocacy groups. The mental health association is a good source of information about mental health resources in your area. The ill person and the family need advocacy groups to voice their rights and to guide and support each other. An important source for practical support is the National Alliance for the Mentally Ill (NAMI). This organization was started by families of mentally ill persons in 1979, and it has become international in scope since then. There are now almost 100,000 members in about 1000 local affiliates in the U.S. alone. The network provides book lists, meeting material, and other educational information for people interested in helping and advocating for the mentally ill and their families. They hold regular local meetings of groups with a focus on different mental illnesses. They also hold regional, state, and national meetings. Not only can your local affiliate of NAMI give information about services, but also the members will be pleased to serve as a sounding board when you feel that your coping skills are at a minimum. And they can give advice on other techniques used successfully with their own mentally ill relatives. The state affiliates of NAMI are listed in the back of this book. There are many similar national organizations, including the National Depressive and Manic-Depressive Association and the Alzheimer's and Related Disease Association. Another national support group with good resources is the Mental Health Association, of which a list of affiliates is also provided in the back of this book.

Self-help groups.   In many communities, affiliates of self-help groups offer the recovering person support and assistance from peers. The oldest and best known probably is Alcoholics Anonymous (AA), which has about 1 million members and meets daily. For those who have problems with drinking and other substance abuse, this may be the best support group possible. There may be a problem because some groups do not want the recovering person to use any drugs, including the psychotropic medication. Please consult with your primary care physician; otherwise, tell your ill family member not to mention that she/he is on medication when attending the meetings. Similar groups for other drug abusers (Narcotics Anonymous, Cocaine Anonymous) and for pathological gamblers, compulsive overeaters, and so on have been formed. In several metropolitan areas, there are also therapeutic communities for drug abusers, which offer services beyond a meeting place.

For the mentally ill, Recovery, Inc., has more than a thousand groups meeting all over the U.S. This organization has a cognitive training schedule; the members learn to exercise control over their thoughts and impulses. Schizophrenics Anonymous is an another community-based self-help group with affiliates nationwide. The members adhere to a nutritional approach in psychiatric treatment (see also chapter 14 for further details). Many self-help groups came together in the National Mental Health Consumer's Self-Help Clearing-house, whose key contacts are listed in the back of this book.

Church, synagogue, or other congregation members. Some people are reluctant to seek help from the members of their place of worship. However, many people are willing to spend extra hours with a troubled person; they need only to be asked. This can be done through an appeal in the weekly bulletin or newsletter. An example would be, "The _____ family is seeking volunteers to spend some time with their daughter Sarah. Sarah likes to take walks, ride a bike, eat ice cream, or just talk with someone other than her family. She and her family would greatly appreciate your charity." (Sarah has not been hidden from worship services, and most members should be aware of her condition.)

Volunteer services. The United Way in your area is a great resource for referral purposes. They do not supply the volunteers, but they will get you in touch with organizations that do. You should explain what you need. From here, you can find out about day care, respite care (temporary care like hous-ing), special camps, special groups, tutoring, etc.

Friends, neighbors, extended family members. All can help. At one time, mentally ill persons were hidden from outsiders. Rumors would start and people began to fear the "crazy" person living in the house next door. Some might be watching, at a distance, for a glimpse of this person. As a result, family members of the recovering individual were shunned and viewed as being strange themselves. Even though some of this stigma may still continue, in many cases, it does not. It is important for families not to be afraid to tell friends and close acquaintances that their relative is experi-encing some emotional difficulty. These people will often be helpful in some way, even if it is only for companionship. Don't disregard those people whom you've depended upon before.

HELP FOR DAILY STRESSES OF HELPING

What About the Caregiving Family?

Establishing a structured environment will greatly help household members to overcome the tyranny experienced when living with a mentally ill person. Remember that it is important to remain in control. The more you give in to the behavior and demands of the person suffering from severe mental illness, the more it may exacerbate the disturbance. However, in spite of having a structured environment, the family will still experience depression, anger, helplessness, anxiety, stress, exhaustion, and despair. Sometimes, life with a mentally ill person is like riding on a rollercoaster, "up and down, round and round." Some people who work with problem people tend to suffer job burnout. This is the reason why the job turnover is so great in the mental health field. Unless the caregiving family's personal needs are provided for, they too can suffer job burnout.

Here are a few ways to handle stress on a day-to-day basis (for what to do in more demanding caregiver crises, see chapter 11):

1. Leave the home regularly to find others to talk with about your experiences.
2. Exercise and otherwise take time out for yourself.
3. Learn to take this situation one day at a time; don't lie awake thinking of tomorrow.
4. If there is a respite center in your community, learn to use it.

13
LONG-TERM PLANNING

Some future day when what is now is not,
when all old faults and follies are forgot.
                    Arthur Hugh Clough, Some Future Day

Families of the mentally ill face the future with anxiety and frustration, and most of all fear, because they do not know what will happen when they are no longer around or are unable to fend for and protect their mentally disabled relative. The thought of their relative living in loneliness and despair, of being forced into a life on the streets haunts them. At one time, it was taken for granted that mentally ill persons could live forever in state institutions. Now that this option is no longer available, families are searching for other ways out. Still, in the backs of their minds is that ray of hope for a cure or complete rehabilitation.

Though the options for long-term support are insufficient and limited, you can plan for your relative's future by following the guidelines listed in this chapter. You also should keep yourself informed about research into severe mental illness;

insight may lead to advanced methods for helping your relative. We also need better services, and you should advocate for reform of the present treatment and care systems by becoming another Dorothea Dix. Not just the mentally ill are victims of this society; we all are.

PLAN AHEAD AS MUCH AS POSSIBLE

Self-sufficiency

One thing that this book stresses is to plan: plan activities, plan schedules, plan doctor visits, plan for crises, plan for setbacks, and plan for the future. The first step is to help the ill person establish as many skills as possible for self-sufficient living. Use a schedule for as long as it takes in order for the skills to become a habit. Under strict supervision (in a hotel or other restricted living situation), let the ill relative try out these learned habits.

For example, teach the relative how to shop for clothing by looking at clothes now owned, and the condition of these clothes, and deciding what articles of clothing need to be replaced. Do basically the same thing when shopping for food. Obviously, these skills cannot be taught until the recovering person is ready (more on this and skill training in Part Three of this book).

Conservatorships and Guardianships

While you are still working to help the recovering person become independent, consider who will be the guardian or the conservator for this person. A guardian is a person who has full responsibility for an individual. A conservator manages the estate of a said person. The guardian or conservator doesn't have to be a member of the family; as a matter of fact, many mentally ill persons do not have other relatives to depend on. There are lots of responsibilities involved in the guardianship or conservatorship, and because each state has its own laws concerning these, it is best to seek the advice of an attorney when decisions are being made for your loved one.

Note: because some of the laws are so vague, make sure you learn all there is to know about this matter; you may have to put other instructions and procedures in writing.

Choose an attorney who is experienced in the area of wills and guardianships. Make sure he/she knows of all arrangements you have made for the ill person, the homecare team, the primary care physician, and so on. The legal planning should take into account the following:

- *Where the ill relative will live.* This could be in a supervised apartment (check the local mental health clinic), with other relatives, in a retirement home, in government-supported facilities, etc.
- *How money will be dispersed* (whether from SSI, Social Security, or an inheritance). Plan how to pay for living expenses such as food, clothing, shelter, utilities, caregivers, doctors, or recreation.
- *Rehospitalization.* Plan for this in case it is needed.
- *Other physical illnesses.* Plan for them.
- *The death of the ill person.* Plan for the type of coffin, clothing, place of burial, and procedures.

BE KNOWLEDGEABLE ABOUT NEW ADVANCES

Areas of concern to the recovering person leaving the hospital for the community were discussed in chapter 6. You were made aware of the problems the individual has to overcome and what you should provide. Plan for everything from the most basic need (a roof over the head) to the teaching of advanced self-care and employment skills, so that the recovering person may be prepared for independent living.

Figure 13.1 shows this hierarchy of needs as the layers of a pyramid. Its base is having a home. The next most important layer is treatment for physical and mental illness. Then comes

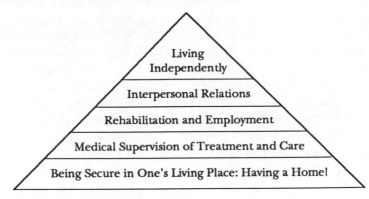

Figure 13.1. The Pyramid of Recovery

the need for daily meaningful activities. Finally, when social relationships have become manageable, the recovering person is ready for independent living!

In any one of these areas, progress may be made through research into mental illness, availability of new community resources, and legislative changes (advocacy is described here later). First comes the best understanding of the illness possible at this time. As we have shown in chapter 1, and discussed as an ongoing process in chapter 4, knowing the most exact diagnosis of the illness is the starting point. The federal government and private foundations are assisting medical researchers to find out more about the severely mentally ill. Unfortunately, the money allocated for this purpose is small as compared to what our society spends on research into cancer, heart disease, cystic fibrosis, and other physical illnesses. Of the total amount of support given for health research (about $11 billion) the government accounts for 60%. But of those billions of dollars, the combined amount of money for mental health, neurological diseases, and alcohol and drug abuse is only $500 million for 1989, or less than 8%! Of this money, only a small amount is targeted for severe mental illness. In terms of the private foundations, only 1% of the almost 5000 listed in the *Foundation Directory* allocated funds for mental health research in the past few years. The percentage of their grant money for mental illness was less than 2% of their total giving of $4.3 billion in 1985!

However, signs of hope for the severely mentally ill are emerging. Congress has designated "Mental Illness Awareness Week" (October 2–8 in 1988), and the National Institute of Mental Health (NIMH) has undertaken initiatives on "Schizophrenia" and on the "Decade of the Brain" (copies of their *National Plan for Research* are available by writing to the Office of Scientific Information, NIMH, 5600 Fishers Lane, Rockville, MD 20857). We hope that readers of this book will express their interest in this area by writing to the authorities and prominent persons in a position to support the cause of helping the chronic mentally ill. The National Alliance for the Mentally Ill petitioned Congress to declare the fight against mental illness a national goal, which President Nixon initiated for cancer!

More about potential helpful future ways of fighting mental illness are presented in chapter 14. Here, we need to review the development of areas of assistance in the community which you should keep in mind when looking for services for your relative. The Community Support Program (CSP) within the NIMH has called on each community to provide the following services, which were mentioned in chapter 12:

1. **Outreach.** Locate the mentally ill, inform them of available services, and assure their access to community resources by providing transportation or by otherwise taking the services to them.

2. **Basic human needs.** Help the mentally ill with shelter, clothing, and food; personal safety; and medical and dental care. Also, provide assistance so that they may apply for income, medical, and housing benefits to which they may be entitled.

3. **Mental health.** Provide adequate care, including diagnostic evaluation, prescription and periodic review of psychotropic drugs, and treatment and counseling services.

4. **Twenty-four-hour crisis assistance.** Both the mentally ill and their families or friends should be provided emergency assistance, thereby making it possible for the recovering individual not to be rehospitalized and to remain functioning in the community.

5. **Rehabilitative and supportive housing.** For recovering individuals not in crisis, who need a special living arrangement, the community should provide housing options. These should be both supervised and nonsupervised apartments. This would make the mentally ill person feel safe and comfortable while being encouraged to assume increasing responsibilities for his/her life.

6. **Psychosocial and vocational services.** Provide places in which the mentally ill can be prepared and trained at their different levels of abilities. Some of these services (a) should be available for an indefinite time and (b) should offer training in daily living skills, as well as sheltered work opportunities. Others should offer the opportunity for vocational training and employment placement. There should also be places where mentally ill persons could develop social skills and interest in leisure time activities.

The CSP mentions additional areas of support needed to reintegrate the recovering individual into the community. We have reviewed some of those in chapter 12 on support from the community. Next, we describe potential continuing improvements for the future of your loved one.

ADVOCATE FOR THE MENTALLY ILL AND THEIR FAMILIES

Another thing to do for long-term planning is to advocate. Seek out the elected officials in your area, and let them know of the deficits in the area of providing for the mentally ill.

Deinstitutionalization, a well-known term, created new freedom for mentally ill people—"new freedom" even though more severely ill persons weren't prepared for it! They were ostracized socially, unprepared for the work force, and lacked basic communication and living skills. And, as related in horror stories across the country, they became a significant portion of the street people. There is little need for more detail on deinstitutionalization; you know the story.

However, *now is the time* to stand up for the mentally ill persons and their families. There needs to be legislation which will ensure lifetime comprehensive services. These services must include better rehabilitation programs (prisoners are offered more services than the law-abiding mentally ill person), improved housing, work experiences, help with future planning, and more positive public awareness about mental illness. All people with government-related jobs (especially police officers and firefighters) should be trained on how to recognize mentally ill persons and to treat them accordingly. This story, in a letter to the editor of *The Nashville Tennesseean*, was written by Joyce Judge, Tennessee President of the Alliance for the Mentally Ill.

Dear Editor:

Two weeks ago, I met a friend. I did not meet her face to face, but through a telephone call from California. Her son had just been arrested on a minor charge in Nashville (when his car had broken down, he had broken into another car), and he was mentally ill and off his medication. The mother had made quick and urgent calls to the jail, to a social worker, to an R.N. at the jail, and to the public defender, informing them that her son had never before been in trouble with the police, that he had been hospitalized several times previously for his illness, and that he was suicidal.

Through a network of the National Alliance for the Mentally Ill, Tennessee has recently formed a committee called H.E.L.P.—M.I. (Help Exists for Loved Ones in Prison who are Mentally Ill). We made contact with our members in Nashville, and they were able to speak with the chaplain at the jail.

Last night, I had another call from California. The young man had committed suicide in his [Tennessee] jail cell. OUR SYSTEM

FOR TAKING CARE OF THE MENTALLY ILL WHO ARE CHARGED WITH LAW-BREAKING IN TENNESSEE HAS FAILED MISERABLY! A young life, brilliant mind but ill, is wasted, and we grieve with his family and are angry with a system that refuses to recognize that mentally ill people do not belong in prisons and jails!

We, families in the Alliance for the Mentally Ill, pledge to bring this story to the attention of all public officials in our state government, in our city governments, and to express it to all elements of the media. We will not be silent any longer [about] a system that fails to listen to our pleas for medical treatment for our ill relatives when their very lives are in danger.

I hope to meet my friend from California at the National AMI Convention. I will cry with her and will extend to her the condolences from all families in Tennessee who, but for the grace of God, might have been suffering the personal tragedy she is experiencing.

May we all have learned a lesson, and may we be diligent in our efforts to avert this kind of tragedy from striking again!

Sincerely,

Joyce V. Judge, President

Tennessee Alliance for the Mentally Ill

This letter was sent to the governor and to all the state officials of the state of Tennessee. The following letter was also sent to the editor of *The Nashville Tennessean.* It was written by Dr. June R. Husted, the mother of the suicide victim.

Dear Editor:

As I write some words about my son for his funeral service, the words and tears spill over, and I wish to share them with the people of Tennessee. Someone must speak out about the terrible flaws in our jails and mental health systems that allowed my son Todd to die. Changes must occur to prevent another such tragedy.

Todd was not a criminal [or] a transient. He was a handsome, formerly brilliant and loving young man, an honor student and a college graduate who, in his mid-twenties, became a victim of schizophrenia. This is a long-misunderstood disease that disorganizes the brain's ability to organize and integrate information, and leaves its victims tormented by hallucinations and delusions. It is a disease that strikes 1% of our population between the ages of 17 and 25, and [it] usually lasts a lifetime. Schizophrenia is not caused by "bad parenting." Todd came from a loving and concerned family. But because of society's misinformation, science's lack of understanding, and the tendency of the media to distort, the stigma of mental illness has interfered with society's efforts to increase research into its cause and cure, and prevented the development of adequate treatment. New research proves schizophrenia is a brain disease, but it will be years before a cure is found. Meanwhile, we must focus our efforts on effective treatment.

When Todd took off across the country with vague hallucinatory commands to visit his father's grave in Washington, D.C., our laws prevented me from stopping him, even though I knew he needed to be hospitalized. The civil libertarians have pushed for laws to give him the choice to be "crazy." They would never give such a choice to a five-year-old child, who has much more sense than an irrational mentally ill person in the midst of a psychosis. So I helplessly let him go, and eventually filed a missing person report, listing him as suicidal.

When Todd's car broke down outside of Nashville, with command hallucinations compelling him to continue on, he saw nothing dishonest in "borrowing" a nearby car, which he intended to return. In the midst of his psychosis, he was incapable of more rational logic to solve his problem. He also left his own car, with all his belongings (including a missing guitar, which I hope someone will return), and the key locked inside.

When I learned [that] Todd was in jail, my first reaction was relief. He was presumably "safe" until I could get him transferred to a mental hospital. Then, as a long-time mental health professional, past president of a NAMI affiliate, advocate for the mentally ill, and consultant to the Los Angeles Sheriff Department, I began to call every involved agency and official to insure his proper transfer and care. During a three week time period, I called Mental Health Association, the crisis line, the highway patrol, the police department, the sheriff department, the medical unit, the social worker, and the public defender. I spoke with nurses, the psychological evaluator, the social worker, and the deputies. I sent the medical records from past hospitalizations, and explained his past history and medications. I warned the staff that his intelligence and paranoia were used by him to hide his illness, requiring careful interviewing. And on at least three occasions someone was informed that Todd was suicidal—the last time on the morning of June 20. On one of these many occasions, a stern male voice informed me "This is a jail, not a hospital!" Did someone really have the audacity to state that there was "No prior warning" of his suicide?

If all of these warnings had so little impact or attention, what hope is there for relatives who are less assertive? The mentally ill do not belong in a jail, where they are isolated, untreated, and vulnerable. The small packages of playing cards, stationery, and treats that I sent Todd were stolen by his more aggressive inmates. We were told on two occasions he could not have visitors, most recently the day before he died. He felt abandoned, hopeless, and tormented by strange voices telling [him] he would die. And so he died. One more statistic in daily tragedies among the mentally ill.

I plead with you to make the necessary changes in your jails and in your mental health system, so [that] his death will not be totally in vain, and so [that] no other families will need to suffer the anguish we have suffered.

June R. Husted, Ph.D., California.

You can be the judge of what needs to be done. Both of these letters stir much compassion and concern. Although Ms. Judge had not even met Dr. Husted, she felt the pain and the concern of the grieving mother. What if all of society had compassion for all those who are saddened? Would there be this stigma against the mentally ill? When groups of people band together in a common cause, action will be taken! Start writing!

14

A LOOK TOWARD THE FUTURE

An old man, going a lone highway,
  Came at the evening, cold and gray,
To a chasm, vast and deep and wide,
  Through which was flowing a sullen tide.
The old man crossed in the twilight dim;
  The sullen stream had no fears for him;
But he turned, when safe on the other side,
  And built a bridge to span the tide.

"Old man," said a fellow pilgrim near,
  "You are wasting strength with building here;
Your journey will end with the ending day;
  You never again must pass this way;
You have crossed the chasm, deep and wide—
  Why build you the bridge at eventide?"

The builder lifted his old gray head;
  "Good friend, in the path I have come," he said,
"There followeth after me today
  A youth, whose feet must pass this way.
This chasm, that has been naught to me,
  To that fair-haired youth may a pitfall be.
He, too, must cross in the twilight dim;
  Good friend, I am building the bridge for him."

Will A. Dromgoole, The Bridge Builder

What is the obligation to the mentally ill for the future? Will someone build a bridge to connect the manifestations of mental disease to its mysteries? The answers to these questions, and a resolution to the persistent grief felt by families rests on research. Too little time and energy has been spent on research into an illness that for so many is a living death.

EXISTING RESEARCH

The scientific study of mental illness began in the nineteenth century. The two world wars, with their need to build up armed forces quickly (thus having to devise tests to exclude the mentally handicapped and the mentally ill from serving) and their countless victims of brain injury and mental instability, have accelerated our concerns with mental health. Until the late 1950s, psychiatrists in the United States have paid almost exclusive attention to psychological explanations for many of the signs and symptoms of severe mental illness. In contrast, this book maintains that a medical approach has to be the basis for treatment, care, and rehabilitation of the mentally ill.

Biological explanations for mental illness do not dismiss psychological and social causes for behavioral signs and symptoms. There is no doubt that particular attitudes, habits, interpersonal conflicts, family and financial problems, and so on may contribute to the ways in which an individual's mental illness reveals itself. But we can think of these negative influences as the periphery of the illness, not its core: *At the center of the illness is a brain that does not function well.*

It is easy to make this point when we are discussing the influence of toxic substances, including street drugs and alcohol, or the clinical picture resulting from damage to the brain, or a progressive dementia. However, many medical doctors and most people have difficulty thinking of the functional psychoses (the schizophrenias and mood disorders) or anxiety disorders and personality disorders in terms of brain malfunction. We argue that the understanding needed to provide a home for the person recovering from mental illness is best served by working from the premise that there is something wrong in the brain of this person. Only after acceptance of this basic explanation for mental illness can we then take into account the considerable knowledge of psychosocial stress factors that shape the behavior and the look of the ill individual's deficit functioning.

The importance of this chain of reasoning should not be underestimated. It determines the future of chronic mental illness. In the first place, it helps the social environment of the ill individual to develop helpful ways of dealing with the undesirable aspects of his/her behavior and making home-care possible: It strengthens our *empathy*. Second, it helps the mental health profession to ignore some aspects of the illness and instead spend more time on improving effective ways of treating the recovering person: It *establishes priorities for goals*. Third, it may shift the focus of research into the causes of mental illness away from those vocal patients who have been called the "worried well" to the chronic mentally ill, whose voices are rarely heard. To do so, researchers must begin to address the rarely asked question of how the human brain interacts with its environment by influencing feeling, thinking, and behavior: It will direct our attention *into researching brain–behavior–environment interactions*.

This final chapter primarily discusses the future directions by which we hope to learn more about the workings of the brain. However, we first enlarge somewhat on the role of empathy for establishing the priorities for research objectives involving brain–behavior–environment interactions.

Empathy Establishes Priorities for Goals

Empathy is the ability to put oneself into the mental frame of reference of another person (its importance was briefly discussed at the end of chapter 1). The caregiver must be able to (1) recognize and identify with the present feelings, thoughts, and behavioral reactions of the suffering individual, and (2) simultaneously understand these intellectually in terms of their importance for the person's future. The aim is to guide the recovering person into learning to develop insight into and eventually to control his/her behavior, no matter how deep, strong, abnormal, or destructive it may be.

Empathy is a part of our intellectual personality that needs constant development. And it takes time and conscious effort to come to an understanding of other people's behaviors. Some of us are born with more tolerance for others, but for all of us, our heritage of empathy is never enough to deal with all that can go wrong for the mentally ill person in the ever-increasing complexity of modern daily life.

Empathy in the homecare of the mentally ill is especially important in light of what we've learned from brain–behavior theory regarding the interactions among persons. Simply put, our communication with one another consists of *projecting ourselves* (that is, the movement outward of our impulses, feelings, and ideas toward another person) in the form of verbal (words) or nonverbal behavior. Parts Two and Three of this book, dealing with scheduling, behavior management, role playing, and other methods of guiding the ill person, have repeatedly emphasized that the choice of both right time and the appropriate approach is the key to success. For instance, we have seen how positive and negative reinforcement and punishment may help develop certain behaviors either for the good or for the detriment of the person. Using only positive reinforcement is not always good: Not saying or doing anything when you see the recovering person steal an item in the store will lead to unmanageable behavior. Punishment also is often counterproductive: Being upset about or punishing inappropriate sexual behavior may lead to worse expressions of the sexual drive. Therefore, success does not rest with the particular guidance technique that you may provide for the behavior of the ill person, but with your capacity for empathy. Your reasoned judgment, based on your empathy for the recovering individual, will determine the right time, occasion, and approach (verbal and nonverbal manner of relating) in which you will attempt to guide his/her behavior. Exactly, how your projection is received by this person will determine whether the message comes across.

The French have a saying about human communication, "C'est le ton qui fait la musique"—that is, literally, "the tone makes the music," and no music reaches deep into the heart unless it is played with love. Basically, positive communication is keeping linkages open to the other person. Our own behavior may build a bridge or dig a ditch between ourselves and the other person. An if we want to think about the future of the mentally ill individual, we have to keep building bridges. The chronically ill person is already inclined to withdraw and think of his/her future as ended. If we dig chasms between us, we will help the process of isolation and destroy any motivation for the recovering person's future.

Once we realize the importance of empathy as a healing attitude toward our loved one suffering from a malfunction of the brain, we have a guideline with which to set priorities. In chapter 13, a set of priorities was illustrated in a pyramid of needs. First, the recovering person needs the security of safe shelter. Therefore, provide this first. Next, look for the best medical attention you can afford. Only when these basics are taken care of can you afford to spend time on the many psychological, family, and social theories that deal with the treatment, care, and rehabilitation of the mentally ill. Look at each of these from the perspective of how it can improve your practice of empathy. In this book, we have shown some basic methods. Our disregard for the insights provided by such important sources as psychoanalytic theories, family interaction theories, or behaviorism and learning theories does not mean that we consider them unimportant. As a matter of fact, there is much to be said for the application of selected methods developed and employed on the basis of such theories. These methods are particularly applicable when working on specific individual problems and also when the ill person already has made great progress toward full recovery. Each recovering person may require different priorities at different stages and times of his/her illness. But regardless of the influences on the *form of the symptoms* that may be explained by these theories, the *cause* of the symptoms must be sought in the malfunction of the brain. And in this respect, our book addresses the *basics* of homecare psychiatric treatment. We give your homecare treatment team our *guidelines* for setting priorities. Further description of successful methods in homecare must be left to another time and another book.

Researching Brain–Behavior–Environment (BBE) Interactions

It has been discovered that mental illness is a disease or other organic cause for malfunction of the brain. Differences have been found between the structure and functioning of the brains of normal persons and those of mentally ill persons. Also, in some cases, specific genetic differences have been located in the cells of persons suffering from particular mental disorders. These findings have led to changing what was called a mental disorder in the past to a physical disorder. One example is the recent decision by the highest court of the state of Arkansas that, for purposes of insurance, manic–depressive illness must be considered a physical disorder, based on finding an abnormal gene in those who suffer from this mood disorder.

Such developments in the changing public perception of mental illness are most important for the future of the severely mentally ill. They will lead to more and more pressure on the part of communities to implement the Community Support Program recommendations, described in chapter 13. After all, if extensive community services exist for the prevention and emergency treatment of heart diseases, why should there not be a crisis intervention center with overnight accommodations in order to help prevent behavior decompensation and possible rehospitalization of the severely mentally ill?

Chapters 12 and 13 offered hope for greater public acceptance of severe mental illness, as well as the resultant development of better services for recovering persons in order to

1. Achieve a quality of life that is better than the ill person experienced in institutional treatment.
2. Find more available housing in the community, as well as respite centers to serve them and their families in times of crisis.
3. Buy into long-term illness insurance plans.
4. Attend motivational centers (clubhouses), state vocational rehabilitation facilities.
5. Have access to job opportunities.

Many more answers to the needs of the chronic mentally ill could be identified. Rereading chapters 6, 12, and 13 should bring countless ideas to mind regarding what should be looked for in terms of resources for planning and implementation of specific individual support services in the community.

BBE Interactions and the Holistic Approach

In this final chapter, we look at some of the promising approaches for the future treatment of mental illness that address the whole person. If we try to make the person *whole*—the original meaning of "healthy"—we must start thinking holistically. This is done by the study of the totality of the person, which is more than the sum of the different parts of his/her body or life.

New Diagnostic Techniques

First, we have to be alert to understand the implications of recent, really incredible, improvements in the study of the brain. Computerization of methods to study structure and function of the brain is changing knowledge rapidly. For instance, CT scans (computerized tomography) and nuclear magnetic resonance imaging (MRI) show brain structures; EEGs (electroencephalograms), in the form of computerized electrical activity mapping (CEAM), record brain function; and other advanced techniques can now contribute to precise localization of abnormalities in areas of the brain. Being able to pinpoint brain defects or malfunction will lead to more precise diagnosis and therefore more effective treatment and rehabilitation. It has been claimed that more elaborate brain imaging procedures, such as positron emission tomography (PET), may reveal details of brain functioning that will speed research into the functional psychoses: schizophrenia and mood disorders. Be this as it may, computer technology has revolutionized the manner in which we begin to understand BBE interactions.

There is another reason to welcome our increased precision of diagnosis. As we discussed in chapter 1, many mental health professionals are reluctant to formulate a diagnosis. This is partially because, as we have seen in chapter 4, making a diagnosis is an ongoing process; every time we learn more about what is wrong with the ill person, the diagnosis may become more refined. Unfortunately, another reason why even psychiatrists may not want to express themselves clearly about a diagnosis in chronic mental illness is the disagreement among them. Some doctors still prefer to think of severe mental illness in terms of psychological explanations while disregarding physical evidence. This is regrettable because, though psychological theories may be extremely helpful in terms of understanding why symptoms take a certain form, they cannot explain why the symptoms are there in the first place. The improved methods of examining brain function will help strengthen the grounds on which a dysfunction of the brain can be demonstrated.

New Discoveries About Etiology (Causes)

Second, the ongoing integration of diagnostic findings with discoveries and developing theories regarding genetic and developmental, biochemical, nutritional, viral, and immunological causation of mental illness will strengthen therapeutic approaches that consider the whole person. Looking at the life history and the total functioning of the person prevents discouragement when a particular treatment modality does not seem to work. A holistic perspective makes it possible to take a look at the facts from a different theoretical perspective and therefore be ready to try another approach. In other words, there is more hope now than ever before in the treatment of mental illness!

This brings us to the concept of BBE—that is, the consideration of mental illness as a defect in the interactions between the brain, the behavior, and the environment. How do BBE interactions apply when we think of homecare? By starting with the brain, we expect to find evidence of malfunction and accept increasingly precise treatment (for instance, psychotropic drugs and biochemicals). Then we try to understand how certain behaviors have changed because of the faulty brain function (for instance, positive symptoms develop based on faulty perception or thinking; negative symptoms arise because the brain can no longer initiate certain normal behaviors). Apart from maintaining medication to counteract positive symptoms, we will care for and rehabilitate the person by maintaining physical health (shelter, food, and clothing) and by providing learning or work to decrease negative symptoms. Finally, we plan to reintegrate the recovering person into the community at large, the environment of our society. We guide the individual into the gradual (re)establishment of social ties, the use of the commercial and cultural environment outside the home, and the meaningful environment of spiritual life, as offered in religious congregation.

It should be clear that success in this type of homecare treatment planning depends on the careful preparation for and monitoring of the interactions between the ill *brain* of the recovering person, the projected *behaviors* of all involved, and the continually expanding *environment* (the home, the neighborhood, community support services, and public places). By now, it should also have become understood why there are *many* possible approaches to studying the ill brain, and therefore many more reasons to try other treatments of behaviors or environments when you have not had success. Just remember, medicine is an experimental science, and healing is an art to be learned during a lifetime. Reread Parts One and Two, and continue to try and try again!

FUTURE RESEARCH PERSPECTIVES

In closing, let us look at some of the following promising perspectives on the treatment of mental illness as a brain disease: (1) developments in psychopharmacology, (2) genetic and developmental theories, (3) nutritional theories and enzyme activation therapy, and (4) environmental stimulation.

Developments in Psychopharmacology

The interest in discovering new drugs began in the 1950s, with the accidental discovery of antipsychotics, what were then called "tranquillizers." Today, research is developing countless new chemicals, following new theoretical guidelines. The majority of the theories about how these psychotropic drugs work involve the study of the nerve endings that are responsible for communication between nerve cells (or neurons, see Figure 14.1).

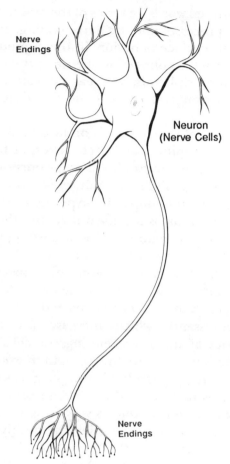

Figure 14.1. Neuron and Nerve Endings

To understand the role of psychotropics, we must examine the most popular model of the functioning of the brain. As some researchers have said, the human brain is "a wondrous organ," the most complex of all that we know to exist. We are far from knowing all of its functions, but for purposes of understanding psychopharmaceutical research, it helps to oversimplify the brain and look at it as a kind of computer. The two main sites of action in a computer would be its central processor and the peripherals, which produce such things as printed words. In terms of the brain, its neurons are the central processor and the nerve endings are the peripherals, which produce behavior. In the computer, electrical signals control the connections between the central processor and the peripherals, whereas neurotransmitters (i.e., chemical messengers) control the function of the nerve endings.

The interest of researchers is on finding drugs that influence neurotransmitters and their action at the nerve endings. For instance, antipsychotic drugs purportedly desensitize nerve endings of specific brain cells in the schizophrenic patient against the dopamine-type neurotransmitters to which the individual is hypersensitive. In other words, positive schizophrenic symptoms are, according to this theory, caused by the overstimulation of nerve endings (and therefore the creation of false and abnormal messages).

Another example would be the theory of depression. Lack of other neurotransmitters is purportedly relieved by the use of antidepressants, which increase the availability of monoamines at the nerve endings of cells that regulate mood. The analogy with the computer would be that in schizophrenia, the peripheral printer garbles the message and produces nonsense, while in depression, a connected monitor would only produce a very faint, dull light.

Indeed, as we have seen earlier, the positive symptoms of mental illness (caused by the "peripherals") respond well to psychotropic drugs. However, the story is different when we consider the nerve cells ("central processors"). One would expect that when the central computer processor shows defects, certain functions of the peripheral equipment might not occur at all. In the analogy, defects in neurons might cause certain mental functions to drop out, which we call the negative symptoms of mental illness. According to the model, it would make sense to say that negative symptoms show *a loss of function in the cells*. Is that consistent with our theories about how psychotropic drugs work? Yes indeed, we have noted repeatedly that negative symptoms are not relieved by commonly used psychotropic drugs, of which the theory says that their action is concentrated on the neurotransmitters and the *disturbed communication between the cells.*

This oversimplified view of the functions of the brain can be applied in looking toward the future of psychopharmacology. In the U.S., some of the new drugs developed and used in Europe are being tried. One that is already available as a so-called "compassionate" investigational new drug is Clozaril® (clozapine). It is related to the dibenzoxapine family and has been successful in treating schizophrenia in Europe and the Far East for many years. A major advantage is that it does not cause the side effect of tardive dyskinesia. Unfortunately, clozapine also has a major disadvantage: Its use must be carefully monitored because of other potentially very serious side effects. Other new antipsychotics are Orap® (pimozide, a butyrophenone) and sulpiride (no trade name yet), of the new chemical family of benzamides. Several drugs that are already used in general medicine for other purposes are being tried as well. Inderal® (propranolol), a beta blocker widely used in the treatment of hypertension; Catapres® (clonidine), also an antihypertensive); as well as, Calan® or Isoptin® (verapimil), used for cardiac conditions), are being tried in psychoses.

But in the case of schizophrenia, the single most pressing need is to find drugs effective against negative symptoms. Although for some of the aforementioned European drugs beneficial effects have been claimed, these have not been substantiated. If fact, it is unfortunate but true that most of the antipsychotics on the market today may actually worsen negative symptoms. We return to a possible novel approach to this problem when we discuss nutritional theories.

Genetic and Developmental Theories

The most basic of the approaches toward improving human life and function is that of genetics. We already know that some mental illnesses are caused by genetic changes, as are some physical diseases. This means that inheritance plays a role in such disorders, as they are passed on from generation to generation. The fact that many of the more severe mental illnesses, as reviewed in chapter 1, seem to run in families certainly lends credence to the theory of genetic transmission. For instance, it is calculated that the offspring of non-schizophrenic parents has a chance of 1% of developing the disease, as compared to a 13% chance for the offspring of one schizophrenic parent, and almost 50% if both parents have the disorder. No *genetic marker* (that is an identifiable abnormality on the gene) has yet been found in people who suffer from any one of the schizophrenias, but recently, such a marker for manic–depressive illness (which runs heavily in families), has been identified. The search for a marker in Alzheimer's disease (another disease noted to occur in certain families) and alcoholism, to mention some frequent causes of severe mental illness, is also quite intense.

In the developmental theory, it is postulated that the disease occurs because of brain damage at some time during development. Although the influence on the brain does not come as early as in genetic change or damage, we know that the brain is particularly sensitive to damage during growth. It is the only organ that matures so slowly that its basic development is not completed until age 2 years.

Many factors other than heredity may be responsible for damage: infectious disease, exposure to drugs, birth trauma, and a host of other causes. Be that as it may, the genetic and developmental theories for the causation of mental disorder would lead us to be extremely careful with the process of human reproduction and early development of human life and argue for preventive measures such as premarital counseling, prenatal clinics, nutritional advice and care during pregnancy, maternal guidance, combating early childhood abuse and neglect, and so on.

Nutritional Theories and Enzyme Activation Therapy

Many biochemical theories assume a genetic basis to mental illness, as well. The best way of thinking about it is the existence of an inherited error in the metabolism of the brain, which, under certain conditions (such as environmental stress or toxicity, or nutritional shortcomings), may lead to defective functioning.

Nutrition Therapy

Neurochemistry (the biochemical theory of brain cell functioning) has not only assisted psychopharmaceutical research, as we saw earlier, but also has sparked the recent increased interest in nutrition, which has developed its own name: *orthomolecular psychiatry*. This means the application of the right molecules for the maintenance of the brain cells responsible for healthy mental functioning. Presumably, if the right biochemicals are not in place and not properly used throughout the brain, mental illness could result.

Ever since the discovery of the role of *vitamins* in the body, the importance of these dietary substances (in particular, those of the B complex of vitamins) has been recognized for nervous system functioning. In the case of schizophrenia, treatment with niacin (vitamin B_3) was started 30 years ago and has spread to include thiamine (vitamin B_1), pyrodoxine (vitamin B_6), vitamin B_{12}, and folic acid. Other vitamins, and such dietary components as *amino acids* (building blocks of the proteins) and *minerals* (magnesium, zinc, etc.) were also added. Control of the diet has been advocated in many mental disorders, especially regarding restriction of sugars, alcohol, and caffeine.

The practice of orthomolecular psychiatry has become very controversial because some of its early proponents made outrageous and extreme statements about its efficacy. Mainstream psychiatrists were taken aback and began to disbelieve the results of improvements supposedly obtained by nutritional means. This was aggravated by other orthomolecular doctors, who proposed the use of these nutritional substances without the benefit of general knowledge of neurochemistry, which would include acceptance of the use of psychotropic medication. However, it is important to note that orthomolecular psychiatrists have the correct basic attitude: Mental illness is a physical disease whose correction lies in providing the brain with the right nutrition for the proper functioning of its cells, as well as the right conditions for the exchange of information between these cells, in order to restore its function.

Enzyme Activation Therapy

In the past few years, another consequence of neurochemical thinking has found application in the treatment of mental illness: enzyme activation therapy. The reasoning here is that it is possible to combine the treatment of biochemical abnormalities at the nerve endings with that of biochemical defects in the neurons themselves. This concept makes it possible to reexamine the controversy between proponents of orthomolecular psychiatry, who thought that their nutritional treatment would not need psychotropic drugs, and mainstream psychiatrists, who believed that psychotropic drugs alone would be sufficient.

Enzyme activation therapy is based on the results of a comparison of the brain's use of *glucose* (a sugar found in human blood) in chronic mentally ill subjects and mentally normal controls. Glucose is the only source of energy for the brain, and when it is broken down, the metabolic products form building blocks for neurotransmitters to be used by the brain cells. In hundreds of experiments, it has been shown that the brain of the chronic mentally ill patient does not use parts of its blood sugar effectively as compared to the normal brain. The defect in the brain cells appears to lie in a certain *enzyme* complex (enzymes bring about the breakdown of foodstuffs): the pyruvate dehydrogenase complex (PDHC). Several studies have shown that the addition of acetazolamide (Diamox®, a widely used drug against many diseases such as glaucoma and seizures) and thiamine (vitamin B_1) to any existing psychotropic drug therapy appears to stimulate some of the mentally ill and improves many of their functions, especially initiative, attention, memory, and thinking. Because it is know that Diamox® improves certain inborn deficiencies of PDHC, and vitamin B_1 is one of the components of PDHC, it is assumed that when acetazolamide and thiamine (A+T) are used in combination, they activate this complex of enzymes. The resulting improvement in the metabolism of the deficient neurons then would obviously assist the action of their nerve endings, on which the simultaneously prescribed psychotropic drugs exert their influence.

If cells in certain areas of the brain are indeed slowed down in their use of glucose, one would expect that particular functions would drop out completely or be insufficiently performed. A loss of function might lead to what we know as negative symptoms in mental illness. But such insufficient function might not completely stop the supply of neurotransmitters to their nerve endings—just interfere with it. The resulting shortage of certain biochemicals would then result in abnormal contacts between the cells. And when wrong messages are being sent around in the brain, the positive symptoms of mental illness appear.

This reasoning brings the claim of orthomolecular psychiatry into agreement with the results of psychopharmacology. As we have seen, antipsychotic drugs are especially effective against the positive symptoms of psychosis. This is in agreement with the theory that they influence the nerve endings. And as the nutritional theorists, especially the orthomolecular ones have it, vitamins and other important food elements are needed to strengthen the cell itself, to provide energy and spark. And indeed, vitamin B_1, one of the most important cofactors of the enzymes needed for the breakdown and utilization of glucose, together with acetazolamide, seems to reverse the negative symptoms of some mentally ill persons! The role of acetazolamide in this process is as yet not entirely clear, but it has been shown that vitamin B_1 alone does not bring about similar success in decreasing mental symptoms; therefore the combination (A+T) appears to be essential.

Further studies regarding enzyme activation involving

other vitamins and foodstuffs used in nutritional approaches to mental illness might improve on this apparent initial success in treating the negative symptoms of mental illness.

Environmental Stimulation

In any holistic approach, the role of the environment in shaping people's mental aptitudes, attitudes, and functioning must be considered. In any psychiatric evaluation, the genetic makeup (the basic genetic inheritance acquired from our parents), the history (the factors that shaped our development), and the present mental functioning (the present condition of our brain) must be accounted for in the final consideration: How does the person function in his/her everyday environment?

Much that is known in environmental psychiatry relies on what we learn from the observation of people's responses to environmental overstimulation, understimulation, and special kinds of natural stimulation.

Overstimulation plays an important role in mental illness. One explanation, suggested earlier, is that when brain cells are not functioning properly, they cannot communicate normally with each other and abnormal perceptions or thoughts will result. Persons suffering from mania or certain forms of schizophrenia are considered to show symptoms resulting from sensory overload. We have seen that recovering individuals must not either be exposed to conditions that lead to overstimulation (see the case of Vera in chapter 6) or experience too many simultaneous changes in their lives.

Understimulation is also responsible for symptoms in mental illness. Like any organ in the body, the brain needs to be used regularly to stay in shape. For elderly persons, who are less able to communicate and therefore often end up being left alone, this may lead to a vicious cycle. Little social stimulation makes them less able to communicate, and this in turn may lead others not to bother with them. The use of systematic sensory stimulation programs (such as music, dance, exercise, being exposed to sights, sounds, smells and touch of plants, animals, and relatives and friends) will do wonders for individuals isolated because of dementia or other chronic mental disorders. New approaches using miniature hearing aids, computers, and video programs, as well as many other prosthetic devices, are creating heretofore unexpected results in the chronic mentally ill who have organic brain disorders or sensory handicaps. For instance, it is exciting to see severely mentally ill persons, who communicated little because of speech or hearing problems, suddenly blossom when exposed to computer-assisted self-help programs! Rehabilitative possibilities in combating the consequences of understimulation are increasing daily.

Natural stimulation of special kinds have proved effective in combating several kinds of mental disorders. The last 20 years (and thousands of years of traditional medical treatment that the West is only lately rediscovering!) have shown that *therapeutic touch* (including massage therapy and attentive holding) can do wonders for mentally ill withdrawn and isolated persons. These methods of direct contact are simple, express our feelings directly, and almost never harm. Any loving parent knows how direct physical contact affects children. How is it that the healing profession generally overlooks this ancient knowledge?

Another age-old healing effect is that of careful *exposure to sunlight.* The oldest scientifically proven example is that rickets, caused by vitamin D deficiency, can easily be corrected by periodic exposure to ultraviolet (solar) radiation. In past decades, the influence of natural light on many diseases has again drawn research interest. Since the beginning of the 1980s, evidence has been accumulating that certain depressive disorders are brought about by the lack of sunlight during the winter. It has been shown that persons who used to suffer from so-called seasonal affective disorder (SAD) during the winter can prevent this by daily 2-hour exposure to *full-spectrum lighting* (i.e., electrical lighting that does not screen out parts of the ultraviolet to infrared spectrum, as provided by the sun). This therapeutic effect is caused somehow by the eye picking up those parts of the light spectrum lacking from ordinary electric lighting and translating this type of visual stimulation into biochemical substances that regulate mood in those individuals susceptible to this type of mood disorder. Presently, the frequency of SAD in depressed people is not known, but estimates range from a small percentage to as much as 10% of those suffering from periodic depression in the Northern latitudes.

It is fitting to end on this humble note that shows us how much we have to (re)discover about the role of natural stimulants such as touch and sunlight. It should encourage us to think of the many ways in which we can improve the life of mentally ill persons, with little financial burden and much kindness and empathy.

APPENDICES

NATIONAL ALLIANCE FOR THE MENTALLY ILL (NAMI)

2101 Wilson Boulevard, Suite 302
Arlington, VA 22201
(703) 524-7600

NAMI is a self-help organization of mentally ill persons and their families and friends. Comprising almost 900 local branches nationwide, loosely organized under state affiliates, its goals are support and guidance, education, and advocacy for the victims of severe and chronic mental illness, especially schizophrenia and the depressions. Referrals to local groups are available from the following state organizations:

Alabama AMI
2061 Fire Pink Court
Birmingham, AL 35244
(205) 987-8338

Alaska AMI
Box 211247
Auke Bay, AK 99821
(907) 463-4910

Arizona AMI
PO Box 60756
Phoenix, AZ 85082-0756
(802) 244-8166

Arkansas AMI—Help and Hope
4313 W. Markham
Little Rock, AR 72201
(501) 661-1548

California AMI
2306 J Street #203
Sacramento, CA 95816
(916) 443-6417

Colorado AMI
1100 Fillmore Street
Denver, CO 80206
(303) 321-3104

Connecticut AMI
284 Pattis Road
Hamden, CT 06514
(203) 249-3351

AMI in Delaware
3705 Concord Pike
Wilmington, DE 19803
(302) 478-3060

Threshold DC AMI
422 8th Street S.E.
Washington, DC 20003
(202) 546-0646

Florida AMI
400 S. Dixie Highway #14
Lake Worth, FL 33460
(305) 582-1835

Georgia AMI
1362 W. Peachtree Street N.W.
Atlanta, GA 30309
(404) 874-7351

Hawaii Friends and Families of AMI
PO Box 10532
Honolulu, HI 96816
(808) 487-5456

Reach AMI
c/o Judith Agenbroad
Mayfield Stage
Boise, ID 83706
(208) 343-1924

AMI of Greater Joliet
125 Robinwood Way
Bolingbrook, IL 60439
(312) 739-6161

AMI Illinois State Coalition
PO Box 4606
Springfield, IL 62708
(312) 297-9966

Indiana AMI
PO Box 5624
Fort Wayne, IN 46895-5624
(219) 483-1190

Iowa AMI
6521 Merle Hay Road
Johnston, IA 50131
(515) 278-2338

Kansas AMI
4811 W. 77th Place
Prairie Village, KS 66209
(913) 642-4389

Kentucky AMI
2001 Catnip Hill Road
Nicholasville, KY 40356
(606) 887-2851

Louisiana AMI
830 Audubon Street
New Orleans, LA 70118
(504) 865-8770

Maine State AMI
PO Box 5057
Augusta, ME 04330
(207) 622-5767

AMI of Maryland, Inc.
2500 N. Charles Street
Baltimore, MD 21218
(301) 235-2511

AMI of Massachusetts
164 Canal Street
Boston, MA 02114
(617) 367-8890

State AMI of Michigan
1602 Granger
Ann Arbor, MI 48104
(313) 663-1150

AMI of Minnesota, Inc.
1595 Selby Avenue #103
St. Paul, MN 55104
(612) 645-2948

Mississippi Gulf Coast AMI
960 Debuys Road #110
Biloxi, MS 39530
(601) 388-5450

Missouri Coalition of AMI
40 E. 107th Street
Kansas City, MO 64114
(816) 941-0285

Monami
PO Box 1021
Helena, MT 59624
(406) 443-7871

AMI of Nebraska
122 Westridge Avenue
Bellevue, NE 68005
(402) 291-9483

Nevada AMI
2923 Congress
Las Vegas, NV 89121
(702) 457-7239

AMI of New Hampshire
PO Box 544
Peterborough, NH 03458
(603) 924-3069

New Jersey AMI
400 Route 1 #10
Monmouth Junction, NJ 08852
(201) 329-2888

Ami of New Mexico
PO Box 9049
Santa Fe, NM 87504-9049
(505) 983-2584

Ami of New York State
42 Elting Avenue
New Paltz, NY 12561
(914) 292-3482

North Carolina AMI
4900 Water Edge Drive #170
Raleigh, NC 27606
(919) 859-2201

AMI Ward County
PO Box 6016
Minot, ND 58702
(701) 838 8005

AMI of Ohio
65 S. 4th Street #305
Columbus, OH 43215
(614) 464-2646

Oklahoma AMI
10404 Sunrise Boulevard
Oklahoma City, OK 73120
(405) 751-2885

Oregon AMI
12955 Southwest Hawthorne Lane
Portland, OR 97255
(503) 297-4350

AMI of Pennsylvania
2149 N. 2nd Street
Harrisburg, PA 17110-1005
(717) 766-8949

AMI of Rhode Island
PO Box 28411
Providence, RI 02908
(401) 621-4588

Ami of Vermont
PO Box 1511
Burlington, VT 05402
(802) 862-6683

South Carolina AMI
PO Box 2538
Columbia, SC 29202
(803) 736-1542

Virginia AMI
PO Box 1903
Richmond, VA 23215
(804) 225-8264

South Dakota AMI
Box 221
Brookings, SD 57006
(605) 692-5673

AMI of Washington State
E. 11115 23rd Avenue
Spokane, WA 99206
(509) 928-1536

Tennessee AMI
1900 N. Winston Road #502
Knoxville, TN 37919
(615) 691-3707

West Virginia AMI
25 Clinton Hills
Triadelphia, WV 26059
(304) 242-8850

Texas AMI (Texami)
400 W. 15th Street #1018
Austin, TX 78701
(512) 474-2225

AMI of Wisconsin, Inc.
1245 E. Washington Avenue #212
Madison, WI 53703
(608) 257-5888

U.A.M.I.
501 Chipeta Way
Salt Lake City, UT 84113
(801) 583-2500

Wyoming AMI (WYAMI)
519 Elk Mountain Drive
Newcastle, WY 82701
(307) 746-9395

NATIONAL MENTAL HEALTH ASSOCIATION (NMHA)

1021 Prince Street
Arlington, VA 22314
(703) 684-7722

NMHA is a consumer advocacy organization devoted to furthering the understanding of mental illness and the advancement of mental health. It provides information on long-term care and rehabilitation, promotes funding for research into improving treatment and rehabilitation, and supports community mental health center programs.

Addresses for any of its 600 local branches can be secured from your state affiliate (where no such statewide mental health association exists, one of the larger regional associations is listed):

Mental Health Association in Alabama
306 Whitman Street
Montgomery, AL 36104
(205) 834-3857

Alaska Mental Health Association
4050 Lake Otis Parkway, Suite 202
Anchorage, AK 99508
(907) 563-0880

Mental Health Association of Arizona
306 E. Pierson
Phoenix, AZ 85012
(602) 323-9383

Mental Health Association in Arkansas
1635 W. Shadowridge
Fayetteville, AR 72701
(501) 521-1158

Mental Health Association in California
926 J. Street, Suite 611
Sacramento, CA 95814
(916) 441-4627

Mental Health Association of Colorado
1391 North Speer Boulevard, Suite 350
Denver, CO 80204
(303) 595-3500

Mental Health Association of Connecticut
20–30 Beaver Road, Suite 101
Wethersfield, CT 06109
(203) 529-1970

Mental Health Association in Delaware
1813 N. Franklin Street
Wilmington, DE 19802
(302) 656-8308

Mental Health Association of DC
1628 16th Street, N.W., 4th Floor
Washington, DC 20009
(202) 265-6363

Mental Health Association of Florida
2337 Wednesday Street
Tallahassee, FL 32308
(904) 385-7527

Mental Health Association of Georgia
1244 Clairmont Road, Suite 204
Decatur, GA 30030
(404) 634-2850

Mental Health Association of Hawaii
200 N. Vineyard Boulevard #507
Honolulu, HI 96817
(808) 521-1846

Mental Health Association in Idaho
715 S. Capitol Boulevard, Suite 401
Boise, ID 83702
(208) 343-4866

Mental Health Association in Illinois
408 E. Devon, Suite 200
Elk Grove Village, IL 60007
(312) 956-0696

Mental Health Association in Indiana
1433 N. Meridian Street, Suite 203
Indianapolis, IN 46202
(317) 638-3501

Mental Health Advocates of Linn
  County
810 1st Avenue, N.E.
Cedar Rapids, IA 52402-5002
(319) 364-6305

Mental Health Association in Kansas
9728 Rosehill Road
Lenexa, KS 66215
(913) 888-5663

Kentucky Association for Mental
  Health
400 Sherburn Lane, Suite 357
Louisville, KY 40207
(502) 585-4161

Mental Health Association in
  Louisiana
6700 Plaza Drive, Suite 104
New Orleans, LA 70127
(504) 241-3462

Mental Health Association of
  Maryland
323 E. 25th Street
Baltimore, MD 21218
(301) 235-1178

Mental Health Association of
  Cambridge
5 Sacramento Street
Cambridge, MA 02138
(617) 354-2275

Mental Health Association in Michigan
15920 W. Twelve Mile Road
Southfield, MI 48076
(313) 557-6777

Mental Health Association in
  Minnesota
328 E. Hennepin Avenue
Minneapolis, MN 55414
(612) 331-6840

Mental Health Association in
  Mississippi
105 Pebble Brook Drive
Clinton, MS 39056
(601) 961-1572

Mental Health Association of Missouri
204 E. High Street
Jefferson City, MO 65101
(314) 635-5979

Mental Health Association of Montana
555 Fuller Avenue
Helena, MT 59601-3302
(406) 442-4276

Mental Health Association of
  Nebraska
4600 Valley Road, Room 411
Lincoln, NE 68510
(402) 488-1080

Mental Health Association in New
  Jersey
60 South Fullerton Avenue, Room 105
Montclair, NJ 07042
(201) 744-2500

Mental Health Association in New
  York State
75 New Scotland Avenue, Room 155
Albany, NY 12208
(518) 434-0439

Mental Health Association in North
  Carolina
115 1/2 W. Morgan Street
Raleigh, NC 27601
(919) 828-8145

North Dakota Mental Health
  Association
PO Box 160
200 W. Bowen
Bismarck, ND 58502
(701) 255-3692

Mental Health Association of Ohio
50 W. Broad Street, Suite 2410
Columbus, OH 43215
(614) 221-5383

Mental Health Association in
Oklahoma County
5104 N. Francis, (Shartel Shopping
Ctr) Suite B
Oklahoma, OK 73118
(405) 524-6363

Mental Health Association of Oregon
325 13th N.E., Suite 402
Salem, OR 97301
(503) 370-4408

Mental Health Association in
Pennsylvania
900 Market Street, Second Floor
Harrisburg, PA 17101
(717) 236-9363

Mental Health Association of Rhode
Island
855 Waterman Avenue, Suite D
East Providence, RI 02914
(401) 431-1240

Mental Health Association in South
Carolina
1823 Gadsden Street
Columbia, SC 29201
(803) 779-5363

Mental Health Association in Nashville
2409 Hillsboro Road
Nashville, TN 37212
(615) 269-5355

Mental Health Association in Texas
1111 W. 24th Street
Austin, TX 78705
(512) 476-0611

Mental Health Association in Utah
3760 Highland Drive #500
Salt Lake City, UT 84106
(801) 273-3944

Mental Health Association in Virginia
5001 W. Broad Street, Suite 34
Richmond, VA 23230
(804) 288-1805

Mental Health Association in West
Virginia
702 1/2 Lee Street, E.
Charleston, WV 25301
(304) 340-3512

Mental Health Association in
Wisconsin
103 N. Hamilton
Madison, WI 53703
(608) 256-9041

NATIONAL MENTAL HEALTH CONSUMER SELF-HELP CLEARINGHOUSE

311 S. Juniper Street, Suite 902
Philadelphia, PA 19107
(215) 735-6367

The clearinghouse is designed to promote and assist the development of consumer-run self-help mental health groups. It provides both information on mental health topics

and referrals to agencies and resources in the community.
Local representatives, called "key contacts," follow:

David & Ann Marshall
PO Box 5453
Tuscaloosa, AL 35486

Barb Green
PO Box 222112
Anchorage, AK 99522-2112

Andrea Schmook
1030 P Street #9
Anchorage, AK 99501

Richard P. Beeman
Survivors on Our Own
6545 N. 19th Avenue Apt. B-42
Phoenix, AZ 85015

Charles B. Simmons
6545 N. 19th Avenue, Apt C-40
Phoenix, AZ 85015

Howie T. Harp
Oakland Independent Support
641 16th Street
Oakland, CA 94612

Christopher Stelian
611 Marion
Denver, CO 80218

Lorenzo Callahan
3415 Oakwood Terrace, N.W.
Washington, DC 20010

Joan Mathis
4921 N.E. 7th Street
Ocala, FL 32671

Devoise Nash
8239 N. Florida Avenue
Tampa, FL 33604

Pippit Carlington
1420 Southland Vista Court, Apt. F
Atlanta, GA 30329

Jane V. Cunningham
197 Hale Street, N.E.
Atlanta, GA 30307

Randolph Hack
Office of United Self-Help
PO Box 4696
Honolulu, HI 96812

Roger D. Black
PO Box 9311
Boise, ID 83707

J. Timothy Brennan
PO Box 247
Huntington, IN 46750-0247

Darline M. Brown
4519 Grand, Unit 1
Des Moines, IA 50312

Paula Davies
1202 W. 19th Street Terrace
Project Acceptance
Lawrence, KS 60046

Phyllis A. Mathis
477 E. Loula, Apt #4
Olathe, KS 66061

David Muchow
1420 College Way, Bldg. #1, Apt. #23
Olathe, KS 66062

Lavaughn White
555 N. Trady
Wichita, KS 67212

Kymberlee Kelly Fuller
MH Association of N. Kentucky
8 Swain Court
Covington, KY 41011

Andrew January Grundy, III
Star Route
Lebanon, KY 40033

Kendall Williams
8060 Stroelitz
New Orleans, LA 70125

Bernice E. Kingdom
c/o Steve Hisch-Moco
114 State Street
Augusta, GA 04330

Philip Kumin
On Our Own
5422 Belair Road
Baltimore, MD 21206

Barbara A. Frenwich
1 King Road, Route 1, Box 536N
Mechanicsville, MD 20659

Brian & Christy Disher
On Our Own/Montgomery
213 Monroe Street
Rockville, MD 20850

Isaiah Uliss
Massachusetts Advisory Council/MH
PO Box 9216
Boston, MA 02114

Bernie Elbinger
10574 Park Terrace
Detroit, MI 48204

Ron Boock
Route 3, Box 618
Bemidgi, MN 56601

Rosalind Artison-Koenning
2739 Blaisdell Avenue S. #202
Minneapolis, MN 55408

Sheryl Lesch
6315 S. Lyndale Avenue
Richfield, MN 55423

Daniel G. Link
13339 Rosebank
St. Louis, MO 63122

Barbara Garrett & Tom Posey
17 W. Meadow
Billings, MT 59102

Wayne Adamson
1035 S. Lincoln
Hastings, NE 68901

Jack Bucher
c/o N.J. Coshap
906 Grand Avenue
Asbury Park. NJ 07712

William J. Butler
906 Grand Avenue
Asbury Park. NJ 07712

Al Michenfelder
906 Grand Avenue
Asbury Park. NJ 07712

Allen Kushner
Voice of Awareness
309A Sutton Towers
Collingswood, NJ 00108

Marilyn Leseke
Emotions Anonymous
48 Maine Court
Matawan, NJ 07747

Diana Romer
New Horizons
739 Wood Street (rear)
Vineland, NJ 08360

Dee Worley
1203 N. Main Street
Clovis, NM 89101

Betty MacIntosh
15 Charles Street #11–4
New York, NY 10014

George Ebert
101 Gifford Parkway
Syracuse, NY 13214

Ron Walters
447 E. Broad Street, Room 108
Columbus, OH 43215

Charles Ford
1038 Roseland Avenue
Dayton, OH 45407

Norman & Jan Fadley
742-B Longmeadow Lane
Findlay, OH 45840

Janice Grewe
519 Ross Avenue, Apt. B
Hamilton, OH 45013

New Beginnings
Box 609
Clinton, OK 73601

Larry A. Woodworth
6230 S. Douglas #210
Oklahoma City, OK 73139-1103

Darlene Jane Russell
562 1/2 S. Youngs
Oklahoma City, OK 73119

Jimmie Davis
New Beginnings
1620 E. 12th Street
Tulsa, OK 74120

Danette Veahman
Box 6, 6th Street
Grapeville, PA 15634

Janet Braunstein Foner
920 Brandt Avenue
New Cumberland, PA 17070

Laura Van Tosh
311 S. Juniper Street #902
Philadelphia, PA 19107

Jack Barry
325 Harrison
Pittsburgh, PA 15202

Jud Trax
Peoples Oakland
223 Coltart Avenue, Apt. #3
Pittsburgh, PA 15213

David Rajotte
5C Pearl Street
Newport, RI 02640

Billy F. Finley
PO Box 2348
Aiken, SC 29802

Bob Long
Chattanooga Bible Institute
1000 Oak Street
Chattanooga, TN 37403

Effie Eubank Washington
1103 S. Cooper, Apt. 3
Memphis, TN 38114

Dian Cox Leighton
Fair Mental Hospital Association
1111 W. 24th Street
Austin, TX 78705

Don Culwell
Reclamation Inc.
2502 Waterford
San Antonio, TX 78217

Peggy Timblin
538 West 1500 North, Apt. P
Layton, UT 84041

David G. Buck
154 W. 5th Street
Logan, UT 84321-5221

Larry McCleery
9895 Poppy Lane
Sandy, UT 84070

Paul Dorfner
VT Liberation Organization
RD #1, 1440-2
Johnson, VT 045656

Jack Daniel Craighead
Route 3, Box 289 E.
Farmville, VA 23901

David Nardi
2190 Reservoir Street
Harrisonburg, VA 22801

Marianne Neff-Daniels
5924 Kireop Road, S.W.
Olympia, WA 98502

John R. Corr
12819 Shorecrest Drive, S.W.
Seattle, WA 98146

Shirley J. Siegel
Stop Abuse by Counselors
PO Box 68392
Seattle, WA 98168

Shirley Bender
I Act
PO Box 1011
3939 W. Spencer Street
Appleton, WI 54911

Antonia Otero Zabeleta
Irlanda Apts. #A-1
Santa Juanita
Bayamon, PR 00621

Tricia Murphy
Project PAL
3957 Wellington
Verdun, Quebec H46-1V6, Canada

RECOMMENDED READING

K.F. Bernheim et al: *The Caring Family*, Chicago: Contemporary Books, 1982.

Primarily psychologically, not medically, oriented.

K. F. Bernheim and A. F. Lehman: *Working with Families of the Mentally Ill*, New York: W. W. Norton, 1985.

Directed primarily toward professional workers in the field of mental health.

J. K. Bouricius: *Dealing with Drugs: Psychoactive Medications and Street Drugs*. Arlington, VA: National Alliance for the Mentally Ill 1987.

Privately produced handbook on the good and bad effects of chemical substances—quite informative and well written.

N. Dearth et al: *Families Helping Families*, New York: W. W. Norton, 1986.

An excellent book about different experiences within families, but lacking medical–biological commentary or advice.

A.G. Hatfield and H. P. Lefley (Eds.): *Families of the Mentally Ill: Coping and Adaptation,* New York: Guilford Press, 1987.

Presents the point of view of families but is somewhat repetitious.

H. R. Lamb: *Treating the Long-Term Mentally Ill,* San Francisco: Jossey-Bass, 1982.

Written for those working in the field of mental health, this book contains valuable advice, especially on rehabilitation.

E. McElroy (Ed.): *Children and Adolescents with Mental Illness,* Kensington MD: Woodbine House, 1988.

An excellent book, focusing on problems of those under 21 years of age.

National Institute of Mental Health: "Schizophrenia: The Experiences of Patients and Families" (accounts from the *Schizophrenia Bulletin*). Schizophrenia Research Branch, NIMH, 5600 Fishers Lane, Bethesda, MD 20852.

One of the many informative publications issued periodically and available at little or no cost from our federal health research facilities.

C.C. Park and L. N. Shapiro: *You Are Not Alone,* Boston: Little, Brown, 1976.

A bit dated, but extensively annotated and must be considered a best buy (but does not make for easy reading!).

F. Safford: *Caring for the Mentally Impaired Elderly.* New York: Henry Holt, Owl Books, 1989.

A thoughtful and compassionate family guide focusing on problems caused by dementia.

E. F. Torrey: *Surviving Schizophrenia: A Family Manual* (rev. ed.). New York: Harper & Row, 1988.

An excellent text (appeared first in 1983) and simply a must for your bookshelf.

INDEX

Abstinence, 26–27
Acquired Immune Deficiency
     Syndrome, see AIDS
Addiction, drugs, 8, 27–28, 57,
     145–147, 199, 153, 220
Adolescence, 124, 178, 184
Advocacy, 51, 64, 71, 132, 219,
     224, 226, 228–232
   groups, 116
Affective disorders, 112 (see also
     Disorders, mood)
Age, 13, 177-178, 184, 186
Aggression, see Behavior,
     aggressive
AIDS, 21, 70, 89, 186-187
Alcohol(ism), 9, 22–28, 33, 43, 53,
     71, 88, 136, 139, 205, 234,
     246, 247
Alcoholics Anonymous, see Self-
     help groups
Allergies, 78, 106
Alliance for the Mentally Ill, see
     Associations, national
Alzheimer's Disease, 19–20, 38,
     48–49, 246
Alzheimer's and Related Disease
     Association, 220 (see also
     Associations, national)

Anger, 24, 36, 42, 51, 68–69, 73,
     131, 222
Anhedonia (inability to feel affect,
     especially enjoyment), 35
Anorexia nervosa (self-starvation),
     25–26
Anxiety, 6, 8, 13–16, 23–24, 27, 32,
     55, 68–69, 118, 128, 205,
     218, 222–223 (see also
     Disorders)
Apathy, 18, 34, 200
Appetite, 15
Assault, 169, 199, 202-203 (see also
     Behavior, aggressive)
Assessment, functional, see
     Functional assessment
Associations, national (see also
     Mentally Ill Chemical
     Abusers; Self-help groups;
     support groups)
   Alzheimer's Disease and
     Related Disease Association,
     220
   National Alliance for the
     Mentally Ill (NAMI), 54,
     174, 219–220, 227, 229–231,
     253
   National Depressive and

(Associations, national: *cont'd*)
Manic–Depressive
Association, 220
National Mental Health
Association, 54, 174,
219–220, 231, 256
National Mental Health
Consumer Self-Help
Clearing House, 221, 259
Attitude, 21, 98, 132, 179, 250
healing 237

Bathing, 19, 95, 109–110, 161, 170,
215 (*see also* Personal care)
Behavior, 6, 9–10, 52, 67–68, 93,
97–116, 188, 197, 210, 216,
218, 234–242
abnormal, 32, 118, 160, 177,
236
abusive, 95, 178, 184
aggressive, 37, 51, 202-203
control of, 5, 236 (*see also*
Negative responses to
behavior; Positive
reinforcement; Time out)
distrustful, 24, 168–169, 172
management or modification,
97–103, 120, 195
panhandling, *see* Panhandling
patterns, 21, 95, 168–169
psychotic (showing positive
signs of highly
inappropriate or "crazy"
behaviors), 6, 34, 41–42,
85–87, 95, 98, 101, 111, 168,
178–182, 195, 236
punishment of, *see* Negative
responses to behavior
sexual, 37, 195, 236 (*see also*
Sex)
undesirable, 24, 29, 37, 98–101
Birth control, 184–185
Blame, 4, 36, 101
Blood
medication levels, 75–78,
136–137, 143–149,
sugar, 85–87, 248–249
tests, *see* Laboratory tests

Brain, 5–7, 9, 17-21, 48, 67-72, 96,
177, 227, 231, 234–252 (*see
also* Disorders)
scans, 240 (*see also* CAT, MRI,
PET)
Brain–Behavior–Environment
Interactions, 235–242
Bulimia (binge eating followed by
purging), 25
Burn-out, 52, 73, 198, 219

Caffeine (coffee), 23, 111,
136–137, 247
CAT (computerized axial
tomography) scan (or CT
scan), 48, 71, 240
Chart (task accomplishment),
165–166 (*see also* Schedules)
Church, 126–129, 175, 223 (*see also*
Spiritual guidance)
Clothing, 170, 189, 224
wardrobe planning, 166-167
Cocaine Anonymous, 220 (*see also*
Self-help groups)
Cognitive
functions, 67, 112
training, 220
Commitment
court, 209
longterm, 53, 59, 217
Community, 13, 32–33, 38–49, 53,
57–58, 118–132, 187, 199,
213–222, 227–228, 238, 241
centers, *see* Mental health,
centers
resources, 81, 97, 123–128, 218,
226, 229
Community Support Programs
(CSP), 218–219, 227, 238
Compliance (with treatment or
medication), 73–78, 115,
137-156 (*see also* Medication,
refusal of)
Computer
assistance, 251
technology, 240
Confidentiality, 56-61, 125, 209
Confusion, 5, 7, 35, 86–87

Consciousness, loss of, 10
Conservatorships, 224–225 (*see also*
     Judicial commitment; Legal
     issues and rights)
Contraception, *see* Birth control
Contracts, 101–103, 169, 195, 200
Conversation, 173–174
Convulsions, *see* Epilepsy
Coping (strategies) 14, 220
Counseling, 184, 227, 246
Crisis, 58–60, 74, 122, 138–139,
     197-207, 224, 228, 239 (*see
     also* Emergencies)
  home, 219
  intervention (center), 116,
     200–209, 239
  residence, 141, 219
Crowded situations, 169, 188,
     191–192, 196

Danger, 4, 43, 101, 116, 201–205
     (*see also* Symptoms)
Decision making, 142, 190, 216
Deinstitutionalization, 229
Delusion(s), 11, 15, 75, 202
Dementia, 7, 18–21, 38, 48–49,
     100, 164, 234, 251
Dentists, 78, 106–107, 116,
     171Depression, 6, 13–16,
     23–24, 55, 67–68, 71, 88,
     145, 200, 213, 251–252 (*see
     also* Disorders, mood)
Detoxification, 22, 28, 57
Diabetes, 85–87, 96, 139, 206
Diagnosis, 27–30, 53, 62–90, 227,
     240–241
Diet, 86–87, 111, 120, 137 (*see also*
     Nutrition)
Discharge plan, 118
Disease (*see also* Disorders)
  cardiovascular, 83–84
  cerebrovascular, 84–85
  infectious, 21, 70, 184–186, 246
  organic or physical, 5, 16–21,
     68–90, 96, 238
Disorders
  anxiety, 8, 14, 25, 53, 126, 135,
     234

developmental, 8
manic–depressive or bipolar, 14
     (*see also* Disorders, mood)
mood (or affective), 8, 13–16,
     26, 126, 147, 234, 238, 240,
     246, 252
organic (mental or brain), 8,
     17–20, 38, 53, 70, 126, 135,
     187, 251
panic, 145
personality, 9, 21–27, 88, 126,
     135, 234
posttraumatic stress (PTSD), 16
schizo-affective, 147
substance use (and abuse), 8,
     21–28, 38, 53, 55, 57, 88,
     126, 135–147 (*see also*
     Addiction)
Driving (transportation), 107, 113,
     138, 174, 205 (*see also*
     Transportation)
Drugs, 67, 70, 72, 83–84, 205
  abuse, *see* Disorders, substance
     use
  antianxiety (anxiolytic), 138,
     143–156
  anticholinergic (to reduce side
     effects),143–156
  antidepressant, 84–88
  antiepileptic (seizures), 17, 147
  antipsychotic (neuroleptic), 75,
     83–88, 143–156, 242-249
  generic or trade, 138, 142-156
  illegal, *see* Street drugs
  psychotropic, 73, 77, 82–88,
     130, 134–156, 220, 227, 241-
     249
  sedatives, 145
  therapeutic, 29, 55

Early symptoms, *see* Symptoms,
     early
Eating, 18, 25, 111, 189–190, 200,
     216
Education, 81, 97, 114
Electroencephalograph (EEG),
     240
Emergencies, 58–60, 82, 89, 104,

(Emergencies: *cont'd*)
106–107, 141, 155, 160, 194, 201, 209, 228, 239 (*see also* Crisis; Identification card; Rehospitalization)
Empathy, 30, 53, 55, 59, 235–252
Employment, 14, 17, 24, 26, 32–33, 37, 42, 47–49, 57, 97, 120, 123–126, 131, 134, 225–228, 239 (*see also* Work)
Entertainment, 192–193
Environmental stimulation, 116, 130, 168, 242, 250
Enzyme activation, 242, 248–249
Epilepsy (convulsion or seizure), 17, 71–72, 86–87, 107, 248
Exhibitionism, 116, 187, 204
Eye contact, 10, 103

Fear, 24, 77, 115, 118, 139, 179, 214, 223
Fire, 206–207
Flashbacks, 16
Full-spectrum lighting, 251 (*see also* Seasonal affective disorder)
Functional assessment, 108–118, 140, 167–168, 200, 207
Future, planning for the, 17, 66, 125–126, 224, 233–252

Generic drugs, *see* Drugs, generic or trade
Genetics, 14, 238, 241–246, 250 (*see also* Heredity)
Glucose, *see* Blood, sugar
Goals, 52, 74–75, 101, 108–109, 214–216, 227, 235
Grooming, 40, 95, 110, 190, 200
Groups, 33, 39 (*see also* Self-help groups; Support groups)
Guardianships, 224–225
Guilt, feelings of, 4, 13–15, 115, 131, 179

Hallucinations, 10, 24, 42, 68, 75, 80, 126, 151, 193, 200, 202, 231

command, 11–12, 200, 231
Heredity, 5, 23, 246
Holistic approaches, 239, 241, 250
Home visits, 97, 108, 128–130
Homicide, 109-202
Homosexuality, 11, 55–56, 178, 187, 205
Hospitalization, 3, 8, 13, 15, 41–43, 60, 94, 117–133, 141, 167, 198, 205, 207–210, 229–232
alternatives to, 44, 132
(in)voluntary, 201, 208
Household chores, 40, 49, 104–105
Housing, 34, 38, 42, 45–47, 175, 225–228, 239
house-sitting, 49, 106
location, 38
Humility, 51, 252
Hygiene, 120, 161

Identification
bracelet or necklace, 80, 160, 171–172
card, 78–80, 84, 106, 136, 155, 160, 194
Illness, *see* Disease; Disorders
acceptance or denial of, 43, 236
physical or medical, 25, 62–90, 122, 141
Inappropriate behaviors (e.g., emotional responses, laughter), *see* Behavior, psychotic
Income, 227
Initiative, 9, 34–36, 39–40, 42, 248
Insight, 43, 224, 236
Insomnia, 27, 69, 111, 145, 199 (*see also* Sleep)
Institutionalization, 32, 39–40, 44, 53, 60, 118–119, 223
Insurance, 3, 44-49, 63, 66, 76, 238–239
Interpersonal relations, 35–36, 46, 75–76, 181–182, 225–226
Isolation, 203, 232, 237, 251 (*see also* Social, withdrawal)

Jobs, *see* Employment
Joint Commission for Accreditation of Healthcare Organizations (JCAHO), 118
Judicial commitment, 208–209 (*see also* Conservatorships)

Laboratory tests, 10, 17, 63, 70–71, 75, 115–116, 123, 137, 171, 217
Legal issues and rights, 26, 51, 208–210, 224–225
Leisure, 228
Libido, 69
Lithium, 143-156
Living arrangements, *see* Housing
Love, as a factor in providing care, 4, 30, 32, 38–40, 131, 160, 179, 237

Machismo, 43
Magnetic Resonance Imaging (MRI), 71, 240
Mania, 13, 71, 147, 238, 246, 250
    manic-depression, *see* Disorders, manic-depressive or bipolar
Manners, *see* Behavior, patterns
Marijuana, 9, 136, 139
Masturbation, 116, 178, 180–184
Medicaid/Medicare, 44–48, 63, 66, 106
Medical care, 227, 230 (*see also* Treatment)
    history of, 65–67, 72, 80
Medication, 3, 17, 22, 35, 43, 46–47, 72–81, 85–88, 104–106, 122, 128, 130, 168, 170, 194, 209, 217, 220, 229–232 (*see also* Drugs)
    change in or interruption of, 60, 136, 141–142, 155, 208
    compliance, *see* Compliance
    long-term injections, 137, 142
    maintenance, 134–156, 241
    refusal of, 168, 170–171, 199, 206, 209 (*see also* Compliance)

right to prescribe, 119
    side effects, 76–77, 82, 136–156, 209
Memory, 67
Menstruation, 163, 186
Mental health (*see also* Disorders; Illness)
    centers, 57, 218, 225
    services, 73, 76, 218, 229–232
    status examination, 57, 67–68, 71
Mental Health Association (MHA), *see* Associations, national
Mentally Ill Chemical Abusers (MICA), 27 (*see also* Self-help groups)
Mental retardation, 8
Money, management of, 94, 108, 114, 124, 171, 189–191, 194
Mosques, 126-127 (*see also* Spiritual guidance)
MRI, *see* Magnetic resonance imaging

Narcotics Anonymous, *see* Self-help groups
National associations, *see* Associations, national
National Institute of Mental Health, 6, 227
Negative responses to behavior (punishment), 99–101, 236 (*see also* Behavior, control of; Positive reinforcement; Time out)
Neuron (nerve cell), 242–249
Neurotransmitters, 244–249
Nicotine, *see* Smoking
Normalization, 96, 159–161, 167, 177, 197, 200
Nutrition, 220, 221, 241, 245–250 (*see also* Diet)

Office
    records, 57
    visits, 75–76, 81
Oral contraceptives, *see* Birth control

Organic disorders, *see* Disease,
  organic; Disorders, organic
Organizations, *see* Associations,
  national
Orthomolecular psychiatry, 247

Panhandling, how to curtail,
  194–195
Panic, 14, 136, 145, 160
Parenting, 24, 39, 183, 229
Part-time employment, *see*
  Employment
Pederasty and pedophilia, 116,
  187
Personal care, 19, 95, 109–111,
  161–163 (*see also* Bathing;
  Clothing; Self-care)
Personality, 9, 20–26, 37, 85, 187
  (*see also* Disorders)
  dual, 9
PET (positron emission
  tomography) scan, 240
Phobias, 14, 145
Planned Parenthood, 101 (*see also*
  Birth control)
Planning, 93–94, 96, 101, 166, 175,
  179, 198, 224
Positive reinforcement, 98–100,
  109, 166, 174, 194, 236 (*see
  also* Negative responses to
  behavior)
Pregnancy, 141, 184 (*see also* Birth
  control)
Prevention of symptoms, *see*
  Symptoms, prevention of
Privacy, 34–38, 44, 57, 95–96, 101,
  130, 178–182, 209
Prognosis, 66
Projection, 11, 236–242
Psychiatric services, *see* Mental
  health, services
Psychoactive substances, 21–23, 67
  (*see also* Drugs)
Psychopharmacology, 71, 134–156,
  242–245 (*see also* Drugs)
Psychosis, 5, 143–156, 231, 245
  episodes of, 24, 130
  functional, 8, 70, 149, 160, 234,
  240

Psychosomatic symptoms, 68-69
Psychotherapy 22, 71, 74, 120
Psychotropic, *see* Drugs;
  Psychoactive substances
Public awareness and perception
  of mental illness, 32, 181,
  188–196, 216, 229, 238–239
Punishment, *see* Negative
  responses to behavior; Time
  out

Quality of life, 39, 47–49, 239

Rape, 116, 187, 205
Reality testing, 5
Record keeping, 60, 78–81, 127,
  138–141
Recovery Inc., *see* Self-help groups
Recreation, 104, 114, 121,
  126–128, 132, 160, 192, 225
Referral, 66, 73–75, 184
Refusal of medication, *see*
  Compliance; Medication,
  refusal of
Rehabilitation, 3, 28–30, 37,
  45–49, 57, 96–97, 124–126,
  218–219, 223, 226, 228–229,
  234, 237, 241, 251
Rehospitalization, 35–37, 42–43,
  78, 116, 128, 139–141, 195,
  199, 207–209, 225, 228, 239
  (*see also* Hospitalization;
  Institutionalization)
Relapse, 36, 42–43, 47, 140
Religion, supportive role of, 30,
  48, 64, 126–128, 132, 141,
  160, 216, 242 (*see also*
  Churches; Mosques;
  Spiritual guidance;
  Synagogues)
Research, 209, 223, 226, 231,
  234–252
Respite (care, center), 96, 219,
  221–222, 239
Responsibility, 24, 101–106, 112,
  214, 224
Retardation, *see* Mental
  retardation
Rights, 51, 209

Risks, 209
Role-playing, 193-194
Routine(s), 94–95, 104, 159, 165, 169, 174
Running away, 171, 199, 204–205 (*see also* Behavior, control of)

SAD, *see* Seasonal affective disorder
Safety, 172–173
Schedule(s), 37, 51, 103–106, 166, 169, 207, 214
    designing, 103–104, 115, 171, 181
    during absences, 106–108
    restricted, 104–105
    unrestricted, 104–106
Schizophrenia, 6, 8–13, 25, 32–33, 53, 55, 64, 75, 83, 126, 129–130, 147, 227, 231, 234, 240, 244–247
    Schizophrenics Anonymous, *see* Self-help groups
Seasonal affective disorder (SAD), 251–252
Seizures, *see* Epilepsy
Self-care, 40, 109, 110, 160–166, 225 (*see also* Personal care)
Self-help groups, 39, 136, 220
    AA (Alcoholics Anonymous), 22, 43, 136, 220
    Cocaine Anonymous, 220
    NA (Narcotics Anonymous), 220
    Recovery Inc., 220
    Schizophrenics Anonymous, 220
Self-mutilation, 199, 203
Self-sufficiency, 108, 224
Sensory stimulation, 250
Setbacks, 168, 182
Sex(uality), 46, 60, 95, 115–116, 127, 132, 153, 176–187, 195, 236 (*see also* Birth control; Venereal disease)
    deviations, 178, 187
    therapist, 179, 181–182
Shopping, 167, 190-191, 224

Side effects, *see* Medication
Signs of mental illness, *see* Symptoms
Sleep, 38, 95, 110-111, 160, 200
    disturbance, *see* Insomnia
Smoking, 12, 22, 83, 85, 136–137, 169–170, 192–193, 216
Social
    field, 32
    guidance, 190, 194
    life, 174–175
    Security, 225
    skills, 189–190, 218, 224
    withdrawal, 116, 168–169, 199, 203
Socialization, 116, 127, 167, 174–175
Somatization, 14, 68, 76, 82
Spiritual guidance for the ill person, 121, 126–128, 160, 242 (*see also* Religion, supportive role of)
Sterilization, 185–186 (*see also* Birth control)
Stigma(tization), 4, 29, 69, 160, 231–232 (*see also* Public awareness)
Stimulation, 127, 250–252 (*see also* Environmental stimulation)
    social 250
Street drugs, 9, 22, 67, 72, 136, 139, 234 (*see also* Drugs; Psychoactive substances)
Stress, 5, 14, 24, 33, 69, 94, 121, 136, 140, 166-167, 188, 190, 197–198, 213, 219, 235, 247
Stroke, 6–7, 18–20, 85–86
    heat, 153
Substance (ab)use, *see* Addiction; Disorders
Suicide, 12–15, 44, 190, 201, 229–232
Sunlight, 251
Support groups, 45, 54, 174 (*see also* Associations, national; Self-help groups)
Symptoms, 5, 13, 15, 17, 21, 35, 60, 63–65, 67–90, 141–143, 234, 238

danger, 140–141
early, 34
positive and negative, 7, 9–13,
    18–20, 34, 40–42, 47, 71,
    126, 134, 138, 143, 241,
    244–245, 248–250
prevention of, 29, 88–90, 141,
    184–186
psychosomatic, 68–69
return of, 34, 41–42, 47,
    139–140, 167
warning, 136, 207
Synagogues, 126–127, 222 (see also
    Spiritual guidance)

Tardive dyskinesia (motor
    dysfunction), 76, 149–155,
    245
Telephone, 127, 172, 200
Tests, see Laboratory tests
Therapeutic touch, 251
Time out, 100 (see also Negative
    responses to behavior)
Trade drugs, see Drugs
Tranquilizers, see Drugs,
    antipsychotic
Transportation, 108, 174, 191–194,
    227 (see also Driving)
Travel, 172–173, 193
Treatment (see Behavior, control
    of; Cognitive, training;

Compliance; Nutrition;
    Psychopharmacology;
    Rehabilitation; Socialization;
    Vocational Rehabilitation)
attention and monitoring to
    assess need for treatment, 8,
    28, 35, 38, 41, 64, 67, 69, 75,
    99, 119, 140, 188, 192, 232,
    235, 248 (see also Hospitaliza-
    tion; Institutionalization;
    Medication; Mental health,
    services; Rehospitalization)

Venereal diseases, 89, 186 (see also
    Birth control; Sex)
Violence, 4, 41, 44, 95, 138, 168,
    179
Vitamins, 71, 247–250, 251
Vocational rehabilitation, 113,
    228, 239 (see also
    Rehabilitation)
Office of Vocational
    Rehabilitation, 124–125
Volunteers, 125, 222
services, 127, 216, 222

Withdrawal, see Social
Work, 15, 18, 20, 32, 44, 57, 67, 75,
    95–97, 113, 118, 123–126,
    132, 160, 228–229 (see also
    Employment)